Global Inequalities and Education

Universities into the 21st Century

Series Editors: Noel Entwistle and Roger King

Further titles are in preparation

Global Inequalities and Higher Education

Whose interests are we serving?

Elaine Unterhalter

Vincent Carpentier

palgrave
macmillan

First published 2010 by
PALGRAVE MACMILLAN

Palgrave Macmillan in the UK is an imprint of Macmillan Publishers Limited,
registered in England, company number 785998, of Houndmills, Basingstoke,
Hampshire RG21 6XS.

Palgrave Macmillan in the US is a division of St Martin's Press LLC,
175 Fifth Avenue, New York, NY 10010.

Palgrave Macmillan is the global academic imprint of the above companies
and has companies and representatives throughout the world.

Palgrave® and Macmillan® are registered trademarks in the United States,
the United Kingdom, Europe and other countries.

ISBN-13: 978–0–230–22351–6

This book is printed on paper suitable for recycling and made from fully
managed and sustained forest sources. Logging, pulping and manufacturing
processes are expected to conform to the environmental regulations of the
country of origin.

A catalogue record for this book is available from the British Library.

A catalog record for this book is available from the Library of Congress.

10   9   8   7   6   5   4   3   2   1
19 18 17 16 15 14 13 12 11 10

Printed and bound in Great Britain by
CPI Antony Rowe, Chippenham and Eastbourne

Contents

List of Tables and Figures

▶ **Tables**

▶ **Figures**

Series Editors' Preface

The series is designed to fill a niche between publications about universities and colleges that focus exclusively on the practical concerns of university teachers, managers or policy makers and those which are written with an academic, research-based audience in mind that provide detailed evidence, argument and conclusions. The books in this series are intended to build upon evidence and conceptual frameworks in discussing issues which are of direct interest to those concerned with universities. The issues in the series will cover a broad range, from the activities of teachers and students to wider developments in policy at local, national and international levels.

The current pressures on academic and administrative staff, and university managers, mean that only rarely can they justify the time needed to read lengthy descriptions of research findings. The aim, therefore, is to produce compact, readable books that in many parts provide a synthesis and overview of the often seemingly disparate issues.

Some of the books, such as the first in the series – *The University in the Global Age* – are deliberately broad in focus and conceptualization, looking at the system as a whole from an international perspective, and are a collection of integrated chapters, written by specialist authors. In other books, such as *Research and Teaching: Beyond the Divide*, the author looks within universities at a specific issue to examine what constitutes 'best practice' through a lens of available theory and research evidence.

Underpinning arguments, where appropriate, with research-based conceptual analysis makes the book more convincing to an academic audience, while the link to 'good practice and policy' avoids the remoteness that comes from an over-abstract approach. The series will thus appeal not just to those working within Higher Education, but also to a wider audience interested in knowing more about an organization that is attracting increasing government and media attention.

Noel Entwistle
Roger King

Acknowledgements

We have worked on this book over 3 years and owe thanks to many people who have contributed to different stages of the project. The conference, at which a number of the papers in this collection were first presented, was a project of the International Student Experience Committee at the Institute of Education. Our thanks to colleagues on that committee and the conference steering group, with particular acknowledgement of the work of Anne Gold and Marcia Beer. Funding for the conference was received from the Higher Education Academy, the Society for Research in Higher Education and the Institute of Education. We are particularly grateful for this, as it enabled a very diverse group of colleagues to come together for a lively and constructive set of discussions.

The authors of the chapters have worked with us over more than a year, engaging with our requests for amendments to papers to reflect on the turbulent contemporary times. We are very grateful for their enthusiasm and commitment to our project. A number of colleagues and doctoral students in the Department of Educational Foundations and Policy Studies attended a Sociology section seminar on the book in October 2009. We benefitted enormously from their searching comments and the opportunity to look at some of their own work in this area. Colleagues and friends in a number of different universities in South Africa, Eastern Africa, the University of Montpelier in France and the University of Sussex in the UK have stimulated us with discussions over many years, and sustained us with their friendship.

Helen Poulsen has helped keep the complex process of reviewing text and corresponding with authors on track and we are most grateful for the work she has done.

We very much appreciate the comments and suggestions of the series editors, Roger King and Noel Entwistle, and owe a deep debt of gratitude to Suzannah Burywood at Palgrave for her patience, encouragement and support.

Lastly we want to thank our grandparents, parents, brothers and sister and record our deepest gratitude to those who live with us and the ups and downs of the book, over many months (Isabelle, Richard, Joe, Rosa, Oliver, Sophie and Filipa).

Elaine Unterhalter and Vincent Carpentier,
London 2010

List of Abbreviations

AAC&U	The Association of American Colleges and Universities
ACU	Association of Commonwealth Universities
APPO	Asamblea Popular de los Pueblos de Oaxaca/Popular Assembly of the Peoples of Oaxaca
BIS	Department for Business, Innovation and Skills (UK)
CRT	Critical Race Theory
CSU	California State University
DEA	Development Education Association
DEED	Dorset Environmental Education and Development
DESD	Decade of Education for Sustainable Development
DETR	Department of the Environment, Transport and the Regions (UK)
DFID	Department for International Development (UK)
DLHE	Destinations of Leavers from Higher Education
DTI	Department of Trade and Industry (UK)
EAUC	Environmental Association for Universities and Colleges
ERASMUS	European Region Action Scheme for the Mobility of University Students
ESD	Education for Sustainable Development
ESL	English as a Second Language
ESRC	Economic and Social Research Council
GATS	General Agreement on Trade in Services
GUNI	Global University Network for Innovation

HDR-PNUD	Human Development Report-Programa de las Naciones Unidas para el Desarrollo/United Nations Development Programme (UNDP)
HEA	Higher Education Academy
HEFCE	Higher Education Funding Council for England
HEI	Higher Education Institute
HESA	Higher Education Statistics Agency
ICT	Information and Communication Technologies
IIE	Institute of International Education
ILO	International Labour Organization
INEE	Inter-Agency Network for Education Emergencies
INEGI	Instituto Nacional de Estadistica y Geografia/National Institute of Statistics and Geography
International EdD	International Education Doctorate
LHT	Liberal Humanist Theory
NGO	Non-Governmental Organization
OECD	Organisation for Economic Co-operation and Development
PPP	Purchasing Power Parity
PUMC	El México Nación Multicultural de la Universidad de Programa/Mexico Multicultural Nation University Programme
RAE	Research Assessment Exercise
RCE	Regional Centre for Expertise in Education for Sustainable Development
REDUI	Red de Universidades Interculturales/ Intercultural Universities Network
RMIT	Royal Melbourne Institute of Technology
SJTIHE	Shanghai Jiao Tong Institute of Higher Education
SSI	South Side Initiative
THE-QS	Times Higher Education-Quacquarelli Symonds

UCAS	Universities & Colleges Admissions Service
UCL	University College London
UKHEIU	UK Higher Education International Unit
UNAM	Universad Nacional Autonoma de Mexico/National Autonomous University of Mexico
UNCED	United Nations Conference on Environment and Development
UNDP	United Nations Development Program
UNESCO	United Nations Educational, Scientific and Cultural Organization
UNITIERRA	Universidad de la Tierra/Non-Government Land University
USAID	United States Agency for International Development
WCED	World Commission on Environment and Development
WDE	World Data on Education
WTO	World trade Organization

Notes on the Contributors

Andrea Abbas completed her PhD on Long Distance Running, Gender and Embodiment in 2000. She is currently a Principal Lecturer in Sociology at Teesside University. She has been working on the sociology of higher education since 1997 when she worked on a funded research project exploring the conditions and work of part-time teachers of sociology in the UK with a view to developing and suggesting effective ways to support their teaching. She is currently co-investigator on a 3-year ESRC-funded project entitled 'Pedagogic Quality and Inequality in University First Degrees' which is a joint venture with colleagues at the University of Nottingham and Lancaster University.

Saleem Badat is Vice Chancellor of Rhodes University, South Africa, and was previously head of the advisory body to the Minister of Education on higher education policy. He holds a PhD in Sociology from the University of York. His research interests include issues in higher education such as policy making, institutional change, social inclusion and exclusion and student politics.

Douglas Bourn was the Director of the Development Education Association and is currently the Director of the Development Education Research Centre, Institute of Education, University of London and Chair of the UNESCO UK Committee on Decade of Education for Sustainable development. He edits the *International journal for Development Education and Global Learning* and has written numerous articles on development education, global citizenship, and education for sustainable development.

Juan Carlos Barrón-Pastor is a PhD candidate from the School of International Development at the University of East Anglia

(UEA), and graduated from the National Autonomous University of Mexico (UNAM). His professional work has been conducted in universities, Non-Governmental Organizations and government institutions in Mexico. His current research is on cultural identities, collective emotional affects and symbolic violence in Mexico.

Harry Brighouse is Professor of Philosophy at University of Wisconsin, Madison and co-director of the Spencer Foundation's Initiative on Philosophy in Educational Policy and Practice. He is author of *On Education* (Routledge, 2006) and is currently working with Adam Swift on a book on the place of the family in egalitarian theory, *Family Values* (to be published by Princeton).

Vincent Carpentier is Senior Lecturer in History of Education at the Institute of Education, University of London. He is the Programme Leader of the MA in Higher and Professional Education and Associate Editor of the London Review of Education. His comparative research on the historical relationship between educational systems, long economic cycles and social change is located at the interface of economic history, history of education and political economy. He has conducted an ESRC-funded research project on the long-term links between funding and access in higher education in relation the Kondratiev cycle. His publications include *Système Éducatif et Performances Économiques au Royaume-Uni: 19ème et 20ème siècles* (L'Harmattan, 2001) and articles in *Economies et Sociétés, History of Education, Paedagogica Historica, the Swiss Review on Education Sciences* and *Higher Education Management and Policy*.

Diana Leonard is Emeritus Professor of Sociology at the Institute of Education, University of London and a Visiting Professor at the University of Sussex. She has published extensively on the sociology of gender and the family, gender and schooling and the long-term consequences of single and mixed sex schooling. Her current interests include diversity in the experiences of doctoral and international students in the UK.

Allan Luke teaches literacy curriculum, sociology and policy at Queensland University of Technology. His books include: *Struggles over Difference: Curriculum, Texts and Pedagogy in the Asia*

Pacific (State University of New York, 2004); *Pierre Bourdieu and Literacy Education* (Routledge, 2008) and *Curriculum, Equity and Syllabus Design* (Routledge, 2010).

Monica McLean is Reader in Higher Education in the School of Education at the University of Nottingham. Her research draws on critical social theory and focuses on pedagogic quality and inequality in higher education policies and practice. Her book *Pedagogy and the University: Critical Theory and Practice* elaborates a theory of pedagogic justice.

Alun Morgan is Co-Director of the Education for Sustainability Masters Programme at London South Bank University and was formerly Lecturer in Geography Education at Institute of Education, University of London. He is the author of numerous articles and chapters on education for sustainability and global citizenship. He is currently involved in creating a Regional Centre for Expertise in Education for Sustainable Development (RCE) in London.

Rajani Naidoo is Director of the Doctoral Programme in Higher Education at the University of Bath. She is outgoing Honorary Secretary of the Society for Research in Higher Education and is on the Editorial Board of a number of journals including the *British Journal of Sociology of Education*. Her research interests include higher education and international development; governance and equity.

Maryam Rab lives and works in Pakistan. She holds the portfolio of the Registrar in the first women's university in Pakistan. She started her career as an English language teacher in 1994 and later moved into higher education management. She holds a Master's degree in Education Management from King's College London and is completing her Doctorate in Education from the Institute of Education, UK. Her research focus is women and leadership, international collaborations and partnerships in higher education.

Elaine Unterhalter is Professor of Education and International Development at the Institute of Education, University of London and the co-ordinator of a number of research projects on gender and education in Africa. She initiated the MA Education, Gender and International Development at the Institute 10 years ago and continues to contribute to teaching on that degree and to the course in International Education on the International EdD. She has published widely on gender, education and questions of equality. Recent works include *Gender, Schooling and Global Social Justice* (2007), which won first prize in the Society of Education Studies book awards in 2008, *Amartya Sen's Capability Approach and Social Justice in Education* (2007, co-edited with Melanie Walker) and the section on postcolonialism in the 2009 *International Handbook of Comparative Education* (edited by Robert Cowen and Andreas Kazamias).

Melanie Walker is Professor of Higher Education in the School of Education at the University of Nottingham in the UK and Extraordinary Professor at the University of the Western Cape in South Africa. She is co-editor of the *Journal of Human Development and Capabilities*. Her research considers the contributions of higher education to human development and capability formation, including in relation to poverty reduction in South Africa.

Introduction
Whose Interests are We Serving? Global Inequalities and Higher Education*

Elaine Unterhalter and Vincent Carpentier

Globalization and the growth of the knowledge economy were leitmotifs for the end of the twentieth century and the beginning of the twenty-first. But so too was growing inequality, both between the richest and poorest countries and within countries. What roles have higher education institutions played in these processes and what possibilities are open to them? Whose interests do they serve? What changes are desirable and feasible?

In 2007, working together in London on the organizing committee for the Institute of Education conference *Learning Together*, we began to discuss the idea of a book based on selected papers. At that point our concerns focussed on understanding how universities did or did not engage with a world marked by vast global inequality. Our discussions ranged across different ways to assess global inequality considering income levels, quality of life, and aspects of discrimination based on race, gender, and disability. But our reflections on these intersecting inequalities came to be overtaken by events. As we engaged with the project of editing the chapters for this book in 2008 and 2009, momentous economic and political changes occurred. Profound crises in the distribution of food, the liquidity of banks, and access to fuel have revealed disasters precipitated by decades of untrammelled globalization. Together we face a predicament for which we have no easy solutions or ready guides from the past.

The initial conference title 'Learning together' and the question of whose interests universities are serving in a world marked by vast inequalities have taken on an altogether more urgent note in what is predicted to be the worst recession since the 1930s. No longer are there easy promises of boundless economic growth – albeit poorly distributed – to fund solutions. The extent of the current crisis was underlined by the IMF writing that 'the global economy is undergoing its most severe recession of the post-war period. World real GDP will drop in 2009, with advanced economies experiencing deep contractions and emerging and developing economies slowing abruptly' (IMF, 2009, p. 1). The G20 meeting in London in April 2009 agreed $1.1 trillion to be made available to developing countries to enable them to weather the crisis. But this finance in the form of loans brings with it the danger of a further period of debt, or constraints on access to loans which limit growth and social spending (Gunter et al., 2009).

This global crisis has brought back to the political agenda the issue of inequalities and their links with economic growth. Inequalities can be defined in the 'space' of opportunities or outcomes. Neither is sufficiently responsive to personal heterogeneities or the actions and values of individuals, which is why we draw on Amartya Sen's concern with considering inequalities in the space of capabilities (1980, 1999), that is valued reasons to do and to be. Capabilities are assessed individually but relate to social or collective relationships and the multiple, intersecting forms these take (Sen, 2009, pp. 245–247). The economic crisis is about inequalities within countries and between countries. Some would argue this is a crisis of the link between globalization or a certain form of globalization and inequalities (Basu, 2006; Stiglitz, 2006; ILO, 2008). Contemporary events confirm the view expressed in a number of studies on inequalities which comment that 'the conditions required for new growth regimes to be sustainable, [are that], they must be lasting and socially balanced, both within national societies and internationally' (Coriat et al., 2006, p. 3).

Higher education has the potential to reduce or increase inequalities depending on the form of policies institutions, governments, inter-government organizations and transnational associations implement. The global economic crisis highlights how interconnected institutions are and those interconnections, many forged in times of boom, now need to be re-examined in particularly demanding conditions. The central question this book examines concerns whose interests are served by the nexus of relations associated with a globalized higher education system and whether relationships formed largely 'going with the flow' of economic globalization can be recast.

▶ Economic growth, equity, democracy and sustainability: The tetralemma of global higher education

One way of viewing the inequalities associated with economic globalization is to set these in the context of a troubling nexus of problems. These present not just a dilemma, but a 'tetralemma', as propositions that might guide what is to be done pull in four different directions. How can we hold together aspirations for economic growth, equity, democracy and sustainability?[1] Economic growth, in all but a handful of countries, has not been associated with equity or concern for sustainability, and its association with participation and democracy has not always been a comfortable one. There are ongoing debates about the interrelationship between economic growth and reduction of poverty and inequalities (Bhalla, 2002; Friedman, 2005; Stiglitz, 2005; Basu, 2006). Kuznets' (1955) research on income and inequality developed the idea that the process of industrialization initially tends to generate inequalities which diminish over the longer term. The hypothesis of a Kuznets' curve has animated intense discussions in relation to national economies and, with the resurgence of international inequalities from the 1980s, has been linked with sharply different positions on globalization (Aghion and Williamson, 1998; Held and Kaya, 2007). However it is clear that, despite the economic growth from the 1990s, levels of poverty and hunger have decreased substantially only in developed regions and in East Asia. Thus the Millennium Development Goals report for 2009 shows the proportion of people in developed regions living on less than $1.25 a day declined from 16 per cent to 10 per cent between 1997 and 2008, but in Sub-Saharan Africa the proportion remained the same (64 per cent), while there was some decline in South Asia (from 55 per cent to 44 per cent) and a substantial decline in East Asia from 38 per cent to 13 per cent (United Nations, 2009b). The number of people living below the FAO minimum level of dietary energy consumption has increased from 826 million in 1990 to 873 million in 2006. Again while numbers fell in developed countries from 19 to 15 million, they rose in Sub-Saharan Africa from 169 to 212 million and in South Asia from 286 to 337 million (FAO, 2009). These totals represent the situation before the sharp swings in food prices in 2008. Such persistent inequalities observed especially in many developing countries but also in high income countries like the USA led Krugman to state that income 'distribution deserves to be treated as an issue as important as growth' (2008, p. 33). Clearly viable economic growth of the future depends on taking distribution and equity seriously and not seeing well-being as a trickle-down effect.

Equity and democracy are often closely related; however, not all arguments for economic growth or sustainability privilege these processes (Bhalla, 2002; Rosenau, 2005; Mishkin, 2006; Okereke, 2007; Finger, 2008). Indeed, discussions of a weakening of the welfare state in response to globalization raise the possibilities of an increase in income inequalities and regressive taxations (Atkinson and Piketty, 2007; ILO, 2008) and the most spectacular increase in economic growth in China took place without a deepening of equity or democracy.

Churchill's epithet about democracy – the worst form of government, except for all the others that have been tried – exposes both the aspirational and the pragmatic dimensions of discussion on the theme, concomitantly revealing how democracy may not always necessarily serve equity or economic growth and may only weakly support sustainability (Persson and Tabellini, 2006; Ross, 2006; Ward, 2008). The fate of affirmative action initiatives in universities often reveals the tensions between democracy and equity, with democratic processes sometimes serving to preserve the historic privileges of dominant groups and arguing there should be no special treatment for particular student or staff applicants (Cahn, 2002).

The tensions between economic and environmental concerns (Boyce, 2002) also generate testing conditions for particular democratic institutions. Processes of public deliberation reveal the long-term harm to all caused by damage to the environment. Although it might be assumed this would translate into protective action by governments and supra-governmental organizations, this has not taken place. Lobbying and the articulation of many sectional interests have led to parliamentary processes being used to slow down action to curb carbon emissions or secure compensation for victims of appalling pollution, such as Bhopal.

Democracy, equity, economy and the environment are thus seen as conflicting agendas (despite a potential benefit for each from the other). Individuals, as producers and consumers, as national and world citizens, all experience these tensions around their actions in relation to the tetralemma. They face a day to day challenge to reconcile their values and their engagement with the economy, democracy, equity and the environment: as do higher education institutions.

Despite these incommensurabilities, the security of our future rests on economic growth, equity, sustainability and democracy being not just necessary or sufficient, but in fact being jointly sufficient. This joint sufficiency places a particular requirement on global systems of higher education in their interface with the world outside the academy, but also raises the question of achieving joint sufficiency within and between higher education institutions. Achieving this is clearly immensely demanding and poses considerable difficulties for universities, governments and civil society organizations. If we cannot have all four together within any particular institution or national system or in relation to the dynamic between higher education and society, must we trade some off against each other, and if so according to which and what criteria? What process could help us decide? Can we revive a form of Keynesian social democracy, or have the institutions that could support this lost their capacity to deliver? Are universities to contribute to assisting the process of tradeoff through developing its ethical, epistemological, institutional and scientific underpinnings, or are they best served by reaching individual institutional conclusions so that each works with its own localized assessment of how it and other institutions should behave? For example, should universities build strategies to increase market share in particular areas in which they have historic strengths and a supportive regulatory regime in particular national contexts? In this way could some support work on economic growth and/or sustainability, regarding democratization and equity as too complex, raising too many obstacles, while others might specialize in democracy and equity? What would be the consequence for contributions to reducing or increasing inequalities of this form of ethical specialization? How might this alter existing forms of interconnection? What would be the costs and benefits to universities of working on all aspects of the tetralemma? What is gained and lost if this work entails not just research, but also relationships with students and staff? If resources are limited because of cuts in the public sector following the recession, how are the investments in universities to engage with the tetralemma to be made? This book examines aspects of these issues, while this introduction presents our preliminary thoughts on how trade-offs between institutions will deepen, not resolve the difficulties associated with the tetralemma.

Apple considers education as 'a site of struggle and compromise. It serves also a proxy for larger battles over what our institutions should do, who they should serve, and who should make these decisions' (2000, p. 58). The implication is that universities will themselves be sites of struggle over the tetralemma. An added tension to this is that, as Giroux points out, the missions of universities entail both the development of individuals and a contribution to public policy: 'higher education should be defended as both a public good and an autonomous sphere for the development of a critical and productive democratic citizenry' (2001, p. 2). We thus need a critical engagement with the tetralemma in terms suggested by Peters and Freeman-Moir regarding Utopianism. This entails 'not a specification of solutions, but rather the opening of the imagination to speculation and open exploration' (2006, p. 4). Thus what is gained by exploratory work in teaching, research and administration with the complexity of the tetralemma not only outweighs aspects of specialization that might be lost, but positively advances both the public good and liberal autonomy rationales for the university.

Milojevic has pointed out 'the success of neo-liberal politics was partially due to their ability to capture the public imagination, to offer a blue-print, a prescriptive and improved imagined state of individual and/or collective being' (2006, p. 28). Neo-liberalism's attempt to ignore or attempt to 'solve' the tetralemma by only focusing on individuals' advantage had disastrous consequences, but this popular appeal needs to be substantively challenged by an alternative imaginary based on regulation, equity, participation and human rights. We can specify general aims for higher education in the face of the tetralemma we confront, given that its effects are evident both inside higher education and in our wider global society. Answering the question regarding whose interests we are serving thus seems both necessary and feasible. In the 1960s, there was a more robust attempt to link higher education with a particular ontology and sense of social obligation. The Robbins Report (1963) defined the aims of higher education as 'instruction in skills; not mere specialists but rather cultivated men and women; Advancement of learning; transmission of common culture and common standards of citizenship'. Not formulating a contemporary response to global inequalities and common humanity seems immensely problematic as these processes are impacting on higher education whether we consider them or not.

The recession has been marked by dramatic decreases in economic growth, coinciding with the battering effects of climate change, often exacerbated by free-market economies and lack of investment in infrastructure for sustainability. There has been a rise in unemployment and widening inequalities within virtually every country in the world, and huge inequalities between countries (Basu, 2006; ILO, 2008). These effects have been felt in universities around the world with some experiencing rapid contractions in income and others having to recalibrate projections of student numbers or other development plans. While the development of the global higher education sector has its own internal momentum, it also reflects some elements of the global economy and thus cannot escape the effects and contradictions of the turbulent market forces of the current period.

Universities are particular institutions with their own histories and social relations, concerned with the content and pedagogy of higher education, the conditions of students and staff and through these institutional relationships with national and global political economic conditions. The questions posed by global conditions and their institutional effects are central, but extremely daunting. Higher education institutions are both profoundly affected by the global recession, but also may impact on the crisis drawing on their potential to foster economic growth, equity and social cohesion, desperately needed in hard times. King's identification of '[the] university as a site for the development of less territorial and more global forms of democracy' (2004, p. 65) and Breton and Lambert's definition of universities as 'new world social actors whose real challenge is to determine their place within international civil society' (2003, p. 234) suggest particular possibilities that are worth exploring taking on board inequalities and the complexity of the tetralemma. This book aims to contribute to elucidating some aspects of these difficulties, reflecting both on how to understand some of the problems universities confront operating as global institutions in uncertain and unequal times, and how to assess some of the solutions that have been attempted.

In trying to assess what possibilities are open to universities we draw conceptually on Amartya Sen's critical engagement with evaluations of justice (Sen, 2009). His argument is that specifying an ideal set of institutional arrangements should not detach itself from a process of assessing whether a particular change would enhance justice. Thus, while ideal theory might focus on enhancing liberty and equality, considering the tensions between distribution and cultural affirmation, or looking at particular forms of prioritization that might resolve the tetralemma we have presented, it is nonetheless immensely important to consider comparative assessments between different alternatives through public discussion. Sen (2009, pp. 408–409) points to the well-meaning rhetoric associated with a call for global justice without appropriate institutions to give this effect, and goes on to set out a framework for his comparative approach. The book sets out an argument for a focus on the choices that are actually on offer, the plurality of principles and interpretations that may be in play, the permissibility of partial resolutions, a stress on public reasoning and attention to assessing human lives in terms of capabilities, that is reasoned values and the significance of agents.

This presentation suggests that the question of joint sufficiency in relation to the tetralemma needs to be examined by those concerned with higher education giving particular concern to widening the space of capabilities, and deepening the educational experiences for whole populations that enhance the expression of reasoned values. The pragmatism of partial resolutions, however, is not traded off against a wider project to see higher education as a capability multiplier. Current conditions in higher education worldwide offer a contradictory space for this reflective public reasoning and assessment of expanding capabilities.

▶ The crisis of capitalism and some effects on higher education

A number of commentators point out that the current period of global crisis is not just one of the financial sector, but a series of interlocking crises (Migiro, 2008; Hanieh, 2009; Scoones, 2009). Most commonly mentioned are the crisis of food (which has mainly affected poor consumers), and of fuel (which has affected distribution because of wildly oscillating prices and has raised problems about sustainability because of the high environmental costs of carbon emissions); the financial crisis and a crisis of inequalities, which have been exacerbated by worsening economic and livelihood conditions and have the potential to shift crises into deeper processes of violence. Associated with all these inter-related crises is a problem of institutions, where, in many countries, governments and associated bodies have been unwilling or unable to provide adequate social protection or regulation. Moreover, organizations associated with the different facets of globalization have more often tended to respond to the developing crises (or exacerbate them), than to anticipate the shocks and help guard against their worst effects.

Each of these crises presents particular challenges to the higher education sector, but in each there are compelling opportunities to contribute to some process of recovery. In discussing the current crisis of capitalism and its effects on higher education we want to draw out some salient features of the financial crisis, the crisis of survival (looking at the fragility of supplies of food and fuel), and point to the ways in which these will have particular consequences for higher education institutions. In each, we show how aspects of the tetralemma we identified above, might play out, and suggest some of the difficult trade-offs associated with inequality that will have to be assessed.

The economic and financial crisis has a number of components in each of which the question of inequalities in higher education is implicated in particular ways. The first feature is a debt culture which grew up from the end of the twentieth century in Western Europe and the USA. Decades of easy credit led to a huge expansion of spending (Brown, 2008). While public spending was slowed down, private debt drove economic growth and masked social inequalities (Carpentier, 2009). Higher education was one area where expanded consumer demand fuelled growth. In a number of countries the agenda for widening participation in higher education was presented not as an expensive and difficult decision for families on a low income, but as an easy option to be funded by low-cost student loans and the promise of higher paid employment on graduation. But this in itself did not solve the problem of inequalities, merely shifting it to take new forms. Some studies in the UK have shown that students from low-income families are more debt averse (Callender and Jackson, 2005). Leathwood and Read reviewing the increasing numbers of women in higher education worldwide in 2005, point out that little is known about their social background, but where there is information, difficulties have been highlighted for students with fathers in blue collar employment or in stigmatized caste or ethnic groups (2009, pp. 33–34). David, however, in reviewing widening participation points to both the ways in which it has remained highly stratified and gendered, but has nonetheless provided opportunities for challenging and creative experiences drawing on inclusive pedagogies that connect meaningfully with students' lives (David, 2009, p. 18). Thus while economic growth, higher education expansion and easy money reduced some inequalities, they were not eliminated. Outside North America and Western Europe, while there was not a comparable expansion of access to money, economic growth and particular government policies led to a significant increase in enrolments in higher education, many in private universities, where study could be combined with work.

Table I.1 shows student numbers increasing between 1980 and 2005; while Table I.2 indicates expansion in enrolment took place at a higher ratio to government investment in higher education.

The social implications of the credit crunch and the dramatic reduction in jobs, particularly those open to younger people, in a period when students and former students are carrying an enormous level of debt in many countries (ILO, 2008) are at the moment largely unknown. We also do not know what the effects

Table I.1 Worldwide enrolment in higher education

Year	Total number of students enrolled in higher education (in thousands)	Total number of students enrolled in developing countries (in thousands)	Proportion of enrolment in developing countries (%)
1970	28,084	6,956	24.8
1980	51,037	16,858	33
1990	68,613	29,125	42.4
1995	81,552	37,743	46.3
1999	92,272	47,229	51.2
2006	143,723	85,331	59.4

Source: UNESCO, 1999; UNESCO, 2008; UNESCO, 2009.

Table I.2 Proportion of government investment in higher education (%)

	OECD average	India	Chile	USA
1995	78.7	99.7	25.1	37.4
1999	79.2	99.7	22.8	
2002	77	77.8	19.3	39.5
2005	73		15.9	34.7

Source: UNESCO, 1999; UNESCO, 2008; OECD, 2009.

of dramatic contractions in growth in emerging economies in Africa and Latin America will be and how this will affect self-financing students or cost recovery schemes, many of which have not been designed to respond to need (Johnstone and Marcucci, 2007; Shen and Ziderman, 2009). The credit crunch has serious consequences for student loans. Some banks in the UK have ceased to offer student loans (Jagger, 2008), and in a number of countries the design of student loan schemes rely heavily on public finance (Shen and Ziderman, 2009), which might contract when governments are balancing many demands on the fiscus. It is likely that anxieties about debt, unemployment and difficulties in accessing finance will alter the nature of the student demographic in many countries and may well reduce student mobility between countries.

This raises a number of questions as to whether universities will continue a commitment to widening participation and equity if this cannot be funded. It is also not known whether a changing student body will limit the engagement of universities with problems of global or national inequality or force new relationships with the state and the labour market. Whether a reduction in student numbers will foster or hinder consideration of questions of sustainability and democracy is also debatable. Current examples of higher education institutions concerning themselves with questions of sustainability, acknowledge the complexity, but are all set in the context of expansion (Lotz-Sisitka, 2004; Everett, 2008; Gough and Scott, 2008), while processes for student and staff participation in democratization and governing universities, albeit recently often under problematic conditions of new public management, are also associated with growth and changing demographics (Morley 2003; Kogan et al., 2006; Welch, 2007). While it may be that improved financial regulation and plans for future economic growth allows a deepening of engagement with equity, democracy and sustainability, it may equally be the case that shallow managerialist forms of governance are used in planning how to survive in a shrinking market and that equity, democracy and sustainability are seen as too expensive of time, money and status.

A second feature of the economic and financial crisis which will impact on universities has been the growth of the Chinese economy built on cheap exports to the rest of the world and accumulation of large trading balances and sovereign wealth funds in Beijing. Many universities in Europe, North America and Australia benefited from this growth of the Chinese economy, as well as that of other emerging economies, such as India, Brazil and Russia. As a huge 'workshop for the world' the Chinese government was able to simultaneously introduce marketization in higher education within China and finance large programmes to expand its own higher education system by sending out thousands of graduates to be educated in other countries (Mok and Lo, 2007). In addition, newly rich young Chinese people found they had the income to contemplate studying abroad. Thus, Chinese students make up a significant proportion of all international students. For example, in 2007, students from China made up almost one-quarter of all international students in the UK (British Council, 2007 cited in UKHEIU, 2009), 13 per cent in the USA in 2008 (International Institute of Education, 2008) and 23 per cent in Australia (Australian Education International, 2009). In 2008, the USA issued 53,000 visas to Chinese students who wanted to study in the USA, a 40 per cent increase on 2007, while the UK government issued 20,000 (Pak, 2008). Students from India were also a key market for these three countries. In 2007, there were more than 23,000 Indian students in the UK, a fivefold increase in less than a decade (British Council, 2007 cited in UKHEIU, 2009); while in 2007–2008, there were 94,563 students from India studying in the USA, the largest group of overseas students in the country (IIE, 2009). There were 93,247 students from India enrolled in universities in Australia at the end of 2008, 17 per cent of all international students and a 54 per cent increase on the number enrolled the previous year (Australia Education International, 2009). What will happen to this vast body of students if the downturn in the Chinese economy or a contraction in growth in India means they can no longer be supported to study abroad? Relatively low incomes for all but the elite in China, and the importance of saving for health and economic downturns, might mean a dramatic reduction in overseas students and the revenue streams to universities in other countries that relied on this. The sharp rise in students from India enrolling beyond their borders might or might not be sensitive to some declines in economic growth. While the changing level of students from emerging economies studying abroad is not known, the high proportions of international students from a handful of countries contributing to expansion of the university sector in other countries show an institutional reliance on fees and economic fluctuations which they cannot really control (Carpentier, this volume).

A third feature of the financial crisis that has a bearing on higher education has been the enormous growth of the process of securitization, that is the bundling up of different kinds of securities, selling them at inflated prices without adequate collateral. For some this process was synonymous with aspects of economic globalization (Elliott and Atkinson, 2009). Toxic securities led to the collapse of a number of banks across the world, emergency bailouts by many governments and dramatic reversals in stock market prices. Many universities were casualties of this process. Some, like Harvard, which had a large part of its endowment invested on the stock exchange, lost heavily in the sharp downturn in share prices associated with the banking crisis (Smith, 2009). The effects on other universities are less well publicized, but a number of them, including some of the most prestigious nationally or globally, have reported assets held in collapsed banks and substantial declines in income (Delbanco, 2009; Healy, 2009). Reported possible outcome are limits on staff recruitment, reduction in development projects and a rise in fees. One consequence of this financial contraction might be that governments, which borrowed heavily to save banks and other financial institutions and now have an enormous level of public debt, will not be able to invest in higher education at the level planned. Universities will seek to increase funding through raising fees, cutting staff and either aggressively competing with other institutions nationally or internationally. A second consequence may be that universities become even more competitive for top rankings in league tables seeing these as *the* mechanism to secure research and fee income. For some this might mean privileging research over teaching or standardizing teaching to minimize the risks of a fall in rankings. In these conditions, engagement with equity, democracy and sustainability may be advanced because they provide a competitive edge, but they could also be overlooked as getting in the way of 'bottom line' processes that assure investment and market share. In either case it is clear that there are likely to be enhanced inequalities between institutions nationally and globally with struggles over resources and status.

The fourth aspect in which the financial and economic crisis impacts on universities entails the form of their engagement with global inequalities and the crisis of survival. In poorer countries, with higher inequalities and a minimal or non-existent welfare state, the food and fuel crises of 2008 exposed the harsh costs of globalization, and the ways in which fluctuations in the price of particular commodities – rice, coffee or oil – could have devastating effects (Nzomi, 2008; Scoones, 2009). According to the 2009 *UN World Economic Situation and Prospects*, 'coming on the heels of the food and energy security crises, the global financial crisis will most likely substantially set back progress towards poverty reduction and the Millennium Development Goals. The tightening of access to credit and weaker growth will cut into public revenues and limit the ability of developing country Governments to make the necessary investments to meet education, health and other human development goals' (United Nations, 2009a, p. ix). It has been estimated that approximately 53 million people will experience the harsh effects of poverty in 2009–2010, with attendant risks to human rights and quality of life (ILO, 2008; Amnesty, 2009).

The nature of the form of responsibility of universities in richer countries for the kinds of analyses and proposed solutions to the problems of poorer countries is complex, enmeshed in relationships of power and control associated with imperial political economies and the particular ideological positions of neo-liberalism (Olssen and Peters, 2005; Sidhu, 2006; Mama, 2007, Mamdani, 2007). While alternate views of globalization have been articulated drawing on an ethics of cosmopolitanism, human rights and participation (Nussbaum, 2006; Pieterse, 2006; Williams, 2008) and while a number of commentators in universities in the global South have outlined visions of the form this engagement should take (Badat, 2006; Mama, 2006; Asare, 2008; Barrón-Pastor, this volume), the crisis of survival, which is clearly also a crisis of inequality, has generally been marked either by differently situated research communities talking past each other, or a failure of universities to engage with the large corporations and the international trade regimes which continue to shape the crisis of survival.

The crisis of survival highlights how important economic growth is to reduce and eliminate poverty, but also how much of the economic growth of the last decade was achieved without equity and only limited forms of democracy, being unequally distributed, with inadequate attention to social provision for the poorest or consideration of sustainability. Universities, which give up on the complexities of the tetralemma or engage in a particular trade-off simply to ensure institutional advantage, may become complicit with cementing existing inequalities. However, discussing forms of institutional participation in collaboration for change, and some of the difficulties entailed by possible solutions, could make a very significant contribution to considering how to overcome inequalities, and attendant problems of democracy, sustainability and their relationship to growth.

Finally, the overarching aspect of this financial and economic crisis which relates to the four features indicated above is inequality within countries and between countries. It may be the case that equality is at the heart of the tetralemma and that at a certain point inequality produces instability which undermines the system. Higher education is both potential source and solution to inequalities which confront us.

Global inequalities in higher education revolve around complex, unstable and often contested concepts, which are not always separate from wider social division. The identification and interpretation of inequalities have been a feature of research on national and global systems of higher education, but many of the major works on inequalities in higher education tend to focus on national contexts (Woodward and Ross, 2000; Allen et al., 2006) with no explicit reference to globalization. Archer and Leathwood, for example commenting on the UK, underline 'the importance of recognizing how multiple identities and inequalities of "race", ethnicity, social class and gender (amongst others) affect the way in which people construct, experience and negotiate different educational opportunities and routes' (2003, p. 175). The critical literature points not only to structures of inequality beyond universities, which they reflect, but also to internal practices that exacerbate inequalities within and between institutions. Thus, despite the expansion of higher education, approaches to admission and pedagogies that fail to engage and support working class students or perpetuate inequities associated with gender, class and caste have been noted in many countries (eg. Bourdieu and Passeron, 1964; Burke, 2002; Bastedo and Gumport, 2003; Morley, 2003; Simpson, 2003; Tomlinson, 2003; Leathwood, 2004; Reay et al., 2005; Allen et al., 2006; Cloete et al., 2006; Duru-Bellat et al., 2008; Gazzola and Didriksson, 2008; Sinha and Srivastava, 2008; Leathwood and Read, 2009).

The interconnection of the global financial, survival and continuing and deep-rooted inequalities poses profound challenges to universities as institutions, but understanding particular features of these requires a consideration of the ways in which the higher education system worldwide engaged with globalization. This is not the first crisis of the capitalist economy and it shares similarities with previous ones (Galbraith, 1954) but it also has specificities because of the higher level of integration of the world economy. Higher education systems and institutions survived previous crises, but their closer dependence not only on government money but also increasingly on private funding in the current era presents more challenges than in previous economic downturns. Moreover, features of global higher education, such as the mobility of students, staff, institutional forms and virtual communication represent as many challenges as opportunities to increase or reduce inequalities within and between countries. The question is therefore how this global system, which grew in more stable economic circumstances, will impact on the tetralemma of higher education in a new context of economic, social and political turbulence.

▶ Global higher education and inequalities

Global higher education offers new forms of organization and new pedagogic and research spaces for negotiation of the tetralemma. It thus both multiplies the challenges of the current era, as well as amplifies its possibilities.

Going global

There is an absence of agreement on the definition of globalization and its manifestations, and alternative interpretations of its impacts (Held and McGrew, 2002). Similar uncertainties apply within the higher education context where terms like 'globalization', 'internationalization' and 'cross-border education' are sometimes employed interchangeably. In this book we consider globalization as a complex process of transformation of economic, political and cultural social relations, underpinned by physical infrastructures, such as transport, ICT and finance, changing normative frameworks steering, for example, trade rules, investment regulation or international relations and symbolic formations of culture and language (Held and McGrew, 2002, p. 3). The driving forces of globalization are evident in the higher education domain, where changing technologies have expanded access making for a more international student body, a wider range of course delivery and new kinds of research co-operation. Shifting rules about intellectual property, competition and the ethics of research have shaped relationships, while particular cultures of pedagogy, scientific exposition, quality assurance and peer review have been both exported and contested. Currie stresses the importance to 'distinguish globalisation as a process that has indeed made communication instantaneous and encouraged people to think in more global terms and a conception of globalisation that combines a market ideology with a corresponding material set of practices drawn from the world of business' (1998, p. 1). The imposition on higher education of trade liberalization regimes associated with GATS commodifies the outputs of the academy with profound consequences for its practices, suggesting these are no different to any other business (Robertson, 2006). All these processes produce differentiated and uneven outcomes, particularly with regard to inequalities and the state. For example, Altbach (2004) and Altbach and Knight (2007) define globalization as 'the economic, political, and societal forces pushing 21st century higher education toward greater international involvement' and see internationalization as the policies and practices of higher education developed to deal with this (2007, p. 290). Globalization can thus be seen as a process entailing particular socio-economic practices and forms of (de)regulation, which in turn require and drive an intensification of internationalization. Thus, while processes of globalization may be agnostic on the presence or absence of the state, internationalization, generally demands some form of state action.

Discussion is sharp as to whether globalization entails a change of scale or a change of nature of socio-economic relations (Held and McGrew, 2002). It is probably both. Thus trends for a higher volume than in previous eras have been noted for numbers of international students (Gürüz, 2008) and the extent of student–staff communication (Ninnes and Hellsten, 2005). In addition, there has been a qualitative shift with regard to, for example, new areas of investigation (eg. global citizenship or international environmental law) and new forms of regulation such as the Bologna process (Bjarnason, 2004). Green claims that 'rather than a full scale globalization of education, the evidence suggests a partial internationalization of education systems which falls far short of an end to national education per se' (1997, p. 171). Altbach and Teichler note that 'universities started as truly international institutions' (2001, p. 6) and that the recent increase of internationalization of higher education is fostering a common academic model worldwide. This is accompanied by an increasing academic marketplace for both staff and students, more extensive use of English in instruction and publication, a growth in distance education and use of the Internet. In addition, partnerships between institutions from different countries, offshore campuses and franchising of educational programmes and degrees are evident. This has been accompanied by efforts to harmonize degree structures and indicators of quality (Altbach and Teichler, 2001, p. 6).

Inequalities

The extent of partial internationalization differs widely between countries, and its effects on existing inequalities are also markedly different. Thus in some countries new technologies and very limited regulation of international competition for students have expanded opportunities, while in others, the same processes have hardened divisions between elite and mass institutions, offering a much slower route to social justice (Clegg et al., 2003; Deem, 2001; Levy, 2003; Mok and Lo, 2007). Stiglitz (2002) and Basu (2006) have pointed to links between globalization and inequalities, highlighting the impact of the Washington Consensus, which focused on trade liberalization, deregulation, privatization and tax austerity on the lives of the poor, contributing both to the expansion of higher education in many countries in the world and widening inequalities within and between higher education systems.

Most research tends to examine the impact of globalization on national higher education rather than considering its impact on forming unequal relationships between countries. Scott underlines the difficulty for universities to articulate equity at national and international levels, implicitly considering inequalities at the global level as a promising agenda (1998, p. 111). But few works have taken up this area of enquiry. While increasing internationalization in higher education has not been primarily driven by concerns with equity, democracy or sustainability, these might sometimes be unintended consequences. The literature on borderless higher education focuses on institutions and international students but does not reflect on inequalities. Jones and Brown's (2007) look at internationalization includes pedagogies, curriculum and identities, but does not look at inequalities. With the notable exception of Ninnes and Hellsten (2005) and Leathwood and Read (2009) most studies refer to international students but not to the influence of globalization on the pedagogic process or dynamics of inequality.

Mobilities

Student and staff mobility as well as partnerships between institutions have increased markedly, sometimes enhancing equity and forms of participation in decision-making, but generally not regulated by concerns with sustainability. Mobility has sometimes been part of a national or institutional economic, political or cultural strategy, sometimes associated with the planned or unanticipated decisions of particular groups or communities. Some countries have exported students and staff abroad to increase human capital without providing additional university places at home, while others encourage mobility to improve their capacity to provide higher education, through enhancing staff development. Student and staff mobility may also be linked with institutional income generation plans, where particular universities set out to recruit international students as a means to inject finance and expertise into their own higher education system as was the case in Australia in the 1990s (Marginson, 2004).

Political connections, such as those associated with the Commonwealth, or the Anglo-American 'special relationship', may encourage mobility, as may strategies for educational integration like the different European exchange programmes (ERASMUS, Socrates).

Over and above the planned strategies of governments and institutions, there are market processes associated with student and staff mobility, where labour market opportunities encourage those who have adequate income and freedom of movement to seek qualifications or employment outside their home country. Lastly there are cultural links between diasporic or other social networks which facilitate student and staff movement around the world.

Student mobility increased from 1.8 million in 2000 to 2.7 million in 2005 (Gürüz, 2008). Table I.3 shows that most education provision for mobile students was in North America and Western Europe, while the least was in South and West Asia, Central Asia and Latin America and the Caribbean. The enormous disparity between the size of student intake into what are generally OECD countries (Larsen and Vincent-Lancrin, 2002, p. 3), located in regions which account for 84.44 per cent of all mobile students, and the rest of the world is clearly evident.

Table I.3 Student mobility in tertiary education by host countries, 2005 (%)

Arab States	2.47
Central and Eastern Europe	7.67
Central Asia	1.50
East Asia and the Pacific	16.60
Latin America and the Caribbean	1.25
North America and Western Europe	67.84
South and West Asia	0.39
Sub-Saharan Africa	2.28

Sources: UNESCO (2007, pp.134–137).

For example, HESA figures assembled by Universities UK International Unit show that there were 223,850 international students (excluding EU) enrolled at UKHEIs in 2005–2006, an increase of 64 per cent in just 5 years (Table I.4). There were a further 106,000 EU students in 2005–2006 (Universities UK International Unit, 2009). In 2007–2008, UCAS figures in the UK showed the number of new international applicants for entry was 68,500, an increase of 7.8 per cent on the previous year. The number of EU applicants rose by 33 per cent (UCAS, 2007 quoted on Universities UK International Unit, 2009). Looking at the countries of origin of migrating students it is evident that the regions with a large number of OECD countries account for

Table I.4 Student mobility in tertiary education by country of origins, 2005 (%)

Arab States	6.63
Central and Eastern Europe	11.55
Central Asia	3.07
East Asia and the Pacific	28.11
Latin America and the Caribbean	5.79
North America and Western Europe	17.33
South and West Asia	7.88
Sub-Saharan Africa	7.07

Sources: UNESCO (2007, pp.134–137).

just under half of mobile students (45.44 per cent), while Africa and South and West Asia, regions with the largest proportions of people living in poverty, account for some of the smallest proportion of mobile students.

However, students from North America and Northern Europe comprise only 17 per cent of all mobile students against nearly 30 per cent coming from East Asia and the Pacific. China is rapidly becoming the most significant source of students studying abroad (sending over 63,000 students to the United States alone in 2002).

> While the popular perception might be to classify mobile students as a homogeneous group, called 'foreign' or 'international' students, a more detailed classification of these students shows marked differences between them, particularly in the way they are treated or 'welcomed' by the chosen country of study, depending on the category to which they belong, but also depending on the personal circumstances which motivate their project. The intrusion of economic priorities over educational ones forces us to ask questions.
> (Byram and Dervin, 2008, p. 20)

According to the report Student Mobility 2025, written at the height of confidence in economic globalization, the global demand for international higher education looked set to grow enormously. Demand was forecast to increase from 1.8 million international students in 2000 to 7.2 million international students in 2025. Asia was believed to dominate the global demand for international higher education. By 2025, it was estimated Asia would represent some 70 per cent of total global demand and increase of 27 percentage points from 2000. 'Within Asia, China and India would represent the key growth drivers generating over half of the global demand in international higher education by 2025' (Böhm et al., 2002, p. 2). It is not clear what the global economic downturn will do to these predictions, but it is evident that a period of economic contraction, demands for reduction in air travel or taxes on carbon emissions might reduce them somewhat.

Unlike students, statistics on staff mobility are not routinely collected. However, the Higher Education Statistics Agency in the UK published data showing that by 2005 more than

20 per cent of staff in UK universities were from abroad, a proportion that had doubled since the mid-1990s; in some disciplines (European languages and electronics) non-UK staff comprised more than a third of appointments, and anecdotal accounts suggested work in the UK was an important career stepping stone (Tysome, 2007). A survey in 2006 by the Association of Commonwealth Universities of 123 institutions in 27 countries found that on average 12 per cent of staff were classed as 'foreign academic staff' with the ratio highest in the UK, Australia and New Zealand and lowest in Africa and Asia (2006, p. 15). Enders and Musselin conclude that 'the national boundaries of academic careers are weakening' (2008, p. 145) but the direction of flow is generally to deepen the inequalities between higher education systems, rather than to lessen them. According to Altbach and Knight, 'international academic mobility...favors well-developed education systems and institutions, thereby compounding existing inequalities' (2007, p. 291).

These mobilities place in a global context Becher and Trowler's view that 'academic tribes, like those of other sorts, are splintered with structural inequalities' (2001, p. 149). Mobilities thus have generally not lessened the problem of inequalities within and between countries with regard to higher education, merely provided a new perspective from which they can be viewed.

Moving programmes: Physically or virtually

Virtual education is another developing area of global higher education. Fielden states that 'many countries, driven by economic development or protectionist motives, are encouraging universities to enter the virtual markets, and some (such as the US, the UK, the Netherlands, Finland and Canada) are beginning to focus on global markets' (2001, p. 50). Moreover, other studies showed that virtual higher education can be used as a cost-effective way of coping with the problems of access in some developing countries and could be seen as an 'opportunity to reduce the North-South knowledge gap' (Kuroda and Shanawez, 2003, p. 565). It has been argued that, like some other major source countries such as Malaysia and Singapore, China may come to view foreign-sourced, in-country provision as more cost-effective (in terms of reducing travel costs and stemming brain drain) (Garrett, 2004). However, Carnoy argues that 'good quality virtual higher education may be more expensive than traditional university education' (2004, p. 13).

Offshore and franchise activities are another developing area of global higher education. Some institutions have the capacity to export their programs or to establish branches in countries where governments are amenable to hosting foreign providers, making funding and buildings available. This is also part of an institutional strategy to generate extra funding. This involves universities which open 'subsidiaries abroad or offering their educational programmes or qualifications via partnership with host-country institutions' (Larsen and Vincent-Lancrin, 2002, p. 21). Australia and Britain have been especially active in establishing transnational programs, while the US came late (Altbach, 2002). According to Bennell and Pearce, 'by 1997 the value of education export from the UK was estimated at £9 billion' (2003, p. 216). A recent study shows the figure is now £28 billion (Lenton, 2007). Garrett and Verbik estimate that UK transnational enrolment was 190, 000 in 2003 (2004, p. 3). According to a report from the World Bank, 'the cost of attending franchise institutions is usually one-fourth to one-third what it would cost to enrol in the mother institutions' (Salmi, 2002, p. 28). The debates on these specific manifestations of global higher education can be linked to those which followed the emergence of the entrepreneurial university (Slaughter and Leslie, 1999). Ball (2010) concludes his examination of the international activities of entrepreneurial universities by noting that 'they are no longer in any straightforward sense national public universities, they are transnational, corporate, profit-oriented, and they are positioned on the boundaries between academia and business – they are hybrids'. This raises the question of the space of action of universities and who they are accountable to. Some universities might have a high profile in addressing equalities at home, but be engaged in inequality enhancing activity abroad, or vice versa. What this raises is that the tetralemma needs to be addressed in relation to governance issues as much as content of research and teaching.

Middlehurst notes that internationalization is not new to universities but that in the context of globalization, new issues are raised: one of these issues is that globalization may be seen as cultural imperialism adding that 'clearly it is the curricula of the West (and particularly cultures linked to the English language) that are being transported around the world' (2001, p. 7). 'Programme and institution mobility carry greater quality risks, because they are new, less stable and often currently do not fall within the scope of quality assurance and accreditation systems' (OECD, 2004a, p. 268). It appears that '(National) quality assurance and accreditation arrangements are commonly restricted to State-recognised "public" institutions, so that foreign and for profit forms of provision are often not covered' (OECD, 2004b, p. 10). Machado highlights that although offshore higher education providers are sometimes subject to the quality insurance mechanism of the country of origin, it is possible that 'an awarding institution is no part of any official system and escapes regulation from the supplier's side' as well as the country of destination (2002, p. 106).

During a UNESCO Meeting of Higher Education Partners, a background paper for the International Association of Universities recommended that 'North-South cooperation in higher education, focusing as it does on human resource development, be recognised as a major instrument of the fight against inequality among nations, people, and groups and be given adequate support and funding by national development agencies, intergovernmental organizations, and private foundations' (International Association of Universities, 2003, p. 27). A number of local and national higher education initiatives engage with inequalities. For example, important initiatives in Argentina, Mexico and Brazil offer 'local solutions to global problems' caused by neo-liberal policies. These entail collaborations between universities, local communities and social movements (Rhoads and Torres, 2006; Barrón-Pastor, this volume). Mollis (2006) in his writing about higher education initiatives for equity in Latin America notes the 'urgent need to recover the social, ethical and humanistic significance of educational quality' (2006, p. 513), while Bernasconi points out that 'traditions of political awareness, social critique, and outreach to the underprivileged seem especially relevant today, in both Latin America and globally, in the face of ideological hegemony and economic inequality' (2008, p. 47). These traditions are particularly generative for new approaches in higher education that engage the tetralemma we have outlined.

These features of global higher education – its selective and diverse engagement with economic globalization, the intensification of mobility for staff, students and technologies, the uneven effects of regulation and the dispersal both of equity and inequity within countries and the entrenchment of inequality between institutions form the background to the chapters in this book. The argument is presented in three parts. The first sets out to map some features of global inequalities in higher education. Allan Luke considers some of the theoretical issues raised by borderless higher education, the questions of culture and different ways of constructing the question as to whose interests we are serving. Drawing out different framings of individual and national identity, he presents a nuanced picture of the ways in which the questions this book examines are inserted into complex histories (Chapter 1). Rajani Naidoo widens the scope to the analysis of the impact of marketized global higher education on inequalities in lower income countries (Chapter 2). She draws out how the emphasis on access to the knowledge economy as the criterion for success in higher education institutions marginalizes important concerns with equity, quality and contribution to development, all of which are necessary for redressing vast global inequalities. Elaine Unterhalter offers a theoretical exploration of some different models of higher education pedagogy, drawing out differences in the way equity and equality are interpreted and the ways in which each pedagogic form positions its relationship with the global level (Chapter 3). All three chapters thus present different perspectives on the problem of inequality, with Luke drawing out its cultural dimensions, Naidoo stressing some of the economic and educational effects and Unterhalter considering some of the social and political relationships that are formed around different formations of inequality in the academy.

In Part II, authors explore the ways in which these broad formations of inequality work, drawing on a range of different forms of data. Saleem Badat (Chapter 4) examines the ways in which league tables of global excellence are constructed, the assumptions about the nature of the relationship between university and society they rest on and how universities engaged in addressing questions of equity and democracy are never likely to score as highly by these measures as those that give this only a cursory consideration. Vincent Carpentier proposes a comparative study of the impacts of funding policies in the US, France and the UK on home and on foreign students over the last century (Chapter 5), showing how the shift from public to private funding for higher education was initially related to inequality in the treatment of international students in the UK. Diana Leonard and Maryam Rab discuss data gathered with students from Pakistan studying in the UK (Chapter 6) looking at aspects of gender inequalities that mobility tends to amplify, unless robustly challenged. Juan Carlos Barrón-Pastor (Chapter 7) focuses on class and ethnic inequalities through an examination of different approaches to widening higher education participation for students from indigenous communities in Mexico. He highlights how forms of inclusion that do not pay sufficient attention to the politics of recognition and participation fall short of enhancing equality. All the chapters in Section 2 alert us to the social complexity which frames inequality and new formations of global higher education. Although, as the chapters show, instituting equalities for one group are not generally accompanied by equalities for another, we do see equity and democracy, either at local or at national level, generally enhancing both growth of institutions and the sustainability of reforms, while partial or exclusive forms of very limited equality (for one group at the expense of another) are either the outcome of evading a concern with democracy or the result of privileging a form of growth that elicits criticism. In the chapters in this section that take a long view of these pro-cesses (Carpentier, Barrón-Pastor) it is suggested these partial forms of equity may not be sustainable.

The third part of the book outlines some initiatives to work within higher education for more equality at the global level: Melanie Walker proposes the inclusion of Sen's notion of capa-bilities at the heart of higher education curriculum and activities (Chapter 8). Andrea Abbas and Monica McLean offer an exam-ination of initiatives that seek to develop quality procedures, suggesting how they could contribute to promoting equalities by taking seriously an assessment of different forms of knowledge (Chapter 9). Douglas Bourn and Alun Morgan outline the history of a range of initiatives to take questions of development and sustainability seriously in higher education (Chapter 10), show-ing that wheels do not have to be reinvented in this process. Harry Brighouse (Chapter 11), in navigating between a Marxist and a liberal vision of higher education, proposes how we might draw on ethics to frame individual and collective actions by academics to consider aspects of local and global inequalities as part of everyday professional concerns.

▶ Conclusion

Our aim in this book has been to examine how higher education has both contributed to widening inequalities under conditions of globalization, economic and financial crisis, and how it might contribute to change. We set up a tetralemma posing the question as to whether trade-offs were desirable or feasible between economic growth, sustainability, equity and democracy and whether global formations of higher education institutions, given particular histories, were better positioned working on particular conditions only or on the problem of joint sufficiency. In concluding, we urge a critical reflection on the insights from the chapters that follow. They point up both deeply entrenched inequalities, but also creative initiatives to change in institutions and in the most personal of relationships linked to family intimacy, language or professional vision and identity. Thus, while the institutional structures laid down for global higher education to drive a knowledge economy may have paid scant attention to poverty or inequality, the lived experience of some (but not all) students, staff and administrators is not so cut off from equity, democracy and sustainability.

The conditions of global economic crisis might provide space to think through concrete strategies for particular organizations and forms of institutional relationship in greater depth, but the exigencies of shrinking resources, panic and assertions of national or institutional supremacy may radically undermine this vision. A clear orientation with regard to the central question this book explores might help with some immediate tactical responses.

Addressing the tetralemma requires an engagement with equality, environment, democracy and economy. Such challenges are so big that one may be tempted to ignore them or offer only a partial response, and it is this which may explain some of the slow progress in world meetings and summits which have set out to address the looming environmental crisis, the problem of financial regulation, the profound tragedy of poverty and inequality and the problem of how to engage with undemocratic states. Just as world statesmen and women cannot meet all the challenges simultaneously, neither can the higher education system do this in isolation. However, there are possibilities to address the tetralemma through processes of participation and cooperation. In these, higher education is positioned as a significant space to develop the skills, imagination and collaborations of academic and non-academic actors across global and local boundaries. There may be many different institutional missions and forms of practice, some of them only oriented to partial resolutions of the problems associated with the tetralemma, but what all have in common would be the orientation of public reasoning to developing actual opportunities for all human lives to benefit from economic growth, equity, sustainability and democratic participation globally and locally. Resolving the contradictions of the tetralemma requires not a ratcheting up of the way different elements stand in opposition to each other, but a development of the space where difference can be explored and different solutions evaluated. Global higher education seems uniquely well placed to serve the interests of redressing inequality, enhancing participatory debate and deliberation. But to do this requires higher education institutions recognizing problems of their past and present in order to contribute to ideas of justice for our future.

▶ Notes

* The title draws on a memorable phrase used by Allan Luke in his keynote address to the conference *Learning Together*. A version of this is published in this volume. We borrow his phrasing with thanks.
1. Thanks to Saleem Badat for distilling this insight.

▶ References

Aghion, P. and Williamson, J. G. (1998) *Growth, Inequality, and Globalization: Theory, History, and Policy* (Cambridge: Cambridge University Press).

Allen, W. R., Bonous-Hammarth, M. and Teranashi, T. T. (2006) *Higher Education in a Global Society: Achieving Diversity, Equity and Excellence* (Amsterdam: Emerald Group Publishing).

Altbach, P. G. (2002) 'Perspectives on Internationalising Higher Education', *International Higher Education*, 27, 6–9.

Altbach, P. G. (2004) 'Globalization and the University: Myths and Realities in an Unequal World', *Tertiary Education and Management*, 1, 3–25.

Altbach, P. and Knight, J. (2007) 'The Internationalization of Higher Education: Motivations and Realities', *Journal of Studies in International Education*, 11, 290–305.

Altbach, P. G. and Teichler, U. (2001) 'Internationalization and Exchanges in a Globalized University', *Journal of Studies in International Education*, 5(1), 6.

Amnesty International (2009) *State of the World's Human Rights* (London: Amnesty International). Online at http://report2009.amnesty.org/sites/report2009.amnesty.org/files/documents/air09-en.pdf (accessed June 2009).

Apple, M. W. (2000) 'Between Neoliberalism and Neoconservatism: Education and Conservatism in a Global Context', in Burbules, N. C. and Torres, C. A. (eds) *Globalization and Education: Critical Perspectives* (New York: Routledge).

Archer, L. and Leathwood, C. (2003) 'Identities, Inequalities and Higher Education', in Archer, L., Hutchings, M., and Ross, A. (eds) *Higher Education and Social Class: Issues of Exclusion and Inclusion* (London: Routledge Falmer).

Asare, A. A. (2008) 'The Ghanaian National Reconciliation Commission: Reparation in a Global Age', *The Global South*, 2(2), 31–53.

Atkinson, A. B. and Piketty, T. (2007) *Top Incomes over the Twentieth Century: A Contrast between European and English-Speaking Countries* (Oxford: Oxford University Press).

Australia Education International (2009) *International Student Data* (Canberra: Australia Education International). Online at http://www.aei.gov.au/AEI/MIP/Statistics/Student Enrolment And Visa Statistics/2008/Monthly_Sum_Nov_pdf.pdf (accessed 5 June 2009).

Badat, S. (2006) 'Our Society, Our University, Our Challenges, Our Responsibilities', *Inaugural Address of the Vice Chancellor of Rhodes University*. Online at http://eprints.ru.ac.za/380/1/vcinauguralspeech.pdf (accessed June 2009).

Ball, S. (2010) 'Global Education, Heterarchies and Hybrid Organisations', in Mok, K. H. (ed.) *The Search for New*

Governance of Higher Education in Asia (New York: Palgrave Macmillan).

Bastedo, M. N. and Gumport, P. J. (2003) 'Access to What? Mission Differentiation and Academic Stratification in US Public Higher Education', *Higher Education*, 46(3), 341–359.

Basu, K. (2006) 'Globalization, Poverty and Inequality. What is the Relationship? What Can be Done?', *World Development*, 34(8), 1361–1373.

Becher, T. and Trowler, P. (2001) *Academic Tribes and Territories: Intellectual Enquiry and the Culture of Disciplines*, 2nd Edition (Buckingham: Society for Research into Higher Education and Open University Press).

Bennell, P. and Pearce, T. (2003) 'The Internationalisation of Higher Education: Exporting Education to Developing and Transitional Economies', *International Journal of Educational Development*, 23, 215–232.

Bernasconi, A. (2008) 'Is there a Latin American Model of the University?', *Comparative Education Review*, 52, 27–52.

Bhalla, S. S. (2002) *Imagine There's No Country: Poverty, Inequality, and Growth in the Era of Globalization* (Washington DC: Institute for International Economics).

Bjarnason, S. (2004) 'Borderless Higher Education', in King, R. (ed.) *The University in the Global Age* (Houndsmills: Palgrave Macmillan).

Böhm, A., Davis, T., Meares, D. and Pearce, D. (2002) *Global Student Mobility 2025: Analysis of Future Labour Market Trends and the Demand for International Higher Education* (Sydney: IDP Education Australia).

Bourdieu, P. and Passeron, J. C. (1964) *Les héritiers, les étudiants et la culture* (Paris, Editions de Minuit).

Boyce, J. K. (2002) *The Political Economy of the Environment* (Cheltenham: Edward Elgar Publishing).

Breton, G. and Lambert, M. (2003) *Universities and Globalization: Private Linkages, Public Trust* (Paris: UNESCO).

Brown, C. (2008) *Inequality, Consumer Credit and the Saving Puzzle* (Cheltenham: Edward Elgar Publishing).

Burke, P. J. (2002) *Accessing Education: Effectively Widening Participation* (Stoke-on-Trent: Trentham Books).

Byram, M. and Dervin, F. (2008) *Students, Staff and Academic Mobility in Higher Education* (Newcastle: Cambridge Scholars Publishing).

Callender, C. and Jackson, J. (2005) 'Does the Fear of Debt Deter Students from Higher Education?', *Journal of Social Policy*, 34(4), 509–540.

Cahn, S. M. (ed.) (2002) *The Affirmative Action Debate* (London: Routledge).

Carnoy, M. (2004) *ICT in Education: Possibilities and Challenges*, Inaugural Lecture of the Universitat Oberta de Catalunya 2004–2005 Academic Year, 1–16.

Carpentier, V. (2009) 'Viewpoint: The Credit Crunch and Education: An Historical Perspective from the Kondratiev Cycle', *London Review of Education*, 7(2), 193–196.

Clegg, S., Hudson, A. and Steel, J. (2003) 'The Emperor's New Clothes: Globalisation and E-learning in Higher Education', *British Journal of Sociology of Education*, 24(1), 39–53.

Cloete, N., Maassen, P., Fehnel, R., Moja, T., Gibbon, T. and Perold, H. (eds) (2006) *Transformation in Higher Education: Global Pressures and Local Realities* (Dordrecht: Springer).

Coriat, B., Petit, P. and Schméder, G. (2006) *The Hardship of Nations: Exploring the Paths of Modern Capitalism* (Cheltenham: Edward Elgar).

Currie, J. (1998) 'Introduction', in Currie and Newson, J. (eds) *Universities and Globalisation, Critical Perspectives* (London: Sage).

David, M. (2009) *Transforming Global Higher Education: A Feminist Perspective*, Inaugural Professorial Lecture, Institute of Education, University of London, 24 November.

Deem, R. (2001) 'Globalization, New Managerialism, Academic Capitalism and Entrepreneurialism in Universities; Is the local dimension still important?', *Comparative Education*, 37(1), 7–20.

Delbanco, A. (2009) 'The Universities in Trouble', *New York Review of Books*, 14 May. Online at http://www.nybooks.com/articles/22673 (accessed 4 June 2009).

Duru-Bellat, M., Kieffer, A. and Reimer, D. (2008) 'International Patterns of Social Inequalities in Access to Higher Education in France and Germany', *Journal of Comparative Sociology*, 49, 347–368.

Elliott, L. and Atkinson, D. (2009) *The Gods That Failed: How Blind Faith in Markets Has Cost Us Our Future* (London: The Bodley Head).

Enders, J. and Musselin, C. (2008) 'Back to the Future? The Academic Professions in the 21st Century', in Organisation for Economic Co-operation and Development (ed.) *Higher Education to 2030, Volume 1: Demography* (Paris: Organisation for Economic Co-operation and Development).

Everett, J. (2008) 'Sustainability in Higher Education: Implications for the Disciplines', *Theory and Research in Education*, 6(2), 237–251.

Fielden, J. (2001) 'Markets for "Borderless Education"', *Minerva*, 39(1), 49–62.

Finger, M. (2008) 'Which Governance for Sustainable Development?', in Park, J. and Corna, K. (eds) *The Crisis of Global Economic Governance* (Abingdon: Routledge).

Food and Agriculture Organisation (FAO) (2009) *The State of Food Insecurity in the World* (Roma: Food and Agriculture Organisation). Online at http://www.fao.org/docrep/012/ i0876e/i0876e00.htm (accessed 9 December 2009).

Friedman, B. M. (2005) *The Moral Consequences of Economic Growth* (New York: Knopf).

Galbraith, J. K. (1954) *The Great Crash, 1929* (Boston: Houghton Mifflin).

Garrett, R. (2004) 'Foreign Higher Education Activity in China', *International Higher Education*, 34, 21–24.

Garrett, R. and Verbik, L. (2004) *Transnational Delivery by UK Higher Education, Part 1: Data and Missing Data*, Report, The Observatory on Borderless Higher Education, 18 July.

Gazzola, A. L. and Didriksson, A. (2008) *Trends in Higher Education in Latin America and the Caribbean* (Paris: UNESCO). Online at http://www.cres2008.org/en/info_ documentos.php (accessed 9 December 2009).

Giroux, H. A. and Myrsiades, K. (2001) *Beyond the Corporate University: Culture and Pedagogy in the New Millennium* (Lanham: Rowman & Littlefield).

Gough, S. and Scott, W. (2008) *Higher Education and Sustainable Development* (Abingdon: Routledge).

Green, A. (1997) *Education, Globalisation and the Nation State* (London: Palgrave).

Gunter, B., Rahman, J. and Haiyan, S. (2009) 'Linking Social Development with the Capacity to Carry Debt: Towards an MDG-Consistent Debt Sustainability Concept', *Development Policy Review*, 27(3), 269–286.

Gürüz, K. (2008) *Higher Education and International Student Mobility in the Global Knowledge Economy* (Albany: State University of New York Press).

Hanieh, A. (2009) 'Hierarchies of a Global Market: The South and the Economic Crisis', *Studies in Political Economy*, 83, 61–84.

Healy, G. (2009) 'University of Sydney's Losses "Threaten Operations"', *The Australian*, 21 May 2009. Online at http://www.theaustralian.news.com.au/story/0,25197,25515031-12332,00.html (accessed 9 June 2009).

Held, D. and Kaya, A. (2007) *Global Inequality: Patterns and Explanations* (Cambridge: Polity).

Held, D. and McGrew, A. (2002) *The Global Transformation Reader*, 2nd Edition (Cambridge: Polity).

International Labour Organization (ILO) (2008) *World of Work. Income Inequalities in the Age of Financial Globalization* (Geneva: International Labour Organization).

International Monetary Fund (IMF) (2009) *World Economic Outlook, April 2009* (Washington: International Monetary Fund).

Institute of International Education (IIE) (2009) 'Leading Places of Origin' (New York: Institute of International Education). Online at http://opendoors.iienetwork.org/?p=131534 (accessed 4 June 2009).

International Association of Universities (2003) 'Internationalisation of Higher Education: Trends and Developments Since 1998: Background Paper Prepared By The International Association of Universities', *United Nations Educational, Scientific and Cultural Organization Meeting of Higher Education Partners*, Paris, 23–25 June.

Jagger, S. (2008) 'US Credit Crunch Hits Education as Banks Abandon Student Loans', *The Times*, 31 March 2008. Online at http://business.timesonline.co.uk/tol/business/economics/article3649021.ece (accessed 2 June 2009).

Johnstone, D. B. and Marcucci, P. N. (2007) 'Worldwide Trends in Higher Education Finance', Paper commissioned by UNESCO Forum on Higher Education, Research and Development. Online at http://portal.unesco.org/education/en/files/53752/11842449745Johnstone.pdf/Johnstone.pdf (accessed June 2009).

Jones, E. and Brown, S. (eds) (2007) *Internationalising Higher Education* (London: Routledge).

King, R. (2004) *The University in the Global Age* (Houndsmills: Palgrave Macmillan).

Kogan, M., Bauer, M., and Bleiklie, I. (2006) *Transforming Higher Education: A Comparative Study* (Dordrecht: Springer).

Krugman, P. (2008) 'Inequality and Redistribution', in Serra, N. and Stiglitz, J. E. (eds) *The Washington Consensus Reconsidered* (Oxford: Oxford University Press).

Kubler, J. and DeLuca, C. (2006) *Trends in Academic Recruitment and Retention* (London: Association of Commonwealth Universities).

Kuroda, K. and Shanawez, H. (2003) 'Strategies for Promoting Virtual Higher Education: General Considerations on Africa and Asia', *African and Asian Studies*, 2–4, 565–575.

Kurosawa F. (2004) 'Cosmopolitanism from Below', *European Journal of Sociology*, 45(2), 233–255.

Kuznets, S. (1955) 'Economic Growth and Income Inequality', *The American Economic Review*, 45(1), 1–28.

Larsen, K. and Vincent-Lancrin, S. (2002) 'International Trade in Educational Services: Good or Bad?', *Higher Education Management and Policy*, 14(3), 9–45.

Leathwood, C. (2004) 'A Critique of Institutional Inequalities in Higher Education (or an alternative to hypocrisy for higher educational policy)', *Theory and Research in Education*, 2(1), 31–48.

Leathwood, C. and Read, B. (2009) *Gender and the Changing Face of Higher Education. A Feminized Future?* (Maidenhead: Open University Press).

Lenton, P. (2007) 'Global Value: The Value of UK Education and Training Exports: An Update', Report to the British Council, September. Online at http://www.britishcouncil.org/global_value_-_the_value_of_uk_education_and_training_exports_-_an_update.pdf (accessed 9 June 2009).

Levy, D. C. (2003) *Expanding Higher Education Through Private Growth, Contributions and Challenges*, Report, The Observatory on Borderless Higher Education, 11 January.

Lotz-Sisitka, H. (2004) 'Stories of Transformation', *International Journal of Sustainability in Higher Education*, 5(1), 8–10.

Machado dos Santos, S. (2002) 'Regulation and Quality Assurance in Transnational Education', *Tertiary Education and Management*, 8(2), 97–112.

Mama, A. (2006) 'Pursuing Gender Equality in the African University', *International Journal of African Renaissance Studies*, 1(1), 53–79.

Mama, A. (2007) 'Is it Ethical to Study Africa? Preliminary Thoughts on Scholarship and Freedom', *African Studies Review*, 50(1), 1–26.

Mamdani, M. (2007) *Scholars in the Marketplace: The Dilemmas of Neo-liberal Reform At Makerere University, 1989–2005* (Dakar: Council for the Development of Social Science Research in Africa).

Marginson, S. (2004) 'Australian Higher Education: National and Global Markets', in Teixeira, P., Jongbloed, B., Dill, D. and Amaral, A. (eds) *Markets in Higher Education: Rhetoric or Reality?* (Kluwer, Dordrecht).

Migiro, R. (2008) 'Remarks by the Deputy Secretary General United Nations to meeting of the African Development Forum' (Addis Ababa: African Development Forum). Online at http://www.uneca.org/adfvi/presentations/DSGspeech.pdf (accessed June 2009).

Milojevic, I. (2006) 'Hegemonic and Marginalised Educational Utopias in the Contemporary Western World', in Peters, M. and Freeman-Moir, J. (eds) *Edutopias: New Utopian Thinking in Education* (Rotterdam: Sense Publishers).

Mishkin, F. S. (2006) *The Next Great Globalization* (New Jersey: Princeton).

Mok, K. H. and Lo, Y. W. (2007) 'The Impacts of Neo-Liberalism on China's Higher Education System', *Journal for Critical Education Policy Studies*, 5(1).

Mollis, M. (2006) 'Latin American University Transformation of the 1990s: Altered Identities?', in Forest, F. and Altbach, P. G. (eds) *International Handbook of Higher Education*, Vol. 2. (Dordrecht: Springer).

Morley, L. (2003) *Quality and Power in Higher Education* (Buckingham: Open University Press).

Ninnes, P. and Hellsten, M. (2005) *Internationalizing Higher Education: Critical Explorations of Pedagogy and Policy* (Dordrecht: Springer).

Nussbaum, M. (2006) *Frontiers of Justice* (Harvard: Harvard University Press).

Nzomi, J. (2008) 'Agriculture and Commodity Price Fluctuations, Poverty and Food Insecurity in Kenya', Paper prepared for Colloquium *Integration des marchés et sécurité alimentaire dans les pays en développement*, University of Auvergne. http://www.cerdi.org/Colloque/IMSA2008/papier/Nzomoi.pdf (accessed June 2009).

Organisation for Economic Co-operation and Development (OECD) (2004a) *Internationalisation and Trade in Higher Education: Opportunities and Challenges* (Paris: Organisation for Economic Co-operation and Development).

Organisation for Economic Co-operation and Development (OECD) (2004b) *Quality and Recognition in Higher Education: The Cross-Border Challenge* (Paris: Organisation for Economic Co-operation and Development).

Okereke, C. (2007) *Global Justice and Neoliberal Environmental Governance* (Abingdon: Routledge).

Olssen, M. and Peters, M. A. (2005) 'Neoliberalism, Higher Education and the Knowledge Economy: From the Free Market to Knowledge Capitalism', *Journal of Education Policy*, 20(3), 313–345.

Pak, J. (2008) 'Overseas Education More Attainable for Chinese Students' *Voice of America 28 April 2008*. Online at http://www.voanews.com/english/archive/2008-04/2008-04-28-voa23.cfm?CFID=217189041&CFTOKEN=68285337&jsessionid=003081ab6fd3107672ad2e304b3495536577 (accessed June 2009).

Paton, G. and Irvine, C. (2008) 'Financial Crisis: Oxford University and Audit Commission Fall Victims to the Banks', *Daily Telegraph*. Online at http://www.telegraph.co.uk/finance/financetopics/financialcrisis/3206491/Financial-crisis-Oxford-University-and-Audit-Commission-fall-victim-to-banks.html (accessed 9 June 2009).

Persson, T. and Tabellini, G. (2006) 'Democracy and Development: The Devil in the Details', *The American Economic Review*, 96(2), 319–324.

Peters, M. and Freeman-Moir, J. (2006) *Edutopias: New Utopian Thinking in Education* (Rotterdam: Sense Publishers).

Pieterse, N. (2006) 'Emancipatory Cosmopolitanism: Towards an Agenda', *Development and Change*, 37, 1247–1257.

Reay, D., David, M. and Ball, S. (2005) *Degrees of Choice: Class, Race, Gender and Higher Education* (Stoke-on-Trent: Trentham Books).

Rhoads, R. A. and Torres, C. A. (eds) (2006) *The University, State and Market. The Political Economy of Globalization in the Americas* (Stanford: Stanford University Press).

Robbins, L. (1963) *Report of the Committee on Higher Education* (London: Her Majesty's Stationary Office).

Robertson, S. L. (2006) 'Globalisation, GATS and Trading in Education Services', in Kallo, J. and Rinne, R. (eds) *Suprana- tional Regimes and National Education Policies: Encountering Challenge* (Helsinki: Finnish Education Research Association).

Rosenau, J. N. (2005) 'Globalization and Governance: Bleak Prospects for Sustainability', in Pfaller, A. and Lerch, M. (eds) *Challenges of Globalization: New Trends in International Politics and Society* (New York: Transaction Publishers).

Ross, M. (2006) 'Is Democracy Good for the Poor?', *American Journal of Political Science*, 50(4), 860–874.

Salmi, J. (2002) *Constructing Knowledge Societies: New Challenges for Tertiary Education* (Washington: World Bank).

Scoones, I. (2009) 'Livelihoods Perspectives and Rural Develop- ment', *Journal of Peasant Studies*, 36(1), 171–196.

Scott, P. (ed.) (1998) *The Globalization of Higher Education* (Buckingham: Society for Research into Higher Education and Open University Press).

Sen, A. (2009) *The Idea of Justice* (London: Allen Lane).

Shen, H. and Ziderman, A. (2009) 'Student Loans Repayment and Recovery: International Comparisons', *Higher Education*, 57(3), 315–333.

Sidhu, R. (2006) *Universities and Globalization: To Market, to Market* (Mahwah, NJ: Lawrence Erlbaum).

Simpson, J. S. (2003) *I Have Been Waiting: Race and U.S. Higher Education* (Toronto: University of Toronto Press).

Sinha, S. and Srivastava, R. S. (2008) 'Inclusiveness and Access of Social Groups to Higher Education', in University Grants Commission (ed.) *Higher Education in India: Issues Related to Expansion, Inclusiveness, Quality and Finance* (New Delhi: University Grants Commission).

Slaughter, S. and Leslie, L. L. (1999) *Academic Capitalism: Pol- itics, Policies, and the Entrepreneurial University* (Baltimore, MD: Johns Hopkins University Press).

Smith, H. (2009) 'The Midas Touch Eludes Harvard', *The Guardian*, 10 March. Online at http://www.guardian.co. uk/education/2009/mar/10/harvard-endowment-financial- reserves (accessed 9 June 2009).

Stiglitz, J. E. (2005) 'The Ethical Economist', *Foreign Affairs, Council on Foreign Relations.* Online at http://

www.foreignaffairs.com/articles/61208/joseph-e-stiglitz/ the-ethical-economist (accessed 9 June 2009).

Stiglitz, J. E. (2002) *Globalization and Its Discontents* (New York: W.W. Norton and Co).

Tomlinson, S. (2003) 'Globalisation, Race and Education: Continuity and Change', *Journal of Educational Change*, 4, 213–230.

Tysome, T. (2007) 'UK's Foreign Legion Set to Continue', *Times Higher Education*, 15 June 2007. Online at http://www. timeshighereducation.co.uk/story.asp?storycode=209325 (accessed 9 June 2009).

UCAS (2007) 'University and College Applications up by 6.4% for 2007' (London: UCAS), 14 February 2007. Online at http://www.ucas.com/about_us/media_enquiries/media_ releases/2007/2007-02-14 (accessed 9 June 2009).

UK Higher Education International Unit (UKHEIU) (2009) *International Student Recruitment* (London: Universities UK) http://www.international.ac.uk/statistics/international_ student_recruitment.cfm (accessed 2 June).

UNESCO (1999) *Statistical Yearbook* (Paris: UNESCO).

UNESCO (2007) *Global Education Digest* (Paris: UNESCO).

UNESCO (2008) *Global Education Digest* (Paris: UNESCO).

UNESCO (2009) *Global Monitoring Report* (Paris: UNESCO).

United Nations (2009a) *The World Economic Situation and Prospects* (New York: United Nations).

United Nations (2009b) *Millennium Development Goals Report* (New York: United Nations).

Universities UK International Unit (2009) *Statistics on Student Recruitment* (London: Universities UK International Unit) http://www.international.ac.uk/statistics/international_ student_recruitment.cfm (accessed June 2009).

Ward, H. (2008) 'Liberal Democracy and Sustainability', *Environmental Politics*, 17(3), 386–409.

Welch, A. (2007) 'Governance Issues in South East Asian Higher Education: Finance, Devolution and Transparency in the Global Era', *Asia Pacific Journal of Education*, 27(3), 237–253.

Williams, G. (2008) *Struggles for an Alternative Globalization* (Farnham: Ashgate).

Woodward, D. and Ross, K. (2000) *Managing Equal Opportunities in Higher Education: A Guide to Understanding and Action* (Buckingham: The Society for Research into Higher Education and Open University).

Part 1
Mapping Inequalities Conceptually

1 Educating the Other: Standpoint and Theory in the 'Internationalization' of Higher Education

Allan Luke

▶ Standpoint

How adequate are current theoretical standpoints, tools, and categories for explaining the flows of international students to Anglo/American/European universities? There is a growing literature on the internationalization of higher education, well represented in this volume. This includes critical policy analyses that attempt to outline the linkages between state, economy, and university institutional strategies (Mok, 2007), the analysis of marketing discourses and strategies (Sidhu, 2003; Mok and Tan, 2004), studies of digital teaching and learning in offshore and external university studies by international students (Doherty, 2006), second language and academic writing studies (Kubota, 2003), and a vast qualitative literature on the cultural and learning experiences of international students and their teachers in the West (Singh and Doherty, 2004; Kettle, 2005, 2007; Marginson et al., 2010). Taken together, this work has begun to provide us with a rich analytic and empirical description of the internationalization of universities in the context of cultural globalization and, indeed, economic crisis.

This essay takes a different analytic tack and historical standpoint to the study of them and us, insiders and outsiders (cf. Foley et al., 2001), in the internationalization of education. It is based on my experience as a senior academic of Chinese ancestry working the field from 'both sides' from 1995 to 2005 – first, as head of an Australian Faculty of Education extending its reach into Asian education, and second, as a member of a senior management team of a leading East Asian university negotiating bilateral agreements with UK, US, and Australian institutions. Throughout, it reflects upon the (my)optics of 'being Asian' in a White-dominated Western university system – and the insider knowledge of 'being Asian' in a Han Chinese-dominated East Asian system (Ang, 2002; Luke, 2009a, 2009b, 2010).

My expository case is that the recent history of Australian involvement in Asia via internationalization has yielded: (1) the emergence of a complex, chaotic, and unpredictable *edubusiness*, whose prioritization of the financial 'bottom line' has supplanted clear normative educational and, indeed, overtly ideological intents; and (2) the construction, along the way, of different versions or 'namings' of the international Others of international student cohorts. This, I argue, distinguishes the current internationalization of universities from that of colonial and Cold War eras.

Yet even as these students and their institutions are structurally positioned, constructed, and reconstructed in this new political economy of higher education, there is ample evidence of their position taking and agency. This is not a one way street of ideological indoctrination, marginalization, or exploitation – but rather an archetypal instance of the push/pull dialectics of cultural and economic globalization (Luke and Luke, 1999; Rizvi, 2000). To make the narrative case, I describe my experience in Australia and Asia, deliberately shifting the optics and standpoint of this piece. First, I raise the class, regional, and cultural interests at work in universities' engagement with Asia – outlining the complex 'differences within difference' (Luke and Luke, 1999) that are brought into play in the development of programs and the relative agency of Asian institutions and students in setting the stage for international programs. Second, I describe how UK, US, and Australian international marketization appears to many academics working in East Asian universities and governments. This is, then, a *double take* on internationalization, with comparative cases of: (1) how our current approaches conceptualize and define the Other of international education; and, (2) how the East Asian Other has come to view the marketing behaviour of Western universities. It is an attempt to flip the dialectics of postcolonial and critical analysis of internationalization by asking how the Other is constructing and defining 'Us'.

Across three decades of my work as an academic in Canada, Australia, and Singapore – there has been one constant. Chinese-American by birth, I have always been a visible 'person of colour' within White-dominated, Anglo-European institutions. My own work has been on the sociology of curriculum and literacy in schools, focusing on issues of social justice and equity, marginalization, and exclusion. As much as minority status within such institutions confers structural positioning and, at times, exclusion – there are instances where White-dominated institutions find it necessary to call upon its Others for strategic institutional purposes. The current press for internationalization is a case in point.

Yet second wave feminist work and critical race theory offer three salient insights about the Anglo/European university: (1) that governance lays principally in and works through the practices of patriarchal masculinity; (2) that these systems of governance are principally institutional representations of White/Anglo/European standpoint; and (3) that the unmarked norm of Western rationality provides a 'naturalizing' device for its regulation of Others of all sorts and kinds (e.g., Brooks and McKinnon, 2001; C. Luke, 2001, 2005). I raise these issues around the optics of universities, then, from yet another oscillating position of Otherness. My intention here is to ask: Who is theorizing and positioning whom, on what grounds, with what historical precedents, and with what educational and material consequences for students, teachers, researchers, and university administrators, as well as for their institutions, communities, and nation states.

▶ **Colonization, aid, and development**

Travelling from 'home' to the North/West for informal and formal cultural and political education has a distinguished and ambiguous history (Robertson et al., 1994). The education of the cultural, linguistic, and racial Other in Anglo/European higher education systems is not a new phenomenon. Its most notable historical precedents were, of course, extensions of the project of colonialism. From the eighteenth to the early twentieth century, British, French, and other European universities established training grounds for colonial civil servants, teachers, the military, missionaries, and, later, technical experts (Pennycook, 1998). The expectation was that they would return to colonies with the requisite bodily disposition, cultural traits, linguistic facility, and technical expertise to represent empire and, where needed, to build colonial infrastructure and operate its institutions. To augment this, colonial universities were established in key outposts, extending the training reach of empire.

In the last century, the Soviet Union and China provided ideological and technological training to nationals from emergent socialist and communist countries in Eastern Europe, Asia, Africa, and the Americas, with the aim of the spread of political ideology and revolutionary consciousness. The United States, likewise, offered further study to expatriates from client states, at times through academic and non-governmental organizations (e.g., Fulbright, Hoover). There were instances where security agencies like the CIA participated in the sponsorship and movement of foreign government officials, intellectuals, military, and technical experts to American study (Reisch, 2005).[1]

In the post-war period, the cross border flows of 'international' students were undertaken principally under the auspices of aid and development funding (Altbach, 1998). Australia's Colombo Plan, the US Fulbright system, and other aid/training models gave scholars and leaders from what was then termed the 'developing' world an opportunity to undertake higher degree studies in major Western universities. While their stated rationale was to improve human capital and intercultural exchange, they were a bid to extend diplomatic and political, cultural and corporate influence internationally. Over the last decade, Australian government officials have consistently raised the effects of the Colombo Plan, noting which East Asia government ministers and corporate leaders received postgraduate training in Australia. The diverse personal, professional and cultural impacts of study abroad on such students are well documented.[2]

Much of the foregoing account is based on specific historical centre/margin political, economic, and military relationships. The idiosyncratic aims and good intentions of academic staff and departments aside, universities have served the extension of state and corporate power through the international dissemination of knowledge, technical expertise, lingua franca, and, indeed, particular forms of ideological disposition (Spring, 1998; Graham et al., 2007). Yet the question of educational effects and consequences is a different matter. As the scholarship and writings, biographies and accounts of those intellectuals and students who travelled to the Anglo/Eurocentric educational centre attest, the educational effects and social consequences of this training have not always aligned with originating state regional geopolitical and economic intents. That is, we find amongst a broad spectrum of political leaders from Nehru to Lee Kwan Yew, and critical intellectuals and artists from Spivak to Ghosh, instances where contact with canonical Western knowledge and culture generated alterior, critical and radical knowledge and practice. There is an as yet emergent history being written on the engagement of Maori, Aborigines, and other indigenous peoples with university education, raising equally vexed questions around intercultural travel, border crossing, and vernacular cultural effects.[3] Yet it is axiomatic that the ideologies of particular trainings, however hegemonic, do not necessarily yield the self-same reproduction of knowledge. In any era, student uptake, use, and transformation of educationally acquired knowledge is, at best, an empirical question and, in other instances, an example of Foucault's (1982) principle of the local unpredictability of discourse at work.

▶ Edubusiness

While the foregoing offers a plausible account of flows of international students East/West, North/South in colonial and neocolonial, hot and cold war conditions, it cannot offer a comprehensive explanation of current contexts. This is in part due to the diminished funding and neoliberal governance structures that have progressively set the context for the internationalization of universities over two decades (Marginson and Considine, 2000). Specifically, while the recruitment and training of international students served and serves the interests of ideological and cultural incorporation by nation states, and the production of specialized technical expertise for globalizing industry – its major function in many American and Commonwealth universities now is revenue generation in the face of declining state and endowment funding.

The rhetoric of universities and governments aside, over the past two decades a complex and chaotic market has been established. Australian, UK, and New Zealand universities currently use overseas student income to cross-subsidize the undergraduate and postgraduate education of domestic students. Further, there has been a major expansion of externally delivered programs via online offerings, offshore campuses, and other modes of distance education, with fierce competition for market share in Asia and the Middle East. This has led to more complicated and diverse student bodies – with university staff encountering new and unprecedented 'aliens': heterogeneous in cultural history and lingua franca, religion and regional, social class and community affiliations, credentials and training histories, background knowledge schemata and motivation structures, and unprecedented professional pathways through globalizing economies.

This is nothing less than a radical change in campus cultural demographics, interactional and educational dynamics – with traditional 'Sandstone' universities like Queensland and Sydney hitting targets of 30 per cent and regional universities like Central Queensland peaking at 45 per cent international students in recent years. All of these institutions historically have evolved as virtual White, English-speaking monocultures, with historically minor cohorts of Aboriginal, Torres Strait Islander, and first-generation Asian and Middle Eastern migrant students.

Australian international education has become a 15 billion dollar 'export' industry, its second largest export industry (Gillard, 2009). Between 1995 and 2006, overall numbers of international students rose from 57,000 to 180,000 (Australian Education International, 2009). This amounts to a shift from 8.4 per cent to 20 per cent of total enrolment, accounting a growth in university revenue from 5.9 per cent to 30 per cent. The number of Chinese students in the post-Tiananmen period, when visas were embargoed centrally by the Chinese government, has expanded from 1500 to 46,000; student flows from the Middle East and India have consistently grown. This expansion has paralleled progressively declining per capita federal funding for Australian students, a matter currently under review by the Labor federal government.

This *international education for profit model* is the principal driver in the current equation – superseding ideological and political, cultural, and economic rationales. Revenue appears to have trumped ideology and culture (Graham et al., 2007). The result is a complex mix of student demographic and cultural variables, with new forms of Otherness entering the Western academy. While governments and universities document the increasing diversity of countries of origin, gender, level, and courses – there is little aggregate data on the socioeconomic, ethnic, religious characteristics of student cohorts, as is available in national schooling data. This massive expansion of overall numbers of international students is a key element of the structural reorganization of universities, a collateral effect of the shift towards technocratic corporatism that began in Australia under the Hawke Labor government in 1988.

During the expansion of international programs, many universities have undergone a wilful deskilling of policy on internationalization. Australian universities in the 1990s moved into a *de facto internationalization as marketization model* – with sophisticated branding, marketing, and advertising, at times assisted by government and statutory agencies. This extended into co-marketing, co-development, and corporate relationships with other countries' universities and governments, and the extensive use of private consultants as marketing and recruitment agents and, in instances, subcontractors in academic recruitment, course administration, and teaching.

There was a failure to include humanities and social science researchers with expertise on the specific countries, regions, and populations that were to be 'internationalized'. Linguists, anthropologists, historians, sociologists, and educationists with relevant knowledge of the country/region were rarely drawn into strategic and operational decisions. Practically, this has entailed an internationalization strategy at the University and Faculty/School level conceived and implemented by higher education managers. This is a distinctive genus of *homo academicus*, typically but not always, former academics from various cognate fields with little specialist expertise on the countries or markets in question. Several Australian universities have filled positions with marketing and public relations professionals with little or no academic teaching and research experience. The failure of university managers to engage with area experts who could advise on the political and cultural context, institutional dynamics, and histories of 'markets' has been parochial and frustrating. There are, of course, exceptions, and in the past 5 years there has been an increasing push to use academic staff who have ethnic, family, and training links to Asia to recruit and market. This has also been an increasing engagement by university planners of critical policy analyses of internationalization – following on from the work of Fazal Rizvi at RMIT University.[4]

But the separation of both 'strategy' and 'marketing' from substantive academic knowledge about the human subjects and contexts involved, akin to Veblen's (1904/1978) separation of 'business' from 'industry', continues. The result is a separation of expertise from both the conception and execution of university policy. Even if judged on its own business terms, to date this approach has led to widely publicized miscalculations in recruitment incentives, off-shore campus development, campus student support infrastructure, curriculum content, and program content delivery.

▶ Psychologizing and culturalizing the Other

These problems have been highlighted in media reports of plagiarism and soft marking, lowered admissions standards, unreliable program quality, credential inflation, and accusations of campus and community racism and discrimination. In response, the Australian and UK governments have established quality audits, ethical guidelines, and operating standards for internationalization. Accordingly, universities have begun rebuilding infrastructure to support what has become a central component of their operations. Many have drawn upon the aforementioned research literature on international student experience.

In her study of international students studying at the University of Queensland, Margaret Kettle (2007) describes three different discourses on international students in Australian universities. The first wave of work, begun in the late 1980s, constructs a version of the Asian international student via discourses of 'lack': specifically, of English language fluency, of specialized academic writing proficiency, and of critical analytic capacity.

In many universities, there were reports of silence and reticence in face-to-face seminars, speech, and writing problems. Many lecturers attributed this to rote learning styles. The stereotype was aptly expressed in the title of a popular book written by a Singaporean scholar: *Can Asians Think?* (Mahbubani, 2006). The first wave of explanation of internationalization thus created a new deficit subject within the Western university – a new minority – precisely when these same institutions faced increased 'market share' of international students and demonstrably inadequate institutional infrastructure and curricular/ pedagogic flexibility.

By the mid-1990s, educational psychologists began to document distinctive cultural approaches to learning that students brought to Australia (e.g., Volet and Renshaw, 1996). This mirrored the parallel shift in explanation of cultural and linguistic minority failure in US and UK schooling from deficit to cultural models, with widely cited work on Asian 'learning styles' from educational psychologists. Case studies and surveys described the difficult everyday transitions in lifestyle, food and dress, institutional procedures and expectations, religious practice, and face-to-face interactional protocols experienced by Asian students studying in Australia. This marked a shift from 'deficit' to 'difference' explanations of international student learning (Kettle, 2007), in effect a move *from psychologization to culturalization of the Other.* This shift has contributed to a strengthening of reception and support infrastructure, improved second language and academic writing support, an emergent debate amongst academics on whether and how to alter curriculum content and pedagogic approach, and an archetypal 'celebratory' approach to cultural diversity. In short, the higher education sector moved to deal with diversity and Otherness precisely as the secular school systems had: embracing a stated rationale and philosophy of liberal multiculturalism.

The third wave of research on international students identified by Kettle is relevant to this volume and the task at hand. Drawing directly from feminist and postcolonial theory, students' lives and experiences were documented and explained in terms of linguistic and cultural marginality. Issues of silence, subjectivity and identity, discrimination, and racism were tabled (e.g., Kubota, 2001; Kettle, 2005). In instances, this led to calls for culturally appropriate approaches to recruitment and support, pedagogy, and curriculum in university programs. The move reconceptualized the international student as marginal, oppressed, and diasporic – adopting concepts of resistance, negotiation, and empowerment from Western discourses of critical educational studies.

Explanations of international students' experience have directly and indirectly drawn on explanatory models from research on cultural and ethnic minorities in mainstream schooling. As Kettle (2007) shows, there is a gradual and subtle borrowing from discourses on migrant, indigenous, and linguistic minority achievement and failure in schools by higher education researchers.[5] But the positioning of cultural and linguistic minorities in mainstream educational systems is closely linked to the intergenerational reproduction of equality and inequality within a specific national or regional political economy. Intersections with social class are key to explaining relative success and failure, and differential treatment and experience by race, culture, and language. By contrast, international students – although visibly culturally Other in Western universities – come from diverse but often middle and upper social class backgrounds, with varied educational histories, and equally diverse motivation, aspirations, and goal structures. They are volitional educational participants. In this regard, a simple culturalization model risks creating a new wave of stereotypes.

We can trace the development, then, of the expansion of international education in Western universities to structural changes in the domestic funding of universities in the UK, Australia, New Zealand, and, more recently, Canada. The marketization of higher education has turned university study for overseas students into a fee-for-service transaction. This has redefined the student as client and the lecturer as service-provider. Increased numbers of cultural and linguistic Others have raised significant practical and educational issues on Australian and UK campuses. The result has been a proliferation of studies of 'overseas' students which, as Kettle (2007) argues, have tended to construct and view international students using vocabulary and explanatory paradigms from educational research on the schooling of cultural minorities.

The Western academy appears to have created a new educational phenomenon for which it lacks explanatory frameworks. Perhaps a shift of optics is in order.

▶ An outsider narrative: But don't exploit the Thai...

In the mid-1990s, I began negotiations with the Rajabhat Institutes, the second tier of 36 teacher training and community colleges in Thailand. Later to achieve 'university' status, many were anchored in provincial and regional centres, chartered to the service of local institutions and communities. I was the newly appointed Dean of a faculty of education that was, by Australian standards, a high status academic unit. The beneficiary of quality 'walk-in' graduate students, it had never systematically engaged with international recruitment. I was given the task of managing a 1.5 million dollar accrued operating debt, a per capita student funding formula in progressive decline, declining graduate teacher training enrolments and a pending generational shift in academic staff. Our involvement with Thailand, Singapore, China, India, and other 'markets', then, was driven as much by economic motives as it might have been by any altruistic engagement with these countries and their educational systems. We were to 'internationalize' as part of a larger university strategic policy.

My initial negotiations to conduct an onshore/offshore graduate program for Rajabhat lecturers took 6 months and successive trips. At the time, my academic work drew on critical and postcolonial theory. Several colleagues and I saw this as an opportunity to expand the scope and relevance of our faculty's research and teaching, directly addressing issues of cultural and economic globalization, cosmopolitanism, and intercultural communication. I was aware of the aforementioned history of internationalization and had supervised PhD students from China, Fiji, Samoa, and Singapore. That supervision foregrounded the conflict between Western 'critical' analyses of education system and the system mandates, scholarship conditions and ideological constraints of students from other countries, cultures and systems. In the late 1980s, several Chinese PhD students had assured me that they could now undertake critical analyses of the People's Republic of China educational system with political impunity. They returned after Tiananmen, facing new constraints on their work as academics.[6]

As a Western-trained, 'critical' educational researcher on the education of working class, and cultural and linguistic minorities in Australia, Canada, and the US, Chinese-American by birth – I considered myself sensitive to international students' issues. I also believed that many paradigmatic tools and approaches to 'critical' educational research were of universal relevance.

Early on, a sympathetic colleague sent me off with the reminder: 'Don't exploit the Thai'. Many of us working in East Asia recognized that the history of colonization, aid, and development had created persisting centre/margin relationships and tensions. To avoid a naïve replication of neocolonial East/West/North/South knowledge relations, our principal concern was to negotiate program content, theses topics, and instruction so that they would optimally benefit local institutions and communities. In hindsight, there were several assumptions at work in his cautionary comments. First, the enjoinder to 'not exploit' was predicated on particular binary power relationships, that is, that we and other Western universities were in the position to exploit. Second, the notion of the 'Thai' as a homogeneous people, culture, social class, and history was at best reductive and at worst, a fundamental misconstrual of the complex politics of difference we would encounter. This remains an unresolved issue in the deployment of Freirian 'point of decolonisation' theory (A. Luke, 2005). Its propensity for binary opposition (e.g., oppressor/oppressed, teacher/student), however accurate a portrayal of conditions of colonization and decolonization, can obscure the complex cultural, linguistic, and historical 'differences within difference' at play in any given social field.

I was mentored by a senior Thai academic, president of one of the colleges, and we embarked on weeks of college tours, spending hours with their staff and students, discussing politics, history, and their institutional goals. We did business over food. During one extended visit, the world began to come apart around us – with the 1997 East Asian economic crash. For my Thai colleagues, it meant severe cutbacks in their operating budgets, job losses, currency devaluation, and a visible destabilization of government. For us, it merely ramped up the competition for scarce Asian revenue.

My understanding of Thailand began to open on several fronts, including a broader understanding of its history and cultural demographics. In terms of higher education, I focused specifically on the hierarchical structure of the university and tertiary education system in Thailand. As in other countries, different institutions were serving distinctive segments of the social class hierarchy and urban/regional population. Hence, involvement with 'second tier' institutions translated into a focus on issues of community engagement, poverty amelioration, teacher education, and local action research-based projects.

Yet the 'reforms' of East Asian tertiary institutions, and the educational content of programs for teacher education that they sought, were driven by conditions placed upon loans by the International Monetary Fund/World Bank, and followed educational program guidelines of the Asian Development Bank and other transnational organizations. Hence, several colleges requested that we provide programs on standardized assessment, accountability systems, school-based management, outcomes-based curriculum, and quality assurance systems. This tension between our normative sense of what was to be done and Thai system imperatives led to difficult negotiations around program and thesis content.

We enrolled 20 students in diploma upgrading and PhD programmes with rotating seminars in Australia and Thailand. Our doctoral completion rate over a 10-year period was 95 per cent, but it required sustained commitment from staff and students. Ironically, while it solved an immediate cash flow problem, with around 12,000 AUD per student flowing into the faculty budget – the real financial and staff costs of extended supervision, second language, and staff travel were substantial and far in excess of fee profits. Nonetheless, the program generated new knowledge, including theses and a series of co-authored articles by Thai students and their supervisors on topics of relevance to the reform of Thai education. Several of our Thai doctoral graduates went on to introduce qualitative research models, theories of globalization, and new pedagogical approaches to their teacher trainees and graduate students.

There were multiple lessons for all. The obvious practical, administrative lesson was that the production of substantial educational outcomes required sustained investment and commitment at all levels, from students, academic staff, and from the university. To do the educational work properly required investment far in excess of ostensible university profits – and sustained institutional commitment beyond quadrennial funding cycles and Deans' terms of appointment. Yet gauging the real and substantive human, fiscal and intellectual investment required for an educationally defensible program was, at the time, impossible.

'Did we exploit the Thai?' was the wrong question. It was predicated on and subliminally reproduced the assumption that colonial centre/margin relationships held – that we, with our paltry budget, limited experience, staff resources, and institutional brand, regardless of our good intentions – were in a position of power to 'exploit'. Further, it treated Thailand as a generic culture, market, and education system – with little understanding of the complex and, at times, difficult tensions within Thai society and institutions. In other words, the 'Don't exploit' enjoinder required a massification of the complexities of Thai culture and history, and a flattening out of hierarchical relations of power within Thai society.

As I learned more about the specific political economic, institutional, and educational context, the dialectical relationship between 'us' and 'them' in the process of internationalization shifted, returning us full circle to the sociological question of: *Whose interests are being served?* Once we grasped more about the histories and power relations of the institutions and students we were working with, it became obvious that we were serving particular social class-based, cultural, regional, and political institutions in Thailand. In the context of edubusiness, further, these institutions had great leverage in making decisions about which Australian programs, partners, and institutions would serve their interests. The program was far from optimal, with mixed results. But at the least we and our Thai institutional colleagues and students had an explicit and ongoing dialogue about whose interests were at play. Insofar as all educational programs operate from stated and unstated normative agendas, an analysis of whose material and ideological interests are at play – however delimited by optics and speaking position – is the minimal requirement for any university engagement with the Other.

▶ An insider narrative: The other side of the table

In 2003, I left Australia to take a position as Dean/Director of a Singapore government-funded educational research centre.

I moved to the other side of the table, meeting with UK, Australian, and US academics interested in bilateral university developments that ranged from collaborative research and higher degree programs, to recruitment of staff and prospective postgraduate students.

This was a radically different culture of university governance and practice. The level of investment and infrastructure development was substantial. Our charter was to develop a research centre on schooling with a 5 year, 49 million (SNG) grant from the government. On a per capita basis, this constitutes an investment of ten times that of agglomerated UK-, Canadian- and Australian-funded research. Comparable developments were occurring in biotechnology, business and commerce, and digital technology in Hong Kong and China, which were reinvesting balance-of-trade surpluses in educational infrastructure. While Australia and the UK were seeking Asian markets to compensate for decreased government funding, the Singapore government was investing at all levels. For example, per capita funding for undergraduate teacher education was three times that of Australian universities. A key element of the East Asian strategy was a reverse 'brain drain' – with active recruitment of overseas 'expatriates', with a strong emphasis in China, Hong Kong, and Singapore on securing the services of senior academics of overseas-Chinese backgrounds. I was part of that global flow.

I represented university management in various closed meetings with senior staff from ranking US, UK, and Australian institutions, who had come to discuss graduate student recruitment, joint research projects and the cooperative delivery of 'offshore' programs in other Asian countries. Many of these encounters were collegial, with robust and honest exchanges of ideas. Yet others quickly lapsed into full-blown marketing pitches, with overtones of moral and cultural condescension. Sitting in boardrooms and the restaurants of five star hotels, I was told that 'Asian students all like the residential colleges', that 'we would accommodate their problems with written English' (many Singaporean students and researchers have demonstrably higher levels of English written competence than Australian and UK counterparts) and that 'we know the students will have trouble with critical and independent thinking'. In another incident, hopefully one of mistaken identity, I was encouraged to enrol in a postgraduate program.

I took these matters back to the boardroom with senior Singaporean colleagues, stating my own moral and political outrage over such treatment. Their advice: simply, smile, tell them we'll be in touch and put them back on the plane – we know which universities rank where, and what they have to offer. The latter was an understatement. The competitive educational environment in Asia has generated a working knowledge of university ranking systems (e.g., *Shanghai Jiao Tong*), the UK, Australian, and Canadian research rankings exercises and universities' field-by-field strengths and weaknesses.

On one instance I commented to officials of the poor quality of an approved offshore program offered by an Australian university – to be told that all were aware of this, and that this institution was providing relatively cheap training for a segment of the tertiary cohort that could not be served domestically. The market knowledge extended to upper and middle class parents, who choose from various publications that rank and cost universities by Departments, Schools, and Faculties.

Complicating this process was the over proliferation of UK, US, Australian, and Canadian degrees across Asia, creating the conditions for credential inflation. In the mid-1990s, the Hong Kong government established an English language requirement for teachers. I was secured as an academic consultant to review teachers' credentials to determine if they represented or guaranteed sufficient English fluency and literacy to meet the new benchmark. I was handed files comprising a bewildering thicket of degrees, diplomas, and certificates with transcripts – some from well-known, reputable universities, others from obscure or unknown sources. It was difficult to discern if their courses had involved residence in another country, online delivery, offshore delivery, course-notes, or the delivery by offshore subcontractors and client institutions. This has led to partial sanctions against specific university degrees by governments and employers. Specific undergraduate degrees are not recognized for government hiring and promotion in Hong Kong and Singapore.

How, then, does the East Asian Other view the marketization of Australian education? As noted, the geopolitical and economic shift of capital flows towards Asia has led to the rapid growth of educational infrastructure and capacity. The intention of many major East Asian universities is to shift the historic centre/margin relationships in the production of knowledge. This serves both strategic geopolitical and economic purposes, with the advanced technology and human capital requisites of expanding Asian economies (Koh, 2003; Mok and Tan, 2007). But a further aim, stated in the Singaporean government's higher education strategy for the past decade, is to fully internationalize its universities – in effect, drawing quality international students and researchers from China, India, Australia, and the UK. Though in its early stages, such a policy marks a turning of the tables of university internationalization, bidding for nothing less than a shift in flows of university-based knowledge/power from West to East.

▶ Whose market will decide?

I began this chapter with a dry, detached account of internationalization of Anglo/European universities, tracing its evolution from political and cultural to economic practice. University authorities and higher education researchers have been suitably naïve about their engagement with the Other, establishing a market with inadequate engagement with the dynamics of national and regional contexts, and, after the students have arrived, drawing explanatory metaphors from research on the schooling of cultural and linguistic minorities. Despite post-Bologna attempts on all sides at regulation, the effect of this expansion has been a chaotic market, with a host of intended and unintended effects. Regardless of its effects on the balance sheets of academic departments and universities, and the stirring testimonials of alumni – Western universities have managed to create a rhizomatic thicket of educational products, paper credentials, and trainings, some coherent and effective, others indecipherable in quality and content.

There are, of course, attempts to superimpose different normative rationales on this development – arguing that as a result universities and their staff are more cosmopolitan, multicultural, and intercultural and more inclined to research and teach about other cultural and national settings. The latter is particularly important, given the current shifts in economic and geopolitical power to China, India, and East Asia. We could ask: How could it be otherwise when a third of your overall student body is visibly different from what was previously a middle and upper class White norm? My view as a participant in the Australian expansion was that these were largely collateral, unintended, and post hoc effects. The result is a range of formal and informal relations with other countries, their institutions, and students – and ever increasing numbers of 'providers' and 'clients' in a transnational educational marketplace of highly variable quality.

There is, simply, no singular Other of the international student or the Chinese student or the Muslim student or the ESL student in our midst. New theoretical models and analytic lenses are in order, many on offer in this volume. These can be built on an understanding and engagement with the complex intersections of social class, gender, cultural, and linguistic differences, students' diverse motivations, and their professional aspirations – mindful of the limits of the situated optics of Anglo/European academics and academies. This is hardly a novel approach. But it has been largely neglected by university administrators, managers and marketers who continue to drive internationalization. Yet my aim here is not to score easy academic or scholarly 'points' against university corporatism. This is not simply a matter of scholarly, political, or cultural rectitude as a redress for histories of colonization and decolonization, aid and trade. There are immediate practical implications for universities' strategic planning, for support infrastructure and curriculum, for those university staff who, rightly, continue to search for a principled rationale for their work, and indeed for those students who travel across borders for education and training, knowledge and credentials.

Western universities' attempts to educate the Other have been limited by an institutionalized Eurocentric myoptics, a standpoint which they remain largely unable to name or understand. Yet if we turn the tables, what is apparent is that the Other is busy studying, theorizing, and analysing our actions, our programs, our constructions of them, and ourselves. Where this is the case, they readily see through our financial motivations, our lack of substantive cultural and intellectual engagement and our limited local and regional knowledge. In the context of the current economic crisis, their institutions are positioning themselves to reclaim these markets – and thereby alter the flows of internationalization of training, knowledge, and scholarship in their countries' interests.

▶ A postscript

I recently spoke with a senior White academic colleague who was considering taking a leadership position in a major East Asian university. He described his motivations and his perspectives, all sincere and altruistic. He intended to engage with and respect 'the culture' during his sojourn, learning the language, customs and enjoying the hospitality of colleagues and students. I raised the question: 'Can you identify all the different kinds and classes of Chinese around you?' His response was: 'What do you mean?' I mentioned the contending and competing tensions between dialect groups, political parties, social classes and religions, the gendered relations of power (C. Luke, 2001), and the position of non-Han Chinese minorities.

Without an undertaking to engage with difference within difference, the risk for university education is the provision of universal truths through generic pedagogies for homogeneously defined cultural subjects. Some readers will find this altogether unobjectionable.

▶ Acknowledgements

Thanks to Margaret Kettle for her insights, Carmen Luke, and the editors for their comments.

▶ Notes

1. In 1997, a Thai colleague reported to me that he and others who had worked for the US on the Thai/Vietnam borders were offered postgraduate positions at major American universities – literally escorted to the plane and to campus by security officials. They returned to establish courses and programs with strong intellectual and programmatic links to those in the US. Many Cold War client states' students studied in the West, but also in Moscow and Beijing under overt and covert aid programs.
2. For a history and overview of the Colombo Plan, see http://www.colombo-plan.org/cp/images/cp_ac/cp_ac_ap.asp?cm=3&cp_num=12.

3. See the outstanding work of Maori scholars and researchers underway at: Ngā Pae o te Māramatanga, New Zealand's Māori Centre of Research Excellence, http://www. maramatanga.co.nz/.
4. Fazal Rizvi's appointment in the early 2000s as Pro-Vice Chancellor of international development was Australia's first senior appointment of an academic of visible cultural minority status with expertise in comparative educational policy analysis.
5. Prototypical higher education teaching and learning research has extrapolated, often uncritically, findings on pedagogy to claims about university adragogy (e.g., Ramsden, 2003).
6. In instances, the issue of government response to theses topics and use of 'critical' approaches became a relevant consideration in my supervision of students from Fiji, Indonesia, China, and Singapore.

▶ References

Altbach, P. (1998) *Comparative Higher Education* (Norwood, NJ: Ablex).

Ang, I. (2001) *On Not Speaking Chinese* (New York: Routledge).

Australian Education International (2009) *International Student Data.* Online at http://www.aei.gov.au/AEI/MIP/Statistics/StudentEnrolmentAndVisaStatistics/2009/Default.htm#Pivot (accessed June 2009).

Brooks, A. and McKinnon, A. (eds) (2001) *Gender and the Restructured University* (Buckingham: Open University Press).

Doherty, C. (2006) *The Production of Cultural Difference and Cultural Sameness in Online Internationalised Education.* PhD thesis, Queensland University of Technology.

Foley, D., Levinson, B. and Hurtig, J. (2001) 'Anthropology Goes Inside: The New Educational Ethnography of Ethnicity and Gender', *Review of Research in Education*, 25, 37–98.

Foucault, M. (1982) *The Archaeology of Knowledge and the Discourse on Language.* Trans. A. Sheridan-Smith (New York: Pantheon).

Gillard, J. (2009) *International Education – Its Contribution to Australia (Speech to the Australian Parliament)* (Canberra: Department of Education, Employment and Workplace

Relations). Online at http://www.deewr.gov.au/Ministers/ Gillard/Media/Speeches/Pages/Article_090527_093411.aspx (accessed November 2009).

Graham, P., Luke, C. and Luke, A. (2007) 'Corporate Consciousness and the Failure of Higher Education', in J. L. Kincheloe and S. R. Steinberg (eds) *Cutting Class: Socioeconomic Status and Education* (New York: Peter Lang).

Kettle, M. (2005) 'Agency as Discursive Practice: From "Nobody" to "Somebody" as an International Student in Australia', *Asia Pacific Journal of Education*, 25(1), 45–60.

Kettle, M. (2007) *Discourse and Academic Practice: Reconceptualising International Students in an Australian University*. PhD thesis, University of Queensland.

Koh, A. (2003) 'Global flows of Foreign Talent: Identity Anxieties in Singapore's Ethnoscape', *Sojourn*, 18(2), 230–257.

Kubota, R. (2003) 'Unfinished Knowledge: The Story of Barbara', *College ESL*, 10, 11–21.

Kubota, R. (2006) 'Unfinished Knowledge: The Story of Barbara' (pp. 107–113), in H. Luria, D. M. Seymour and T. Smoke (eds) *Language and Linguistics in Context* (Mahwah: Lawrence Erlbaum).

Luke, A. (2005) 'Two Takes on the Critical', in B. Norton and K. Toohey (eds) *Critical Pedagogy and Language Learning* (Cambridge: Cambridge University Press).

Luke, A. (2009a) 'Another Ethnic Autobiography: Childhood and the Cultural Economy of Looking', in R. Hammer and D. Kellner (eds) *Media/Cultural Studies* (New York: Peter Lang).

Luke, A. (2009b) 'Race and Language as Capital in School: A Sociological Template for Language Education Reform', in R. Kubota and A. Lin (eds) *Race, Culture and Identities in Second Language Education* (New York: Routledge).

Luke, A. (2010) 'On this Writing: An Autotheoretic Account', in D. Nunan and J. Choi (eds) *Language and Culture: Reflective Narratives and the Emergence of Identity* (New York: Routledge).

Luke, A. and Luke, C. (1999) 'A Situated Perspective on Cultural Globalisation', in N. Burbules and C. Torres (eds) *Globalisation and Education* (New York: Routledge).

Luke, C. (2001) *Globalisation and Women in Academia: North/ South/East/West* (Malwah: Erlbaum).

Luke, C. (2005) 'Capital and Knowledge Flows: Global Higher Education Markets', *Asia Pacific Journal of Education*, 25(2), 159–174.

Luke, C. and Luke, A. (1999) 'Theorising Interracial Families and Hybrid Identity: An Australian perspective', *Educational Theory*, 49(2), 223–250.

Mahbubani, K. (2006) *Can Asians Think?* (Singapore: Times Books).

Marginson, S. and Considine, M. (2000) *The Enterprise University* (Cambridge: Cambridge University Press).

Marginson, S., Nyland, C., Sawir, E. and Forbes-Mewett, H. (2010) *International Student Security* (Cambridge: Cambridge University Press).

Mok, K. H. (2007) 'Withering the State: Globalisation Challenges and Changing Higher Education Governance in East Asia', in W. Pink and G. Noblett (eds) *International Handbook of Urban Education* (Dordrecht: Springer).

Mok, K. H. and Tan, J. (2004) *Globalization and Marketization in Education* (Cheltenham: Edward Elgar).

Pennycook, A. (1998) *English and the Discourses of Colonialism* (London: Routledge).

Ramsden, P. (2003) *Learning to Teach in Higher Education* (London: Routledge).

Reisch, G. A. (2005) *How the Cold War Transformed the Philosophy of Science* (Cambridge: Cambridge University Press).

Rizvi, F. (2000) 'International Education and the Production of Global Imagination', in N. Burbules and C. Torres (eds) *Globalisation and Education* (New York: Routledge).

Robertson, G., Mash, M., Tichner, L., Bird, J., Curtis, B. and Putnam, T. (eds) (1994) *Travellers' Tales: Narratives of Home and Displacement* (London: Routledge).

Singh, P. and Doherty, C. (2004) 'Global Cultural Flows and Pedagogic Dilemmas: Teaching in the Global University Contact Zone', *Teaching English to Speakers of Other Languages Quarterly*, 38(1), 9–42.

Sidhu, R. (2003) *Selling Futures: Globalisation and International Education*. PhD thesis, University of Queensland.

Spring, J. (1998) *Education and the Rise of the Global Economy* (Malwah: Erlbaum).

Veblen, T. (1904/1978) *The Theory of Business Enterprise* (New York: Transaction).

Volet, S. E. and Renshaw, P. D. (1996) 'Chinese Students at an Australian University: Adaptability and Continuity' (pp. 205–220), in D. Watkins and J. Biggs (eds) *The Chinese Learner: Cultural, Psychological and Contextual Influences* (Comparative Education Research Centre, The University of Hong Kong/ Australian Council of Educational Research).

2 Global Learning in a NeoLiberal Age: Implications for Development

Rajani Naidoo

Since the 1990s, higher education has been positioned as one of the most important powerhouses for development in low-income countries. This signals a policy inversion on the part of international organizations such as the World Bank which for decades declared that there should be little investment in higher education. The rationale is that in the context of the knowledge economy, the ability to generate, transmit and access information rapidly across the globe has the potential to transform countries that are materially poor into 'information-rich' ones with the ability to utilize knowledge for economic development. In this context, higher education has become a crucial incubator for economically productive knowledge and is expected to impart to students the skills, knowledge and dispositions to participate in the global economy.

While this new-found appreciation is welcome, what is of concern is that the rationale for the rebuilding of higher education has become almost exclusively linked to the narratives surrounding the idea of the knowledge-based economy. What is of equal concern is that the development of higher education in low-income countries has been framed in general by a neoliberal paradigm. This chapter begins by exposing some of the dangers of the uncritical and often simplistic linking of higher education to the perceived characteristics of the knowledge economy. It then illustrates how pressures to implement a neoliberal paradigm may compound these difficulties, particularly in relation to the transformation of higher education into a global commodity. Areas that may be adversely affected include equity, quality and the development of education and research that contributes to developmental strategies. It concludes by developing a research agenda for the reshaping of higher education systems which may be in greater alignment with developmental goals.

▶ Higher education and the knowledge economy

The 1990s marked a dramatic overturning of the view, long held by the World Bank and Western governments, that investment in higher education would bring limited social and economic benefits to developing countries. The new orthodoxy is that the ability of a country to compete successfully in the global knowledge economy relies on the production of value-added products and services, which are in turn dependent on scientific and technological knowledge, and on innovation (see for example, Castells, 2001). In this context, the ability to generate, utilize and transmit information rapidly across the globe will enable developing countries to utilize knowledge to 'leapfrog' over intermediate developmental stages and improve their positions in the global economy (Castells, 2001). Higher education has therefore been positioned as a crucial engine for development, with a particular role in producing, disseminating and transferring economically productive knowledge, innovation and technology (Carnoy, 1994). There is also the sense that value-added production through innovation and technology requires a configuration of skills that is at a substantially higher level and of a more generic kind than the technical competences required to perform specific occupational roles in the past (Brown et al., 2001). Higher education is therefore expected to impart to students the academic, technical, social and managerial skills perceived to be essential in meeting the requirements of dynamic international markets.

While the recognition of the importance of higher education can only be seen as positive, what is of concern is that the revitalization of higher education has occurred within the straitjacket of what Jessop (2008) has termed the 'master economic imaginary' of the knowledge economy. By this he means a hegemonic discourse closely linked to the idea of global competitiveness that frames political, intellectual and economic strategies as well as a wide range of government policies. This results in the tight coupling of higher education to the requirements of the knowledge economy which in turn poses many dangers for developing countries. First, it is not clear to what extent the interests of developing countries are served by an uncritical acceptance of the prescriptions and predictions encapsulated within the knowledge economy discourse. A number of analysts have argued that the rise of the knowledge economy to the status of master narrative was at least in part a response to the 1970s crisis of the post-war model of economic growth. An economic strategy based on knowledge and intellectual property as a new source of competitive advantage was needed to enlarge and protect the dominance of American capital for the next long wave of capitalist development (Jessop, 2008; Robertson, 2009). If this analysis is accepted, then the advantage that powerful countries already have as well as continuing unequal power relations and structural barriers are likely to impede the development prospects of the majority of low-income countries.

A further difficulty is that the faith in higher education as a motor of development relies on the high-skills thesis which contends that for states to remain competitive in current economic conditions, a change in the nature of skills and its relationship to productivity is required. Higher levels of skill are perceived to be a pre-requisite for economic activity to shift from the old Fordist and Taylorist paradigms into a new high-skills mode of working. However, this thesis, which is linked with the role of higher education in development, has come under criticism by researchers who have pointed out that even in high-income countries, high-performance production systems and high-skills regimes are not all-pervasive and widely distributed (see, for example, Kraak, 2004). They assert that in reality in most countries Fordist mass producing manufacturing, as well as low-skill labour intensive production, exist alongside high-skill production techniques. Other analysts such as Keep (1999) go further to argue that Fordist and post-Fordist modes of production continue to flourish in advanced economies particularly in the United States of America and the United Kingdom as they are based on the expansion of low-skilled, low-cost jobs which give a certain competitive advantage. According to these analysts, the reality of high-skill production strategies is that it only occurs in a few sectors mainly in the leading advanced economies. The high-skills rhetoric of the knowledge-based economy also prophesizes that the growing importance of knowledge work would significantly raise the demand for educated workers, who would enjoy greater autonomy in their work. However, as Lauder et al. (2008) show, bursts of creativity in capitalist countries are followed by the routinization of work to enable profits to be made. Innovations are therefore translated into sets of routines that do not require the creativity and independence of judgement that are often associated with the knowledge economy rhetoric. The authors suggest that rather than changes leading to greater creativity and autonomy for the majority of knowledge workers, 'permission to think' has only been given to a minority. The majority of knowledge workers are faced with routinization, surveillance and exploitation.

If this is the case in advanced economies, then the uncritical acceptance of the high-skills thesis for developing countries, where skills polarities are even greater, is highly problematic. Indeed, as Ashton (2004) has pointed out, the incorporation of a low-skills development strategy may be viewed positively in developing countries since it could lead to labour intensive forms of employment and help alleviate mass unemployment. A development strategy built around the interlocking potential of low, intermediate and high skills to allow for greater variability and unevenness is thus a persuasive one (Kraak, 2004) and has implications for a mixture of investment strategies in higher and other levels of education, including vocational training.

▶ NeoLiberalism as a global template

While it is important to challenge the restrictive roles prescribed for universities in developing countries, it is also necessary to state that higher education in its wider social, economic and political roles is vital to development. However, a range of factors have contributed to a crisis in higher education in many low-income countries. These include policies of 'disinvestment' in higher education developed by international organizations such as the World Bank (Task Force on Higher Education in Developing Countries, 2000), political instability, the colonial and post-colonial origins of the university system, the effects of structural adjustment policies and the migration of skilled academics to Western higher education systems (see Sawyerr, 2004; Mamdani, 2006). The response to this crisis has in general been fixed within a neoliberal framework. In the next section, I will present a brief analysis of how neoliberalism can be seen to be an attempt to restructure all areas of society along market lines before analysing the particular impact on higher education.

As Peters (2001) has illustrated, neoliberalism has spread rapidly from a theory of economic behaviour to a framework for governing all aspects of society. Deregulation, competitiveness and privatization feature prominently in the transitions towards neoliberal forms of governance (Kelsey, 1993). However, unlike classical liberalism with its central philosophy of the freedom of the individual from state interference, neoliberalism envisions a positive role for the state in facilitating the workings of a market and in developing institutions and individuals that are responsive to market forces. The state develops into what Cerny (1990) has termed the 'competition' state which sees its primary objective as one of fostering a competitive national economy by promoting and maximizing returns from market forces in international settings while abandoning some of the core functions of the welfare state. There is greater functionality between the state and the market with the state establishing conditions for the quasi-market but also actively mobilizing market mechanisms to attain political goals.

Neoliberalism has also become embedded in low-income countries with some important contemporary exceptions such as Cuba, Venezuela and Bolivia. In general, neoliberal tenets have dominated policy making through a number of factors including policy diffusion as well as the training of policy elites in Western, pro-market university faculties. In addition, international organizations such as the World Bank and the International Monetary Fund have played a key role in embedding neoliberalism through structural adjustment programmes, austerity packages and conditions attached to loans. Governments in low-income countries have been persuaded to roll back state control, deregulate domestic markets and open up to international trade and competition. More recently, there has been a shift to what Stiglitz (1998) has termed the 'post Washington consensus'. Fine (2004) has argued that this is not a rejection of neoliberal policy but rather its widening to encompass social and non-market arenas. While market solutions are still perceived as central to effective development strategies (Kempner and Jurema, 2002), the negative conception of the state's role in development has more recently been replaced by a more positive conception of the state in creating the appropriate conditions for the market to function. Rather than providing public services, the state is expected to act as a facilitator for global market integration. This shift has enabled international organizations to address both economic and social policies in developing countries, particularly around issues of good governance (Fine, 2004; Griffin, 2006). In the next section, I will turn to how neoliberalism has transformed higher education into a global commodity.

▶ Higher education as a global commodity

The global template of neoliberalism has also impacted on higher education. In many countries, the 'social compact' that evolved between higher education, the state and society over the last century (Marginson and Considine, 2000) has been eroded. The perceptions of higher education as an industry for enhancing national competitiveness have begun to eclipse the social and cultural objectives of higher education generally encompassed in the conception of higher education as a 'public good'. In relation to governance, the belief that universities require a relative independence from political and corporate influence to function optimally, which was in turn linked to the need for guaranteed state funding and professional autonomy, has been eroded. These changes may be seen to be part of a broader policy shift away from the Keynesian welfare state settlement towards a neoliberal one which introduced mechanisms of the market and New Public Management techniques into higher education (see Deem, 2001; Naidoo, 2003). The assumption is that competition within and between higher education institutions for limited resources will produce a more effective and efficient higher education system. In the present time, this competition will be intensified by what many consider as the worst financial crisis since the Great Depression in the 1930s as illustrated by the failure of several major financial institutions, widespread credit squeeze and large drops in stock prices. While well-resourced universities may be able to weather the financial turmoil and may even improve their standing, smaller, less well-resourced universities that are dependent on tuition fees may face closure. The further assumption of this new mode of governance is that the monitoring and measuring of professional work will enhance performance. New Public Management techniques have been introduced which rely on performance measurement, audit systems rather than tacit self regulation, entrepreneurial and hierarchical management rather than collegial mechanisms and a shift of power from academics to consumers and managers (Ferlie et al., 2008). Neoliberal market-oriented reform, particularly in the form of privatization and commercialization, has also been implemented in higher education in developing countries. Torres and Schugurensky (2002) have pointed out how international organizations can act as 'parallel governments' as a result of conditionalities attached to loans and structural adjustment programmes. A reduction in public spending, de-regulation, privatization, user fees and the attraction of private and foreign higher education providers has been prescribed.

NeoLiberal policies and management frameworks result in the transformation of higher education into a global commodity. Rather than merely stipulating new procedures to enhance the functioning of higher education, these changes may be seen to introduce new modes of rationality and value systems to fit a framework of market relations. The work of the French social theorist, Pierre Bourdieu, who has attempted to analyse the 'inner' life of universities in the nineteenth century makes an important contribution to understandings of the global commodification of higher education. In Bourdieu's own research conducted in France and the application of his work to other national contexts (see, for example, Robbins, 1993; Naidoo, 2004) institutions of higher education are located in a 'field' of higher education which is presented as a conceptual space with a high degree of autonomy in that it generates its own organizational culture consisting of values and behavioural imperatives which are relatively independent from forces emerging from the economic and political fields. The activities in each field revolve around the acquisition and development of different species of capital, which may be defined as particular resources that are invested with value (Bourdieu, 1988). The 'capital' historically invested with value in the field of higher education is termed 'academic capital' and consists in the first instance of intellectual or cultural, rather than economic or political, assets. According to Bourdieu, acts of cognition are implemented to select and consecrate what is classified as 'academic' and therefore what counts as valid criteria for entry and success in higher education. Professional practice in the field of higher education has therefore been traditionally shaped by deeply ingrained rules, values and professional protocols that revolve around a belief in, the struggle for and the acquisition of academic capital (Bourdieu, 1988, 1996).

Neoliberal mechanisms have resulted in the structural and the ideological undermining of academic capital. Economic forces have begun to impact more powerfully, and more directly, on universities than in previous decades. In addition, changes in funding policy which require institutions to generate surplus income have led to the undermining of academic capital. The concept 'commodification', which refers to the development of a product or process specifically for exchange on the market rather than for its intrinsic 'use' value, captures the shift from activities aimed at the acquisition of academic capital to activities intended for income generation. Forces for commodification therefore impact on universities by altering the nature of rewards and sanctions operating in higher education and are likely to impact on the social and academic missions of universities. Success shifts from being measured according to academic principles to being measured according to income generation such as the numbers of student customers captured and courses sold, the extent of involvement with commercial interests and the degree of financial surplus created. While some benefits have accrued, I would like to turn the stick in the other direction by focusing in the next section on some potential dangers of the transformation of higher education into a global commodity.

▶ The erosion of equity

The new managerialist and marketized frameworks adopted within neoliberal paradigms are likely to erode the potential of higher education to contribute to equity. In many countries, competitive frameworks apply pressure on universities to achieve a type of productivity which can be measured by quantifiable outputs such as the progression rate of students, the number of postgraduates and staff producing publications of 'good standing'. Such output-based numerical measures do not differentiate between different categories of students, different systems or the different means required to produce a successful 'outcome'. As such, the model is inevitably blind to social and educational factors associated with equity measures. Funding regimes also demarcate between research and teaching and accord greater status to research. The logic of the policies, which require institutions to maximize research output and demonstrate student success and progression in the shortest time possible, mitigates against the development of a more inclusive higher education system. Institutions which have not traditionally included widening participation in their missions are unlikely to develop admission strategies to recruit students from under-represented groups. As shown in other national contexts (Marginson, 1997; Naidoo, 1998), students from non-traditional constituencies are viewed by elite universities to be time- and resource-intensive. Such students are therefore perceived to threaten institutional arrangements around activities, such as research, through which academic status and financial resources are accrued. In addition, such students are unlikely to enhance the institution's 'output' indicators. Institutions absorbing students from groups that are traditionally excluded from higher education are likely to be financially penalized, since such frameworks do not differentiate between categories of students with regard to social disadvantage and differences in prior educational attainment. While neoliberal measures are presented as devices for drawing diverse institutions into a high quality system, in reality, the impact will be to encourage the development of a university sector in which status and resources are likely to be inversely proportional to institutional and student disadvantage.

Example of such trends can be found in Chile and India. Espinoza (2008) indicates that as a result of the reduction of public social expenditures imposed by the International Monetary Fund/ World Bank structural adjustment programs, universities in Chile have sought to generate institutional revenue sources by increasing the level of sale of services and tuition fees. While acknowledging that the Chilean higher education system was always more biased towards students from upper income groups, the author argues that the new model of high tuition fees and partial vouchers and loans has resulted in even greater difficulties for lower income students. In particular, students who study in fields with low private returns are in effect denied loans. Inequitable access to higher education is also reported by Kamat and colleagues (2007) who assert that the Indian government is withdrawing from its role as a grand equalizer of society. In relation to technological education the state has responded to the global labour market by providing a high quality technological education for an elite who join the research and development wings of US corporations. Technology education for the masses is left mainly to unregulated private providers who concentrate on income generation in the shortest time possible. They have abandoned a broad-based education and instead focus on a narrow set of skills condensed into short certification programmes. According to the authors, this strategy has led to the reproduction of caste and class inequality. The super elites – the highest castes continue to have access to the best quality comprehensive technological education while the ascendant middle castes are deployed as the new labour the in the globalized service sector. The marginalized communities, on the other hand, have little or no access to the dream of technological modernization. The current financial crisis which already shows signs of impacting on financial aid packages and the ability of students and parents to take out loans in high-income countries has the potential to exacerbate these trends in inequity.

▶ The bifurcation of quality

The transformation of higher education into a global commodity has many implications for quality. According to Altbach (2002), older rationales for transnational higher education including capacity building in low-income countries have been replaced by the aim of generating revenue at the institutional level and trade surpluses at the national level. This has led to developing countries being seen as attractive new markets. Developing countries are also likely to become attractive arenas for private and for-profit institutions. Enrolments are rapidly increasing in Africa, Jordan, Malaysia, Vietnam, China, Thailand and Indonesia. The sector is also growing throughout South America, with approximately 44 per cent of all institutions in Brazil being for-profit ones (McCowan, 2004). In addition, technological advances associated with globalization, which have given rise to virtual higher education, are a further important factor in the growth of new providers.

Despite the faith of advocates of marketization that the market itself will control quality (see, for example Tooley, 2001), indications are that the proliferation of for-profit institutions may lead to an increasing number of low-quality 'diploma mills' (Knight, 2003). In India, private higher education institutions have been growing more significantly than government institutions. While estimates are that about a quarter of private higher education institutions are of high quality, the majority do not meet minimum standards and indulge in malpractice relating to admissions and fees (Anandakrishnan, 2006). In addition, it is also important to bear in mind that demand is not merely related to quality but also to affordability and availability. McCowan (2004), for example, has argued that in Brazil, a number of institutions that are widely regarded to be of low quality, such as *Estácio de Sá* and *UniverCidade*, have achieved growth simply because there is no geographical or financial alternative for large numbers of the population.

The decline in funding and other pressures on publicly funded universities in high-income countries are also likely to impact negatively on their provision of higher education to developing countries. There are indications that higher education in Northern nations is becoming increasingly hierarchized and stratified as a result of government policies which are reconfiguring systems in a marketizing milieu. Marginson (2006) has indicated that this has resulted in the bifurcation of the system with, at one end, elite institutions where demand always exceeds supply and where expansion is constrained to maximize status and, at the other end, mass institutions which strive to expand numbers. Between these two poles are intermediate universities. These divisions are happening at two levels: one within advanced capitalist countries where a small number of elite universities are being separated out from the rest, and the other between the education offered in high- and low-income countries.

In this scenario, publicly funded universities that are being financially squeezed by their governments may seize on opportunities to produce low-cost teaching. These could include reputable universities who may devise strategies to protect their core on-campus provision in their home countries while viewing developing countries with weak regulation as mass markets for lower-cost learning (see, for example, Noble, 2002). In a similar vein to that which operates in other parts of the global economy, the reduction of costs may be achieved primarily by focussing on scale. The temptation will therefore be to produce standardized products and generic content which are easily and cheaply transferable across borders. In these circumstances, e-learning is seen as a viable and lucrative learning mode. Many virtual learning providers, who have made the required investment in e-learning including heavy investment in the technological infrastructure, borrow mass production techniques to deliver teaching and assessment in an effort to expand their virtual student numbers and spread their costs.

A model of learning predicated on the need to deliver information more quickly and more cheaply to the students is likely to be employed. This is likely to lead to a number of pedagogical arrangements which may impact negatively on the development of high-level intellectual skills, necessary for the successful participation of developing countries in the global knowledge economy. Studies on effective learning have indicated that students need to engage in modes of active learning, and most importantly teachers need to constantly adjust what they do to the needs of learners. This is in significant contrast to a model of learning which sees the task as one of essentially adding knowledge to students. In higher education students tend to already possess cognitive maps of the fields of knowledge which they are studying, however rudimentary. The process of learning therefore involves confronting those 'maps' with new models and information so that they may be developed and in some cases completely changed (Mezirow, 1991).

Teachers thus have a crucial role in getting students to reveal their understandings and hold them up for 'public' scrutiny in a manner which is both supportive yet ultimately challenging. This is both a time-consuming and skilled process. However, in commodified forms of learning, there is likely to be a large reliance on learning resources which simply provide information to students rather than require the active engagement of students in their own learning. There may be an attempt to 'teacher proof' delivery which becomes important if institutions are attempting to use less qualified, less experienced and thus cheaper staff, as would be the case in nations that have already had other parts of their public sector infrastructure deregulated. The process of feedback to students may also be altered. Rather than the use of a variety of feedback mechanisms to help students learn in a developmental way, formal assessment systems including computerized multiple choice tests may be used.

Foreign providers who are primarily motivated by profit are likely to offer programmes in disciplines which are profitable rather than disciplines that are expensive or difficult to teach. This includes reputable universities such as Harvard. In its educational initiative called 'Harvard in India' the university focuses on technical training. Since comprehensive universities often function on the basis of cross-subsidization where expensive courses like Medicine are taught alongside cheaper ones like Business Studies, indigenous universities may lose students to the new providers, especially in the very disciplines that generate important revenue for cross-subsidization (Teixeira and Amaral, 2001). Disciplines such as Medicine, Engineering and Music, as well as the Humanities and Social Science which are crucial to development may thus be placed in a vulnerable position. In addition, little interest has been shown in offering programmes to build indigenous research capacity such as research degrees at postgraduate level or doctoral level work. In a marketized higher education system, fee-based Masters and postgraduate Diploma programmes based primarily on coursework hold the promise of economies of scale. Marginson (2001) has argued that such courses are often hard to distinguish from undergraduate courses and may in fact be augmenting credentialism rather than developing national capacity through the training of new generations of indigenous researchers. They may in turn lead to a shortage of programmes and graduates in key strategic areas which may be detrimental to development strategies.

The lucrative nature of higher education as a global export, particularly in the context of weak regulation, may lead to developing countries becoming markets for the mass dumping of low quality knowledge. Rather than gaining access to powerful forms of knowledge, many students in developing countries may therefore receive an education that has been reduced to narrowly defined core competencies. Such initiatives are likely to stunt indigenous capacity in higher education in developing countries and maintain global institutional hierarchies.

▶ Whose knowledge?

The potential for education and research to contribute to development is also compromised by a particular hegemonic view of knowledge. The master narrative of the knowledge economy combines with neoliberal templates to lay down the criteria for what is meant by high quality and relevant higher education. In addition, the globalization of higher education, the hegemony exerted by universities in the US and Western European and the advent of global league tables all exert pressure on universities in developing countries to adhere to a highly restricted form of knowledge. The generation and dissemination of knowledge that can be utilized for national competitive advantage is valued. Slaughter and Rhoades (2004) drawing on the work of Michel Foucault (1980) have characterized these trends in the growing commodification of knowledge as the 'capitalist knowledge regime.' This is a regime which values the profit potential of knowledge and in which interests such as corporations have claims that come before those of the public. As a regime of power it operates as a set of norms and practices in which universities find themselves in competition for increased revenues resulting in revenue-generating fields taking on greater relevance, with other less profitable areas of academic life becoming more or less second- or third-class. Furthermore, as Jessop (2008) has shown, knowledge is increasingly commodified, subjected to closure and treated as intellectual property. He gives the apposite example of commercial enterprises expropriating knowledge that has been collectively produced by indigenous communities and indicates how this is mirrored in the growing pressures for the privatization and patenting of publicly financed work in higher education.

These effects have the potential to exclude the important social, political and cultural functions of higher education. This includes a broad liberal education to give students the skills and the dispositions for lifelong learning, an understanding of national culture and history and its interrelationship with hegemonic cultures and the preparation for citizenship. While these omissions are important in all countries, it has been argued that in developing countries, particularly those which have undergone social transformation, the contribution of higher education to non-economic areas of the public good, such as building democracy and social cohesion, increasing and widening participation and developing expertise to address local needs and problems, is vitally important (see for example Badat, 2001). Researchers in Latin America have also argued that the prioritization of research for commercial development has led to the displacement of research leading to the generation of knowledge by an 'exaggerated adaptation to market demands' (Orozco, 1998, cited in Arocena and Sutz, 2005). Researchers from developing countries have also argued against the imposition of hegemonic models such as the 'triple helix' model developed in the context of high-income countries which advocates relations between universities, industry and government. They suggest that in the context of developing countries, particularly in national contexts where industries are unwilling to fund research and training and may not have sufficient capacity to utilize research findings or knowledge workers, universities will face pressures to perform low-level routine activities with the aim of generating income (Arocena and Sutz, 2005). Research conducted in Malawi has also indicated that in a national context where Mode 1 knowledge was never thoroughly institutionalized, high market demand for knowledge for narrow utilitarian purposes has already constrained research and education to the point of squeezing out explanatory questions (Holland, 2008). Such analyses indicate that universities can more appropriately correspond to the developmental goals of their countries by also developing strong relationships with other stakeholders including the public sector and community organizations (see, for example, Subotsky, 1999; Arocena and Sutz, 2000).

The sections above have indicated that the interlocking of the 'master economic imaginary' of the knowledge economy with neoliberal governance mechanisms show little potential to contribute to developmental goals capable of eroding current disparities between high- and low-income countries. Indeed, analysis would suggest that inequalities in access, quality and knowledge disparities in the previous industrial era, are likely to be compounded in the present era of the knowledge society. In the following section, I present some key issues that may contribute to the development of a research agenda on higher education and its role in development.

▶ A research agenda for higher education and development

Greater research attention is required to understand the relationship between development and higher education systems in low-income countries. Theoretical frameworks such as those developed by Simon Marginson and Gary Rhoades (2002) which emphasize the simultaneous significance of global, national and local forces on the development of higher education offer a powerful conceptual frame. However, while this provides an understanding of the relationships between systems of higher education and globalization, it does not explicitly address the role of higher education in development. Such theories therefore need to be linked to broader theories of development, including some of the important concepts of Amartya Sen. His 'human capabilities' concept, which measures development by the capacity of people to do and be what they value, as counterposed to merely focussing on narrow measures of income, offers important possibilities (See Sen, 1999). A critical appraisal of newer theories such as world polity (Meyer, 2000) and world order (Cox, 1981) and older development theories such as 'world systems' (Wallerstein, 2004) and dependency theory (Amin, 1976) which acted as important correctives to theories of modernization needs to be conducted to determine whether they have any purchase under changing contemporary conditions. Given research findings which indicate that the orientation and effectiveness of the state are critical variables in explaining successful development, it is also important to develop further analyses on the concept and practices of 'developmental states'. While state-led development in a number of Asian countries has been documented, it is not an easy model to emulate since it is as a result of different historical, social, political and, importantly, geopolitical structures. Such states have also often been characterized as autocratic (Fritz and Menocal, 2007). There thus remain significant gaps in knowledge about the role of the state in development and its steering of higher education.

Given the existing state of crisis of higher education in many countries and the fact that it would be difficult to overturn the provision of higher education within a market milieu, attention on how policy can shape the relationship between the domestic, foreign, public and private sectors in order to build capacity is vitally important. An important area for research consideration is the extent to which policy fosters collaboration, competition or functional differentiation between the different sets of providers. In addition, the assumption that publicly funded institutions by their very nature are likely to contribute to the public good is misplaced. Studies on the role of universities in industrialized, developing and transitional countries have indicated that universities have played multiple roles, sometimes contributing to the transformation of societies and at other times reproducing unequal relations in society (Brennan et al., 2004). Research therefore needs to be conducted on which functions of the higher education system need to be publicly funded and protected. In addition, if markets are deemed necessary, much closer attention needs to be paid to developing policy to shape the operation of markets in higher education so that higher education can contribute to citizens of developing countries rather than merely providing income for universities in high-income countries. Many developing countries are exploring various regulatory mechanisms (see King, 2003; Verbik and Jokivirta, 2005) aimed at protecting national higher education systems and students from the potentially adverse effects of transnational higher education. There are also initiatives by for example, the World Bank and UNESCO, to develop international forms of regulation (King, 2003). This may be particularly beneficial to low income, vulnerable countries with insufficient capacity to develop appropriate regulatory systems. However, the question that is likely to emerge is whether the sort of model advocated by the World Bank, which is based on simple licensing procedures with minimum thresholds, merely strengthens neoliberal frameworks rather than helping protect developing countries. While regulation normally operates through rules and sanctions, it might also be useful to look at the provision of incentives so that institutions contribute to developmental goals. An argument that has been presented in the South African context is that just as publicly funded universities are urged to become more entrepreneurial, foreign and private providers could also be required to contribute to the public good (Kruss and Kraak, 2003). In most countries, governments have responded to the perceived insularity of higher education by implementing mechanisms to open up higher education to economic forces, to encourage higher education to contribute more directly to economic development and to foster closer relations with industry. However, while there has been a great deal of policy rhetoric, there has in general been little corresponding link between financial or performance incentives and the provision of public goods.

However, perhaps the most important strategy for the sustainable development of higher education in low-income countries is to develop 'country ownership' of the higher education and development agenda. As indicated above, governments are hindered from devising policies that are appropriate to the local socio-political and economic context and relevant to developmental goals because of pressures imposed by dominant countries and powerful international organizations. Kempner and Jurema (2002) have indicated that the concept of 'developmental association', used by powerful governments and international agencies, assumes that all developing countries are cultural variations of the same problem and require the same general solutions. They point out that this is potentially erroneous as a strategy because development is not necessarily linear and each nation does not follow the same path. Rather than relying on a one-size-fits-all approach or on ideal type solutions, the opportunities and constraints that different countries face must be recognized. In addition, the constraining of policy in developing countries within the boundaries of the neoliberal/knowledge economy complex requires a radical interrogation of the assumptions, prescriptions and predictions underlying this model. Bourdieu (1998) has referred to neoliberalism as a 'doxa' or an unquestionable orthodoxy that operates at all levels of society, from individual perceptions and practices to state policy, as if it were the objective truth. It is thus vital to develop theoretical and empirical research that challenges this doxa, and to restate that there is at present a lack of evidence to support the assumption that an unregulated global market will lead to the development of high quality higher education. More crucially, the positioning of this doxa as an 'objective truth' prevents policy makers and researchers from thinking about development strategies that have worked in the past and others that could work in the future. Finally, there needs to be a wider acknowledgement that the imposition of models of governing higher education by external actors in the absence of commitment and ownership by governments and communities within low-income country has little chance of success.

▶ References

Altbach, G. P. (2002) 'Knowledge and Education as International Commodities?', *International Higher Education*, 28, 2–5.

Amin, S. (1976) *Unequal Development: An Essay on the Social Formations of Peripheral Capitalism* (New York: Monthly Review Press).

Anandakrishnan, M. (2006) *Privatisation of Higher Education – Opportunities and Anomalies.* Paper presented at a seminar on 'Privatisation and Commercialisation of Higher Education', organized by the National Institute of Educational Planning and Administration, New Delhi, India, May 2006.

Arocena, R. and Sutz, J. (2000) 'Interactive Learning Spaces and Development Policies in Latin America', DRUID Working Chapter No 00-13, www.druid.dk/wp/pdf_files/00-13.pdf (Last accessed 20 August 2006).

Arocena, R. and Sutz, J. (2005) 'Latin American Universities: From an Original Revolution to an Uncertain Transition', *Higher Education*, 50, 573–592.

Ashton, D. (2004) 'High Skills: The Concept and Its Application to South Africa', in McGrath, S., Badroodien, A., Kraak, A.

and Unwin, L. (eds) *Shifting Understandings of Skills in South Africa: Overcoming the Historical Imprint of a Low Skills Regime* (Pretoria: Human Science Research Council Press).

Badat, S. (2001) 'Transforming South African Higher Education: Paradoxes, Policy and Choices, Interests and Constraints', Paper presented at the Salzburg seminar symposium on Higher Education in Emerging Economies, Salzburg, Austria, 7–11 July.

Bourdieu, P. (1988) *Homo Academicus* (Cambridge: Polity Press).

Bourdieu, P. (1996) *The State Nobility* (Cambridge: Polity Press).

Bourdieu, P. (1998) *Acts of Resistance: Against the Tyranny of the Market* (New York: The New Press).

Brennan, J., King, R. and Lebeau, Y. (2004) *The Role of Universities in the Transformation of Societies: Synthesis Report* (London: Association of Commonwealth Universities and the Open University).

Brown, P., Green, A. and Lauder, H. (2001) *High Skills: Globalisation, Competitiveness, and Skill* (Oxford: Oxford University Press).

Carnoy, M. (1994) 'Universities, Technological Change and Training in the Information Age', in Salmi, J. and Verspoor, A. M. (eds) *Revitalising Higher Education* (New York: Pergamon/International Association of Universities Press).

Castells, M. (2001) 'Information Technology and Global Development', in Muller, J., Cloete, N. and Badat, S. (eds) *Challenges of Globalisation: South African Debates with Manuel Castells* (Cape Town: Maskew Miller/ Longman).

Cerny, P. G. (1990) *The Changing Architecture of Politics: Structure, Agency and the Future of the State* (London, Newbury Park, CA, New Delhi: Sage).

Chossudovsky, M. (1998) *The Globalisation of Poverty: Impacts of IMF and World Bank Reforms* (New York: Zed Books Ltd.).

Cox, R. (1981) 'Social Forces, States, and World Orders: Beyond International Relations Theory', *Millennium*, 10, 126–155.

Deem, R. (2001) 'Globalisation, New Managerialism, Academic Capitalism and Entrepreneurialism in Universities: Is the Local Dimension Still Important?', *Comparative Education*, 37(1), 7–20.

Espinoza, O. (2008) 'Creating (In)equalities in Access to Higher Education in the Context of Structural Adjustment and

Post-Adjustment Policies: The Case of Chile', *Higher Education*, 55, 269–284.

Ferlie, E., Musselin, C. and Gianluca, A. (2008) 'The Steering of Higher Education Systems: A Public Management Perspective', *Higher Education*, 56(3), 325–348.

Fine, B. (2004) 'Examining the Role of Globalisation and Development Critically: What Role for Political Economy?', *New Political Economy*, 9(2), 214–231.

Foucault, M. (1980) *Power/Knowledge: Selected Interviews and Other Writings 1972–1977* (New York: Pantheon).

Fritz, V. and Menocal, A. R. (2007) 'Developmental States in the New Millennium: Concepts and Challenges for a New Aid Agenda', *Development Policy Review*, 25(5), 531–552.

Griffin, P. (2006) 'The World Bank', *New Political Economy*, 11(4), 572–581.

Holland, D. G. (2008) 'Discipline in the Context of Development: A Case of the Social Sciences in Malawi, Southern Africa', *Higher Education*, 55, 671–681.

Jessop, B. (2008) 'The Knowledge Based Economy', Article Prepared for Naked Punch, eprints.lancs.ac.uk/1007/1/Microsoft_Word_-_I-2008_Naked_Punch.pdf – (Accessed 10 April 2009).

Kamat, S., Mir, A. and Matthew, B. (2006) 'Producing Hi-Tech: Globalization, the State and Migrant Subjects', in Lauder, H., Brown, P., Dillabough, J. A. and Halsey, A. H. (eds) *Education, Globalization, and Social Change* (Oxford: Open University Press).

Keep, E. (1999) 'UK's VET Policy and the Third Way: Following a High Skills Trajectory or Running Up a Dead End Street?', *Journal of Education and Work*, 12(3), 323–346.

Kelsey, J. (1993) *Rolling Back the State* (Wellington: Brigit Williams Books).

Kempner, K. and Jurema, A. L. (2002) 'The Global Politics of Education: Brazil and the World Bank', *Higher Education*, 43, 331–354.

King, R. (2003) *The Rise and Regulation of For Profit Education* (London: Observatory on Borderless Higher Education).

Knight, J. (2003) *GATS, Trade and Higher Education: Perspective 2003 – Where Are We?* (London: Observatory on Borderless Higher Education).

Kraak, A. (2004) 'Rethinking the High Skills Thesis in South Africa', in McGrath, S., Badroodien, A., Kraak, A. and Unwin, L. (eds) *Shifting Understandings of Skills in South Africa: Overcoming the Historical Imprint of a Low Skills Regime* (Pretoria: Human Science Research Council Press).

Kruss, G. and Kraak, A. (eds) (2003) *A Contested Good?: Understanding Private Higher Education in South Africa* (Boston, USA: Boston College Center for International Higher Education and 'Perspectives in Education', South Africa).

Lauder, H., Brown, P. and Ashton, D. (2008) 'Globalisation, Skill Formation and the Varieties of Capitalism Approach', *New Political Economy*, 13(1) 19–35.

Levis, K. (2003) 'Universities Online. The New Business Model?' Paper presented at 'Universities Challenged: New Strategies and Business Models' Conference, London, 4 December.

Mamdani, M. (2006) 'Higher Education, the State and the Marketplace'. Talk presented to the Conference of Commonwealth Ministers of Education, 12 December 2006. Cape Town, South Africa.

Marginson, S. (1997) 'Competition in Higher Education: Intended and Unintended Effects', Paper presented at Australian Institute of Tertiary Education Administration (AITEA) Queensland Branch 12th Annual Conference, Surfers' Paradise, 22–23 May.

Marginson, S. (2001) 'Knowledge Economy and Knowledge Culture'. Paper presented at National Scholarly Communications Forum, ANU, 9 August.

Marginson, S. (2004) 'Global Education Markets and Global Public Goods'. Keynote address, Australian and New Zealand Comparative and International Education Society Conference, Australian Catholic University, Melbourne, 3 December.

Marginson, S. (2006) 'Putting "Public" Back into the Public University', *Thesis Eleven*, 84, 44–59.

Marginson, S. and Considine, M. (2000) *The Enterprise University: Power, Governance and Reinvention in Australia* (Cambridge: Cambridge University Press).

Marginson, S. and Rhoades, G. (2002) 'Beyond National States, Markets, and Systems of Higher Education: A Glonacal Agency Heuristic', *Higher Education*, 43(3), 281–309.

Meyer, J. (2000) 'Globalization: Sources and Effects on National States and Societies', *International Sociology*, 15, 233–248.

Mezirow, J. (1991) *Transformative Dimensions of Adult Learning* (San Francisco: Jossey-Bass).

McCowan, T. (2004) 'The Growth of Private Higher Education in Brazil: Implications for Equity and Quality', *Journal of Education Policy*, 19(4), 453–472.

Moja, T. and Cloete, N. (2001) 'Vanishing Borders and New Boundaries', in Muller, J., Cloete, N. and Badat, S. (eds) *Challenges of Globalisation: South African Debates with Manuel Castells* (Cape Town: Maskew Miller/ Longman).

Naidoo, R. (1998) 'Levelling or Playing the Field: The Politics of Access to Post-apartheid South Africa', *Cambridge Journal of Education*, 28(3),369–384.

Naidoo, R. (2003) 'Repositioning Higher Education as a Global Commodity: Opportunities and Challenges for Future Sociology of Education Work', *British Journal of Sociology of Education*, 24(2), 249–259.

Naidoo, R. (2004) 'Fields and Institutional Strategy: Bourdieu on the Relationship Between Higher Education, Inequality and Society', *British Journal of Sociology of Education*, 25(4), 446–472.

Naidoo, R. and Jamieson, I. M. (2004) 'Knowledge in the Marketplace: The Global Commodification of Teaching and Learning', in Innes, P. and Hellsten, M. (eds) *Internationalizing Higher Education: Critical Perspectives for Critical Times* (Dordrecht: Springer/ Connecticut Economic Resource Center).

Noble, D. F. (2002) 'Rehearsal for the Revolution', in Robins, K. and Webster, F. (eds) *The Virtual University* (Oxford: Oxford University Press).

Orozco, L. E. (1998) 'La Reforma de la Educacion Colombia: Balance Critico', in Mendes, C. (ed.) *Novas Perspectivas nas Políticas de Educacao Superior na America Latina no Limiar do Seculo XXI* (Campinas: Autores Associados).

Peters, M. A. (2001) *Post-structuralism, Marxism and Neoliberalism: Between Theory and Politics* (New York: Roman and Littlefield).

Robbins, D. (1993) 'The Practical Importance of Bourdieu's Analyses of Higher Education', *Studies in Higher Education*, 18(2), 151–163.

Robertson, S. L. (2009) 'Education, Knowledge and Innovation in the Global Economy: Challenges and Future Directions'.

Keynote Address at Launch of Research Centres, VIA University College, Aarhus, Denmark, 6 March 2009.

Sen, A. (1999) *Development as Freedom* (Oxford, Oxford University Press).

Slaughter, S. and Rhoades, G. (2004) *Academic Capitalism and the New Economy: Markets, State and Higher Education* (Baltimore, MD: Johns Hopkins University Press).

Stiglitz, J. E. (1998) 'Towards a New Paradigm for Development; Strategies, Policies and Processes', Prebisch Lecture at United Nations Conference on Trade and Development, Geneva, 19 October 1998.

Subotsky, G. (1999) 'Alternatives to the Entrepreneurial University: New Modes of Knowledge Production in Community Service Programs', *Higher Education*, 38(4), 401–440.

Sawyerr, A. (2004) 'Challenges Facing African Universities: Selected Issues', *Association of African Universities*, http://www.aau.org/rc/asa-challengesfigs.pdf (Accessed 28 May 2009).

Singh, M. (2001) 'Reinserting the Public Good into Higher Education' *Council for Higher Education Discussion Series*, 1, 7–22.

Task Force on Higher Education in Developing Countries (convened by UNESCO and the World Bank) (2000) 'Higher Education in Developing Countries: Peril and Promise', http:///www.tfhe.net/report/overview.htm (Accessed 20 August 2006).

Teixeira, P. and Amaral, A. (2001). 'Private Higher Education and Diversity: An Exploratory Survey', *Higher Education Quarterly*, 55(4), 359–395.

Tooley, J. (2001) *The Global Education Industry: Lessons from Private Education in Developing Countries* (2nd edn) (London: Institute of Economic Affairs).

Torres, C. A. and Schugurenky, D. (2002) 'The Political Economy of Higher Education in the Era of Neoliberal Globalisation: Latin America in Comparative Perspective', *Higher Education*, 43, 429–455.

Uvalic-Trumbic, S. and Varoglu, Z. (2003) *Survey of the 2002 Breaking News and the UNESCO Global Forum on Quality Assurance, Accreditation and the Recognition of Qualifications* (London: Observatory on Borderless Higher Education).

Verbik, L. and Jokivirta, L. (2005) *National Regulatory Frameworks for Transnational Higher Education: Models and Trends, Part 1 and Part 2*, Briefing Notes, 22 and 23 February and March (London: Observatory on Borderless Higher Education).

Vincent-Lancrin, S. (2005) *Building Capacity Through Cross-border Tertiary Education* (London: Observatory on Borderless Higher Education).

Wallerstein, I. M. (2004) *World Systems Analysis: An Introduction* (Durham, NC: Duke University Press).

3 Considering Equality, Equity and Higher Education Pedagogies in the Context of Globalization*

Elaine Unterhalter

Discussions of globalization by both advocates and critics accept the salience of the question of inequalities. The enormous growth, from the mid-1990s, of financial flows and trade, and of the movement of people, ideas, information, and technologies often took place with little regard for, and indeed masking, attendant inequalities (Castells, 2000). Indeed, a number of writers have disputed the assessment that globalization has been associated with increasing inequality; sharp debates rage concerning whether numbers in poverty have risen or fallen (Bhalla, 2002; Hoekman and Olarreaga, 2007). Critics of globalization remark the inequalities of race, class, gender, and the legacies of colonialism which it reproduced (eg. Sassen, 1996; Stiglitz, 2001 Hobsbawm, 2007). Others note the diminution of inequalities for some groups, and an entrenchment for others (Chen and Ravaillon, 2000; Wade, 2003). This has been a characteristic identified by writers on globalization and education, where differential processes of incorporation into the knowledge economy are noted, both at a national level and for particular groups (Green, 1997; Carnoy, 2000; Lauder, 2001; Brown, 2003; Blackmore, 2000; David, 2009). The discussion of the nature of the effects of globalization turns partly on the meanings ascribed to poverty, inequality, and knowledge economy. In this chapter, I want to set this debate, which has sometimes been conducted as a matter of technical definitions and disputes about data, within a wider context looking at the process of knowledge production within universities. Thus, partly through looking at accounts of higher education institutions engaging with the question of global inequalities, and partly through a reflection on some of the philosophical literature on equality, I want to try to understand the forms of pedagogical response to globalization and inequality. In this I am particularly interested first, in distinguishing forms of shifting relationships in relation to knowledge production, and second, in pedagogies that in some way have been oriented to changing inequalities. Through this discussion I want to return to consider the definitional debate.

My reflections on these issues draw on experiences of teaching, since the 1970s, in contexts where global inequality was both the everyday context of work and simultaneously the topic of discussion between differently positioned interlocutors. My first introduction to this was as a student volunteer on a literacy programme in Johannesburg, my home city, in 1971. At that time (and as distressingly remains the case today) Johannesburg was so sharply divided by geographies of race and class that it was not at all remarkable that I could have started a university degree, but not yet set foot in neighbourhoods just a few miles from the university, and know nothing at all of the lives of my contemporaries who lived there. What I knew in dimly understood fragments was a compressed excitement we attached to the ideas of Paulo Freire, which circulated as a kind of semi-legitimate shorthand for a means to effect the huge social and political change we wished for. Sitting in a youth club to plan a literacy programme, I heard for the first time about the lives of other volunteers and the people who would attend the classes, and wondered what, if anything, I could bring to the relational dynamic of a Freirean discussion. Our lives had a similar outward form, in that we had all been to school, read books, or listened to the radio, but the society constructed such vast inequalities in how we were treated in public spaces, what might be happening to our parents or school friends, and how we dared to think about the future. I was deeply perplexed regarding the relationship of learner and teacher, and the ways in which education articulates with social change, both in the sense of trying to name it and also connect with it. In some ways those concerns have only deepened over decades. While my opportunities to hear about different lives and participate in other kinds of education practices have widened, the complexities of the problem of addressing inequality and education have only become more puzzling. The deep rifts and misunderstandings, so evident amongst different groups living in Johannesburg in the 1970s, continue to play out again and again through global economic cycles of boom and bust, but so too does Freire's illumination that through understanding some of the processes at work we have a possibility to build towards social change. In some ways this attempt to clarify some aspects of a pedagogical engagement with inequality is a considered response to the questions posed by that long-ago literacy project with its combination of enormous division and fragile aspiration.

In thinking about equality, equity, and higher education pedagogies, I want to step off from a number of arguments very cogently put forward in Melanie's Walker's (2006) work on the capability approach and education. Her analysis proposes that thinking about higher education pedagogies is an ethically informed process in which we are alert to questions of equitability, a humane justice, and what we want students to be and become. Such a project is not a simple matter of organizing higher education institutions to respond to requirements for a knowledge society, be these imperatives couched in terms of efficiency, human capital, or cost-benefit. She also argues for a transformative view of higher education pedagogies that stretches beyond the bounded formal institutional places in which teaching and learning take place. This entails a critical engagement with knowledge, interwoven with the processes of freedom entailed in student and staff identity formation, organizational change, and support for student well-being and agency development. In conclusion she makes the case that this approach to changing higher education pedagogies, which draws on ideas about justice and capabilities, is a practice of 'guarded optimism', a practical project animated by hope. In this she seems to suggest that higher education pedagogies are an extremely generative space in which to understand, not just the problem of differently and unequally situated groups talking past each other and making completely opposing assessments of, say the effects of globalization, or the purposes of literacy, but also the possibilities that changes can be effected through differently inflected higher education pedagogies.

In developing her ideas I want to distinguish three views of higher education pedagogy, which I have termed: (1) Pedagogies of consequence; (2) Pedagogies of construction; (3) Pedagogies of connection. I use the more political term 'pedagogy', rather than the technical term 'teaching and learning' because, as a number of critical commentators note, seeing higher education merely as a space for the production of highly skilled 'human resources' who do no more than augment stocks of capital, overlooks the ways in which processes in higher education entail a critical engagement of trying to understand the world in which we live, an examination of hidden, as well as clearly defined problems, and a consideration of practices for change (Darder et al., 2003; Morley, 2003; Giroux and Giroux, 2006; Lambert et al., 2007). An underlying assumption is thus that the production of knowledge is enmeshed in social relations, which can be reproduced or changed, through contributory actions in universities.

I thus want to develop some themes in relation to the equality and equity questions entailed in thinking about justice, agency, and higher education's international dynamic. In looking at three different views of higher education pedagogies, I want to suggest some of the epistemological assumptions associated with each, some of the ways in which equality comes to be positioned, and some of the assessments that are made about global relations. I want to look at the implications for thinking about opportunity and process freedoms, core ideas in the capability approach as elaborated in the work of Amartya Sen and Martha Nussbaum and used by them and others to discuss aspects of higher education (Sen, 1992; Nussbaum, 1997; Sen, 1999; Nussbaum, 2006; Walker, 2006; Deprez and Butler, 2007).

As in any taxonomy used as a heuristic device, the boundaries between categories are somewhat tentative. They are intended to map a field and explore a range of positions, rather than to set up a hard set of divisional categories. It is thus highly likely that empirical work in particular institutions or of specified forms of global relationships will reveal an interplay between the different pedagogies I distinguish.

▶ Pedagogies of consequence

Pedagogies of consequence are, I think, the default position in much higher education, and the term may indeed not denote any critical pedagogical relationship, but in fact describe the more technical position on teaching and learning. However, the complexity of the processes occurring within higher education, even those that appear to use technical approaches (David, 2007), I think merits the consideration that these are pedagogies and not just techniques.

This formulation of pedagogies of consequence is associated with the view that the purpose of higher education is primarily to develop human capital and improve economic growth. Sometimes these pedagogies are linked with the idea that the purpose of higher education is to develop social stability or a sense of national pride or appropriate understandings of international and global processes. Thus pedagogies of consequence are linked with an instrumental view of higher education and knowledge production.

The view tends to be associated with what Michael Young (2008) and Joe Muller (2000) have termed 'an insular view of knowledge', that is that there are boundaries between different fields of knowledge and between theoretical or disciplinary knowledge, learned in higher education, and everyday knowledge, acquired somewhere else. In this view knowledge is somehow independent of the conditions of its production and the purpose of higher education pedagogy is immersion or induction into those knowledge systems, either through a particular form of teaching or a combination of research and teaching (Brew, 2006).

In the UK, the perception that pedagogies of consequence will 'harness' talents and promote economic and global growth were linked with initiatives for widening participation in higher education. These elements are evident elsewhere in the world, for example in initiatives in South Africa and India, to expand access to higher education and include groups once barred. But in all the three countries an expanded exposure to pedagogies of consequence, which might entail establishing new institutions or larger classes, admitting students with more diverse school backgrounds, and utilizing new technologies, has been effected without any full dismantling of the hierarchies between institutions, and long entrenched inequalities in the ways in which different groups of staff and students experience their education (Cloete et al., 2006; Kapur and Mehta, 2007; David, 2009; Leathwood and Read, 2009).

Thus equality and equity figure in pedagogies of consequence in limited ways. Pedagogies of consequence are associated with the view that some forms of social and economic inequality are inevitable. People will inherit different amounts of capital, have different school histories, and will earn differently depending on various rankings of professions or the pay scales within organizations. The countries of the world make different levels of provision for the wealth and well-being of the people who live there, and within different countries there are wider or narrower social divisions. People will live lives that are differently marked by happiness or personal fulfilment or levels of ethnic affiliation, themselves associated with different status levels. For pedagogies of consequence these inevitable inequalities are moderated by the policy and practice of meritocracy. Through widening access, the provision of what are assumed to be equal opportunities the worst excesses of these differences will be mitigated.

This approach, while noted as a means to address national social divisions in access to higher education and participation in the process of knowledge production, is neutral on the lifestyle and assumptions of what E. H. Hobsbawm has called 'pure, stateless, market capitalism, a sort of international bourgeois anarchism' (Hobsbawm, 2009), in which the promise of widening opportunities (whether or not these are realized) is articulated unproblematically side by side with the notion that no scrutiny should be given to the basis of wealth in the inequalities of others. This global bourgeoisie, unlike nationally embedded bourgeois classes of previous eras, may have a particularly problematic relationship with the country in which its members hold citizenship. Many may have stronger loyalties to the companies that employ them or the lifestyle they aspire to than to a nation state. They may thus evade or resent paying taxes, not enrol their children in local schools, not consider it a matter of course that they would attend a national university, and assess that only the less talented work in the public sector or address questions of inequality (Ball, 2003;

Connell, 2005; Reay et al., 2005; Kapur and Mehta, 2007; Longlands, 2009).

The global bourgeoisie is highly mobile and its members, or those who seek to enter its ranks, make up a high proportion of international students around the world (Ninnes and Hellsten, 2005; Takagi, 2009). One condition of this mobility is a guarantee of equal access to higher education to anyone who has the intellectual capacity and financial means for university study. For pedagogies of consequence whatever barriers exist are considered 'external', material, and relatively easy to overcome. Thus pedagogies of consequence are associated with no outward discrimination in admission or progression or access to the curriculum. This has been particularly useful in marketing higher education globally and helping develop frameworks for borderless or articulated higher education systems (Marginson, 2004; Ninnes and Hellsten, 2005; Bjarnason, 2004). Visas can be issued, satellite campuses can be established, technologies for communication can be put in place, academic literacy courses can be provided, and conventions associated with learning in higher education can be explained and de-coded. While within particular countries widening participation to pedagogies of consequence has meant barriers based on fees may be dismantled or repackaged in terms of student loans, internationalizing the drive for expanded access and equality of opportunity requires particular technologies and forms of regulation, but not a questioning of substantive pedagogical assumptions.

Pedagogies of consequence affirm that erroneous assumptions about the ways race or gender or class prohibit access to knowledge or wealth will be challenged and dismissed because all will have opportunities and the falsity of assessments based on prejudice will be revealed through the rigour of intellectual debate. Here is an extract from the Mission Statement of University College London, which encapsulates a combined commitment to equality of opportunity, global leadership, and academic excellence:

We are
a world-class centre of research and teaching, dedicated to developing and disseminating original knowledge to benefit the world of the future.

We believe
in engaging fully with the world around us; in breaking new ground through challenging convention; in progress through partnership....

We are committed
to pursuit of excellence and sustainability; to maintaining rich academic diversity embracing the Arts and Sciences; to equality of opportunity and fulfilment of potential for all our staff and students.

We strive always
to lead; to inspire; to achieve. (UCL, 2008)

Pedagogies of consequence are often monitored by looking for indicators of equal amounts, that is equal numbers of women or men, proportions of racialized groups in higher education, equal to the proportions in the population, and equal amounts of tutorial time given to each student, regardless of her or his background or country of origin. This is a view that stresses equality of opportunity. Pedagogies of consequence may come either in a weak form, that is they entail removing discriminatory barriers rooted in economic or geographic conditions or prejudices, or they may come in a strong form that attempts to redress forms of structural disadvantage associated with exclusion and discrimination, transforming conditions of work, schooling, and housing and health conditions (For further discussion of this distinction see Marshall, 2007). The extract from the UCL Mission Statement quoted above seems to express a weak form of equality of opportunity for staff and students. A strong form may be associated with active university engagement with, for example participation in campaigns to promote gender equality in schools and higher education worldwide, and support for refugee students that generated participation in the assessments of the social conditions driving their displacement.

In recent work on equity in education I have developed a topographical metaphor for distinguishing between three different forms of equity (Unterhalter, 2009). What I have called 'equity from above' is concerned with rules, regulation, and establishing a system of fairness. I see 'equity from below' as ensuring a fair process of participation and representation in discussion and I outline 'equity from the middle' associated with processes that facilitate fair forms of flow of information, resources or esteem between different settings of education. I associate a pedagogy of consequences with equity from above as this form of pedagogy rests on rules that have been decided as fair and reasonable by some widely recognized body of opinion. The rules that govern disciplines, regulate admission to higher education, and govern the award of certificates for teaching in higher education all might comprise this form of equity. Both national and supranational forms of system regulation have been developed with the Bologna process and a range of regional schemes worldwide for recognition of prior learning epitomizing notions of expanding access. Equity from above appeals to rules and notions of public good and it is these 'higher' processes that guide the pedagogy of consequence.

Within the pedagogy of consequence the assumption made about global relations appears to be that linked with many celebratory accounts of globalization that point to the expansion of trade, improved levels of economic growth and communication, and the impact of these processes on addressing poverty (Held, 2002). Thus pedagogies of consequence are concerned to overcome the outmoded boundaries of nation states, draw on the cultural and intellectual diversity they offer for knowledge production and enhancement, and work within a global regulatory regime that will enhance excellence and assist with mitigating against harm.

Pedagogies of consequence, thus, offer opportunities but not opportunity or process freedoms. They do not in and of themselves consider the ways in which freedom from hunger, poor schooling, or limited social protection in health are required to effect equality of opportunity. Moreover, the rather bland notion of 'progressing through partnership' expressed in the UCL Mission Statement quoted above does not take on board the long history of inequality between universities within particular countries and between countries that will affect the process freedoms in directing the participation in knowledge production. For pedagogies of consequence, the end of global economic expansion or sustainability or excellence in research will always trump the means.

▶ Pedagogies of construction

Pedagogies of consequence are concerned with the outcomes of higher education and their relationship with equality and equity both globally and nationally, and tend not to comment in too much depth on the process of knowledge construction, teaching, and learning so long as this is efficient and produces the requisite level of skill. By contrast, pedagogies of construction are associated with the view that higher education is intrinsically valuable in establishing the dispositions which can in Martha Nussbaum's terms 'cultivate humanity' (Nussbaum, 1997). There are particular virtues which can be nurtured in higher education which can tend towards abolishing oppression and building a democratic community. Unlike pedagogies of consequence, which are tolerant of some forms of inequality, providing there are no barriers to equality of access, pedagogies of construction assert and practice the importance of moral equality as a supreme value. For these pedagogies a key aspect of higher education is the inculcation of this idea. It may find expression in subject matter and teaching practices that instil an understanding of the moral worth of each and every person in the practice of medicine or the delivery of schooling or the assessment of economic harm. Whatever the discipline or profession, a concern with equality lies at the heart of pedagogic practice. The implication of this approach, in a context of global interconnections and responsibilities, is that pedagogies of construction are concerned with the worth of people in places that are geographically and socially far away as well as those that are close to home.

Pedagogies of construction regard the knowledge developed in higher education as a particular mix of disciplinary knowledge constructed and reconstructed through the lens of everyday knowledge. This is both generative of new insights and particularly effective, in, for example, enhancing disciplinary knowledge and facilitating a reflective appreciation of how forms of disciplinary knowledge have set up processes of exclusion and marginalization of various knowledge forms. In various formations associated with Vygotsky's work or post-structuralism knowledge is seen to be relational both to particular contexts and particular discursive formations. Some higher education pedagogies associated with this concern with what Bernard

Williams (2002) has termed 'truthfulness' to distinguish it from the assumptions of truth generally found in pedagogies of consequence. These stress the significance of stripping away the 'magical relations' that pretend to 'truth' and exposing the relational and contingent formations of truthfulness. I think that while this is a well-documented process in pedagogies of construction, the substantive concern with equality I place at the heart of the position entails more than balancing one set of relational approaches against another.

In order to illustrate this pedagogy at work, I want to quote from Yvette Abrahams' essay 'Ambiguity is my middle name. A research diary' (Abrahams, 2007). The work, written by a historian at the University of Cape Town, is an engagement with ideas about moral equality as a supreme value. It starts

> In 1996 I was requested to write up the historiography of Sarah Bartmann, a task I had up to then always managed to avoid. In fact, even in the face of a pointed request, I found the task impossible. I began writing this diary in order to understand why this was so. This chapter deals with my relationship to the academic world of knowledge surrounding the Sarah Bartmann story. It is a quest for self understanding and self-retrieval from the obscurities of a language not created for my benefit, a turnaround polemic against racist and sexist cultural texts which silenced me through their animosity, and a contribution towards the communal project of creating a more hospitable mental environment for African creativity. (Abrahams, 2007, 421)

The story of Sarah Bartmann is about one woman who experienced the immense cruelty and violence of racism, sexism, and inequalities between countries. Born in slavery in the Eastern Cape in the late eighteenth century, she was shipped to London and exhibited naked there and in Paris as an example of what was considered a particular racial type. After she died in 1815, her body was dissected and displayed in the Musée de l'Homme. A formal request for the return of her body to South Africa was made in 1994, but only effected in 2002, where she was buried near her home.

Yvette Abrahams comes from the same community as Sarah Bartmann. Her essay ranges across a critique of some of the writings about 'Auntie Sarah'. At points she counterposes her academic knowledge with the 'unschooled' everyday knowledge of her mother. At other points she reflects on the process of teaching this very personal and painful history in classes still marked by race and gender subjugation and about how black women can talk about a history of rape and sexual abuse. The chapter ends:

> I have always believed that, in trying to understand the world, the answers are only as important as the way you phrase the questions. Let me endeavour again: is there a 'right' history to be written about the crimes which were committed against us? This may be a strange question for a historian, but I am starting to see my elders' reasoning. My elders chose, often, not to tell me of my history because the pain, anger and hatred were considered not suitable for children. Only with the attainment of a certain age and seniority have I, cautiously, been allowed to hear the stories. I wonder still, and often, if all this were not better forgotten. My grandmother-in-law used to try to teach me to forgive my enemies. For years I shrugged this off as turn-the-other-cheek stuff which had no place in our struggle. Then I began to think about this clever woman who is never too old to learn. My grandmother-in-law has certainly survived a life I would be too frightened to live. Now, I have come to understand that it is the other tradition of my people – that side by side with our struggle to be free, there lived a struggle to remain human. Forgiving your enemies is not about them – they can see to themselves – it is about us.
>
> To write the history of pain, hatred and anger, without replicating and passing on the heavy burden of those unresolved emotions, would be a truly human story of Africa. (Abrahams, 2007, 450)

The pedagogic practice I want to draw out here is not only the postcolonial relationality, so that the past is in the present, the agency of the historian is always partial and fractured, but also, I want to stress the substantive concern with equality and the notion of being human that frames the analysis.

Higher education pedagogies of construction which stress substantive equality as a value in the centre seem to link with the notion I delineated of equity from below (Unterhalter, 2009). In this meaning equity in education entails some acknowledgement of pedagogy as a space of deliberation in which particular concerns of groups or individuals on, say, the curriculum content or the form of assessment or the treatment of men or women or the approach to management are negotiated. These negotiations take place not on the basis of majority rule, or the intensity of one person's view with regard to another, but through a process of reasonableness and reflection that considers each person participating in the discussion has a valuable opinion, which draws on multiple knowledge forms. But what is most valued is the process of establishing the considerate and fair relationships that support negotiation, questioning, and discussion. Equity from below seems to align with the emphasis in the capability approach on agency and process freedoms. Central to higher education pedagogies that draw on equity from below are knowledge forms and processes that establish dispositions for participation, exploration of different forms of experience, and respect. They might nurture a critical reflection on structures that inhibit dialogue, and would be oriented to develop a practice engaged with concern for equality. In the context of international and global higher education they would be particularly attentive to developing curricula that do not only frame issues in the perspectives of the minority world. They would also assess criticisms from beyond those frameworks, and come to reasoned conclusions about the different positions of diverse actors.

Martha Nussbaum has written both about cosmopolitan principles and higher education pedagogy. She defends her view of global obligations in terms of the entitlements all people in the world have to capabilities to function (Nussbaum, 2006, 271–324). All have entitlements to education, irrespective of gender or other social divisions. This does not mean everyone in the world has a duty to provide education for all, but we have a collective duty to think about how we can provide that education up to an appropriate threshold established by using the capabilities approach to focus on what valued aspects of doing and being can be secured (Nussbaum, 2006, 281). Nussbaum identifies a provisional list of central capabilities to function to guide this assessment. In its current form this list includes many areas where education is central – life, health, bodily integrity, senses, imagination, thought, emotions, practical reason, affiliation, play, relation with other species, and control over one's own environment (Nussbaum, 2000, 78–80; 2006). In Nussbaum's work the thin cosmopolitan boundaries drawn by nation states, although important for establishing ties of affiliation, are not adequate to secure gender equality in education or any other aspect of equality as a substantive moral goal. A contract among citizens may not adequately secure enough education or adequate equality. In these instances governments are manifestly not able to provide for education or other capabilities and a thick cosmopolitan statement of entitlements that goes beyond minimal provision holds up values not just to governments, but to many forms of social organization. In Nussbaum's view these ideas form part of the institutional architecture of a global structure which can make demands of governments and societies, including higher education organizations to provide for capabilities up to a minimum threshold (Nussbaum, 2006, 322). It is thus not enough for universities to offer equal opportunities in access, there is an additional commitment to social justice that is required.

Nussbaum thus welds thinking about global entitlements secured by global action, together with an appreciation of the importance of working within existing forms of citizenship and social contract provided by the nation state and diverse notions of the inter-national. She is particularly attentive to the complexities of cultural discussion, arguing that it is through building a capacity to see the world through the eyes of others that we can learn some of the dispositions associated with global social justice (Nussbaum, 1997). The space of education and forms of pedagogies of construction are particularly generative sites for cultural appreciation, contestation, and expansion into cosmopolitan spaces where equality is a central moral idea.

The Mission statement of the Institute of Education, University of London, expresses some of this idea of a guiding concern with justice:

> The Institute of Education's mission is to pursue excellence in education and related areas of social science and professional practice. In undertaking this mission the Institute will adhere to the highest standards of academic rigour in all its

work, be guided by a concern for truth and justice, and make a positive contribution to the development of individuals, institutions and societies facing the challenges of change. To this end, it will engage in:

- research and scholarship of national and international significance
- high quality, research-informed postgraduate and post-experience learning and teaching programmes
- the promotion of new ideas in policy and professional practice grounded in its research and teaching expertise
- consultancy and other services to support and develop the quality of educational systems and related fields of policy and practice (Institute of Education, 2003)

The statement makes a strong commitment about 'truth and justice' and the institution's 'positive contribution' to 'the challenges of change', which are implied to be not only national but also international. It does not assert it will lead this, but 'support and develop', and promote new ideas 'grounded in research and teaching expertise'. The pedagogy of constructing a shared, dialogic space guided by a particular set of values thus seems to be set out in aspiration.

▶ Pedagogies of connection

Pedagogies of construction consider how to develop dispositions that tend towards equality and justice. I want to distinguish these from a third form of pedagogies associated with equality that I have termed 'pedagogies of connection'. While pedagogies of construction express a notion of the good – and there might be many different variants of such a notion – pedagogies of connection are concerned with building engaged conceptual, empirical, and professional practices that allow for the evaluation of different situations and guide action. In developing the notion of pedagogies of connection I am drawing on ideas advanced by Amartya Sen (2008) on the importance of comparative ideas in making assessments about justice, trying to consider the kinds of connections that are important in establishing the kinds of rankings he suggests might be an important component of taking decisions on justice.

Pedagogies of connection I think can be associated with prag-matist and experientialist ideas about knowledge found in John Dewey's work. His argument that philosophy must be practical and step off from the problems of human activity generates a concern with ideas that socialize and humanize knowledge or truth. This process of making evaluations on the basis of under-standing the nature of knowledge production, the aspirations of everyday life, and how knowledge is different from belief are brought together in an approach to education that engages with ideas of active learning, critical reflection, and democratic participation (Dewey, 1916, 1938).

Thus pedagogies of connection have as one important com-ponent developing practices of evaluation. One key practice of evaluation is understanding the plurality of types of advantage and equality. Another form entails what Harry Brighouse and I (Brighouse and Unterhalter, 2010) have argued is a key impli-cation of some of the writings on the capability approach and education. We suggest that one purpose of education should be to support an individual to develop capabilities for a conception of the good and sense of justice. This suggests that educators should seek to inculcate capabilities for other-interestedness, for some degree of self-control, and for scrutinizing evidence and argument. Forms of evaluation are implicit in all these processes. Thus equality is not given the status of supreme value as in pedagogies of construction, but the concerns of justice require a consideration or evaluation of questions of equality, together with other issues such as liberty, fairness, and human rights. These evaluations cannot happen only through expanding opportunities or deepening process freedoms and participation; although these are important conditions to make this evaluation not purely academic, they need to call on addi-tional values with regard to deliberation about human rights, the notion of obligation, more general forms of social justice, and sustainability. This pedagogy of connection is associated with a third meaning of equity I have termed 'equity from the middle' (Unterhalter, 2009), which considers how fairly infor-mation or money or recognition might flow so that there are not distributional blockages, deficits, or hierarchies established or reproduced.

A recent example from teaching on a Masters programme in London illustrates some of these pedagogical practices. The module 'Gender, education and development' at the Institute of Education enrols a large number of students from many different countries, with a wide range of academic and professional backgrounds. In a session on gender, education, and empowerment the course team took up the issue of female circumcision to illustrate some of the diverse ways in which empowerment has been viewed. Using film interviews with women who carried out circumcisions, advocated for it, and activists who campaigned against it, very graphic material was presented side by side with academic debates on empowerment. While in earlier versions of the course this material had sparked sharp antagonisms between students from different regions, a pedagogy that set out both to inform students in advance of the upsetting nature of some of the detail, opened a space for students to talk about their own experiences, and allowed a debate to progress, considering both personal reflection and the nature of some conceptual framings. Reflecting on the quality of the discussion as one of the teachers, I had the feel of a particularly generative form of connection and evaluation. This is illustrated by one student's response, extracted from the course evaluation:

> We need to be aware of the values we export to other cultures through development. Of course, there are some universal values at play, but equality/empowerment looks to us different in different contexts. We also should be more aware of the forces that shaped female emancipation in Europe because ethics/gender mainstreaming/rights alone do not result in equality/emancipation for women. (IoE, 2009)

What are the issues of global relationship entailed by equity from the middle and pedagogies of connection? I think that considering cosmopolitanism not just as a substantive value, associated with the ideas I have grouped under pedagogies of construction, but as a means of making particular evaluations may be a generative way of framing global pedagogies engaged with questions of equality. Anthony Appiah (2007), in making an argument for cosmopolitanism, questions the boundaries made by culture, while acknowledging ties of identity and affiliation. He argues for the importance of conversation across national and cultural difference, kindness to strangers, and global obligation underpinned by an idea of justice. He stresses the importance of evaluating how aid or recognition is disbursed. It seems to me there is equity from the middle here. There are flows of language, stories, ethical relationships, and redistribution which attempt to move to overcome the hierarchies of history or the power of money. The implication is that cosmopolitan higher education pedagogies are concerned with global obligations. Thus they do not mark boundaries around culture or citizenship. Their mode is a process of flow or conversation through which they assess, evaluate, and revise. Appiah draws on Adam Smith to describe a process of responding to strangers because of 'reason, principle, conscience, the inhabitants of the breast'. The pedagogy of connection links these all together.

The changing world relations associated with a recession in which needs cannot only be met nationally, be these for food, fuel, control on climate change, financial stability, or improved economic relations that build towards equality, all seem to call for an ethical orientation to strangers animated by listening, exchanging, and assessing one's own aspirations in relation to the needs of others. Universities can provide an important semi-detached space in which such pedagogies can be developed and enhanced.

▶ **Conclusion**

I have tried to distinguish three forms of higher education pedagogies each differently concerned with a form of equality and equity and different views of global relations. In concluding I want to make an argument for complementarity. I think that each of the three pedagogic forms are often presented as all-encompassing. Hence each is seen as the only valuable way to expand capabilities, achieve equality, equity, or global social justice. But I think that pedagogies of consequence that do not take seriously a substantive notion of equality quickly become detached and co-opted by political economies that are hostile to any ideas of equality. They have been associated with the most destructive forms of globalization and lack of regulation which corrupt some of their core ideas associated with skills, inclusion, and institution building. Pedagogies of construction that are primarily concerned with feeling, experience, and the elaboration of the value of equality may find they have ample space in the most elite institution, regulated only by equity from above, and no dynamic to move into practical policy or the evaluation of global inequalities associated with equity from the middle. Pedagogies of connection with their stress on comparative evaluation and the link between theory and practice, which do not take seriously the deep hurts and injustices identified by the concern with emotion facilitated by equity from below and expressed through pedagogies of construction, may find their evaluations work on a narrow range of indicators. Their concerns with a comparative approach to justice may be construed as merely rhetorical, technical, or limited by the rules and principles enacted by equity from above. Thus I want to stress the importance of a pluralist egalitarianism, the complementarity of different higher education pedagogies, and the significance of understanding particular socio-cultural and political-economic contexts in articulating forms of equity and global obligation. Articulation has a sense both of making a statement and a connection and thus appears to express some of the ideas about talking and listening I could not name 30 years ago.

▶ Note

* Versions of this chapter were presented at the conference *Learning Together* which took place at the Institute of Education, University of London, in July 2007, and at a colloquium on Higher Education Pedagogies at the University of Nottingham in May 2008. I appreciate the questions from those who participated in both events and am grateful for very helpful comments on drafts from Vincent Carpentier, Melanie Walker, and Louise Morley.

▶ References

Abrahams, Y. (2007) 'Ambiguity is My Middle Name: A Research Diary', in N. Gasa (ed.) *Women in South African History* (Pretoria: Human Sciences Research Council Press).

Appiah, A. (2007) *Cosmopolitanism: Ethics in a World of Strangers* (London: Penguin).

Ball, S. J. (2003) *Class Strategies and the Education Market: The Middle Class and Social Advantage* (London: Routledge Falmer).

Bhalla, S. (2002) *Imagine There's No Country: Poverty, Inequality and Growth in the Era of Globalization* (Washington: Peterson Institute).

Bjarnason, S. (2004) 'Borderless Higher Education', in R. King (ed.) *The University in the Global Age* (London: Palgrave).

Blackmore, J. (2000) 'Globalisation: A Useful Concept for Feminists Rethinking Theory and Strategy in Education?', in N. C. Burbules and C. A. Torres (eds) *Globalisation and Education: Critical Perspectives* (Abingdon: Routledge).

Brew, A. (2006) *Research and Teaching: Beyond the Divide* (London: Palgrave).

Brighouse, H. and Unterhalter, E. (2010) 'Education, Primary Goods and Capabilities', in H. Brighouse and I. Robeyns (eds) *Measuring Justice: Primary Goods and Capabilities* (Cambridge: Cambridge University Press).

Brown, P. (2003) 'The Opportunity Trap: Education and Employment in a Global Economy', *European Education Research Journal*, 2(1), 142–178.

Carnoy, M. (2000) *Sustaining the New Economy: Work, Family and Community in the Information Age* (Cambridge, MA: Harvard University Press).

Castells, M. (2000) *The Rise of the Network Society: Economy, Society and Culture* (London: Blackwell).

Chen, C. and Ravaillon, M. (2000) *How Did the World's Poor Fare in the 1990s?*, World Bank Working Paper (Washington: World Bank).

Clarke, C. (2003) *Foreword to White Paper on Higher Education: The Future of Higher Education* (London: Department for Education and Skills).

Cloete, N., Fehnel, R., Massen, P., Moja, T., Perold, H. and Gibbon, T. (eds) (2007) *Transformation in Higher Education: Global Pressures and Local Realities* (Cape Town: Juta and Company).

Connell, R. W. (2005) 'Globalization, Imperialism and Masculinities', in M. S. Kimmel, J. Hearnand and R. W. Connell (eds) *Handbook of Men and Masculinities* (Thousand Oaks, CA: Sage).

Darder, A., Baltodano, M. and Torres, R. D. (eds) (2003) *The Critical Pedagogy Reader* (New York: Routledge Falmer).

David, M. (2007) 'Equity and Diversity: Towards a Sociology of Higher Education for the Twenty-First Century?', *British Journal of Sociology of Education*, 28(5), 675–690.

David, M. (ed.) (2009) *Improving Learning by Widening Participation in Higher Education* (London: Routledge).

Deprez, L. and Butler, S. (2007) 'Higher Education and Well Being', in M. Walker and E. Unterhalter (eds) *Amartya Sen's Capability Approach and Social Justice in Education* (London: Palgrave).

Dewey, J. (1916) *Democracy and Education: An Introduction to the Philosophy of Education* (London: Macmillan).

Dewey, J. (1938) *Experience and Education* (London: MacMillan).

Foucault, M. (1977) *Discipline and Punish: The Birth of the Prison* (London: Allen Lane).

Giroux, H. and Giroux, S. (2006) 'Challenging Neo-liberalism's New World Order: The Promise of Critical Pedagogy', *Cultural Studies. Critical Methodology*, 6(1), 21–32.

Green, A. (1997) *Education, Globalisation and the Nation State* (London: Palgrave).

Held, D. (2002) *Globalization/Anti-Globalization* (Cambridge: Polity).

Hobsbawm, E. (2007) *Globalization, Democracy and Terrorism* (London: Abacus).

Hobsbawm, E. (2009) 'Socialism has Failed, Now Capitalism is Bankrupt. So What Comes Next?', *The Guardian*, 10 April, online at http://www.guardian.co.uk/commentisfree/2009/apr/10/financial-crisis-capitalism-socialism-alternatives (accessed 2 June 2009).

Hoekman, B. and Olarreaga, M. (eds) (2007) *Global Trade and Poor Nations* (Washington: Brookings Institute Press).

Institute of Education (IoE) (2003) 'Mission Statement of the Institute of Education, University of London' (London: Institute of Education). Online at http://www.ioe.ac.uk/about/760.html (accessed 11 December 2009).

Institute of Education (IoE) (2009) 'Institute of Education, University of London Module Evaluation: Gender Education and Development, Summer term 2008/2009' (London: Institute of Education).

Kapur, D. and Mehta, H. (2007) 'Indian Higher Education Reform: From Half-Baked Socialism to Half-Baked Capitalism', Paper presented at the Brookings National Council of Applied Economic Research Policy Forum, New Delhi.

Lambert, C., Parker, A. and Neary, M. (2007) 'Teaching Entrepreneurialism and Critical Pedagogy: Reinventing the Higher Education Curriculum', *Teaching in Higher Education*, 12(4), 525–536.

Lauder, H. (2001) 'Innovation, Skill Diffusion and Social Exclusion', in Brown, P., Green, A. and Lauder, H. (eds) *High Skills: Globalisation, Competitiveness and Skill Formation* (Oxford, Oxford University Press).

Leathwood, C. and Read, B. (2009) *Gender and the Changing Face of Higher Education. A Feminized Future?* (Maidenhead: Open University Press).

Longlands, H. (2009) 'Breadwinners or Caregivers? Masculinities and Fatherhood in Global Corporations', Paper presented at the Gender and Education Association Conference, 25 March 2009, Institute of Education, University of London.

Marginson, S. (2004) 'Global Education Markets and Global Public Goods'. Keynote address, Australian and New Zealand Comparative and International Education Society conference, Australian Catholic University, Melbourne, 3 December.

Marshall, G. (2006) *Equality* (Cambridge: Polity Press).

Morley, L. (2003) *Quality and Power in Higher Education* (Maidenhead: McGraw Hill).

Muller, J. (2000) *Reclaiming Knowledge: Social Theory, Curriculum and Educational Policy* (London: Routledge).

Ninnes, P. and Hellsten, M. (2005) *Internationalizing Higher Education: Critical Explorations of Pedagogy and Policy* (Dordrecht: Springer).

Nussbaum, M. (1997) *Cultivating Humanity: A Classical Defense of Reform in Liberal Education* (Cambridge: Harvard University Press).

Nussbaum, M. (2000) *Women and Human Development: The Capabilities Approach* (Cambridge: Cambridge University Press).

Nussbaum, M. (2006) *Frontiers of Justice: Disability, Nationality, Species Membership* (Cambridge, MA: The Belknap Press of Harvard University Press).

Reay, D., David, M. and Ball, S. (2005) *Degrees of Choice: Social Class, Race and Gender in Higher Education* (Stoke-on-Trent: Trentham Books).

Sassen, S. (1996) *Losing Control? Sovereignty in an Age of Globalization* (New York: Columbia University Press).

Sassen, S. (2001) *The Global City* (New Jersey: Princeton University Press).

Sen, A. (1992) *Inequality Re-examined* (Oxford: Oxford University Press).

Sen, A. (1999) *Development as Freedom* (Oxford: Oxford University Press).

Sen, A. (2008) 'The Idea of Justice', *Journal of Human Development*, 9(3), 331–342.

Stiglitz, J. (2001) *Globalization and its Discontents* (London: Penguin).

Takagi, H. (2009) 'Internationalisation of Undergraduate Curricula: The Gap Between Ideas and Practice in Japan', *London Review of Education*, 7(1), 31–39.

University College London (2008) 'Mission Statement: University College London', online at http://www.ucl.ac.uk/academic-manual/part-b/b2 (accessed 2 June 2009).

Unterhalter, E. (2009) 'What is Equity in Education? Reflections from the Capability Approach', *Studies in Philosophy and Education*, 28(5), 415–424.

Wade, R. (2003) 'Is Globalization Reducing Poverty and Inequality?', *World Development*, 32(4), 567–589.

Walker, M. (2006) *Higher Education Pedagogies* (Maidenhead: Society for Research into Higher Education/Open University Press).

Williams, B. (2002) *Truth and Truthfulness: An Essay in Genealogy* (Princeton: Princeton University Press).

Young, M. (2008) *Bringing Knowledge Back In: From Social Constructivism to Social Realism in the Sociology of Education* (London: Routledge).

Part 2
Some Dimensions of Inequalities

4 Global Rankings of Universities: A Perverse and Present Burden

Saleem Badat

> Not everything that can be counted counts and not everything that counts can be counted. (Albert Einstein)

> A farmer wanting to breed a big cow should focus more on nutrition than the weighing scales (President of a Japanese University, cited in Charon and Wauters, 2007)

> Indices 'rarely have adequate scientific foundations to support precise rankings: typical practice is to acknowledge uncertainty in the text of the report and then to present a table with unambiguous rankings.' (Andrews cited in Saisana and d'Hombres, 2008)

▶ Introduction

While national rankings of universities have existed for some decades, in recent years the phenomenon of the global rankings of universities has come into prominence. The Times Higher Education-Quacquarelli Symonds (THE-QS) 'World University Rankings' and the Shanghai Jiao Tong Institute of Higher Education's (SJTIHE) 'Academic Ranking of World Universities' are the best known of such rankings.

This chapter engages with the phenomenon of global rankings from the perspective of higher education in the global South and informed by a particular conception of universities and higher education. It addresses five issues: what credence should be given to rankings; the value of rankings; what is at stake in terms of educational and social purposes; the social determinants of rankings; and the future of rankings.

▶ Defining universities

For good reasons, national higher education systems tend to evince highly differentiated and diverse institutions, with universities characterized by different missions, goals, and differing size, configurations of academic programmes, admission requirements and academic standards, as appropriate to specified purposes and goals. This implies that the meaning of a university cannot be found in the content of their teaching and research, how they undertake these or their admission policies. Instead, the core purposes of a university reside elsewhere.

The first purpose is the production of knowledge which advances understanding of the natural and social worlds, and enriches humanity's accumulated scientific and cultural inheritances. Boulton and Lucas pithily summarize the myriad responsibilities of universities in this regard:

> [U]niversities operate on a complex set of mutually sustaining fronts – they research into the most theoretical and intractable uncertainties of knowledge and yet also seek the practical application of discovery; they test, reinvigorate and carry forward the inherited knowledge of earlier generations; they seek to establish sound principles of reasoning and action which they teach to generations of students. Thus, universities operate on both the short and the long horizon. On the one hand...they work with contemporary problems and they render appropriate the discoveries and understanding that they generate. On the other hand, they forage in realms of abstraction and domains of enquiry that may not appear immediately relevant to others, but have the proven potential to yield great future benefit. (2008, p. 3)

A second purpose of universities is the dissemination of knowledge and the cultivation of the cognitive character of students. The goal is to produce graduates that, ideally: 'can think effectively and critically'; have 'achieved depth in some field of knowledge'; have a 'critical appreciation of the ways in which we gain knowledge and understanding of the universe, of society, and of ourselves'; have 'a broad knowledge of other cultures and other times'; are 'able to make decisions based on reference to the wider world and to the historical forces that have shaped it'; have 'some understanding of and experience in thinking systematically about moral and ethical problems'; and can 'communicate with cogency' (The Task Force on Higher Education and Society, 2000, p. 84).

The final purpose of universities is to undertake community engagement. Here, it is important to distinguish between a university being responsive to its political, economic and social contexts and community engagement. Being alive to context does not mean that a university is necessarily engaged with communities. Sensitivity to economic and social conditions and challenges is a necessary condition but not a sufficient condition for community engagement.

Community engagement encompasses community outreach, student and staff volunteer activities and more recently 'service-learning'. Service-learning seeks to build on the core knowledge production and dissemination purposes of the university and has sought to become a 'curricular innovation' infused in the teaching and learning and research activities of the University (Stanton, 2008, p. 2). As has been noted

> Service-learning...engage(s) students in activities where both the community and student are primary beneficiaries and where the primary goals are to provide a service to the community and, equally, to enhance student learning through rendering this service. Reciprocity is therefore a central characteristic of service-learning. The primary focus of programmes in this category is on integrating community service with scholarly activity such as student learning, teaching, and research. This form of community engagement is underpinned by the assumption that service is enriched through scholarly activity and that scholarly activity, particularly student learning, is enriched through service to the community. (CHE, 2006, p. 15)

To effectively undertake its diverse educational and social purposes, a university must have a commitment 'to the spirit of truth' (Graham, 2005, p. 163), and must possess the necessary academic freedom and institutional autonomy. However, while academic freedom and institutional autonomy are necessary conditions, they are also rights in which duties inhere (Jonathan, 2006). In formerly colonial contexts, we must recognize, as Andre du Toit urges, 'the legacies of intellectual colonisation and racialisation as threats to academic freedom' (2000); and that 'the powers conferred by academic freedom go hand in hand with substantive duties to deracialise and decolonize intellectual spaces' (Bentley et al., 2006). Other duties on the part of universities include advancing the public good and being democratically accountable. They also encompass bold engagement with economic and social orthodoxies and public policies that may seriously misunderstand and distort the purposes of universities, stripping them of their substance and leaving them 'universities only in name' (Boulton and Lucas, 2008, p. 6).

It is not necessary here to deal with the roots, emergence or central doctrines of neo liberalism, the dominant orthodoxy of recent decades. Suffice to say that neo-liberalism holds that 'the social good will be maximized by maximizing the reach and frequency of market transactions, and it seeks to bring all human action into the domain of the market' (Harvey, 2008, p. 3). Importantly, 'if markets do not exist (in areas such as land, water, education, health care, social security, or environmental pollution) then they must be created, by state action if necessary' (ibid., p. 2).

Neo-liberal thinking and ideas, whether embraced willingly or imposed through the coercive or disciplinary power of powerful international economic and political institutions, have reshaped economic and social policies, institutions and practices. For one, instead of development as 'a process of expanding the real freedoms that people enjoy' (Sen, 1993, p. 3), the conception of development has been economized and reduced to economic growth and enhanced economic performance as measured by various indicators. Not surprizingly, 'the logic of the market has...defined the purposes of universities largely in terms of their role in economic development' (Berdahl, 2008, p. 48). Public investment in higher education has come to be justified largely in terms of economic growth and preparing students for the labour market. For another, neo-liberalism has come to define universities as 'just supermarkets for a variety of public and private goods that are currently in demand, and whose value is defined by their perceived aggregate financial value' (Boulton and Lucas, 2008, p. 17). As a recent monograph notes, 'to define the university enterprise by these specific outputs, and to fund it only through metrics that measure them, is to misunderstand the nature of the enterprise and its potential to deliver social benefit' (ibid., p. 17).

The notion of higher education as simply another tradable service and a private good that primarily benefits students has influenced public financing, which in turn has impacted on the structure and nature of higher education. As public universities have sought out 'third stream income' to supplement resources, this has often resulted in 'at one end, the commercialization of universities [which] means business in education. At the other end, the entry of private players in higher education means education as business' (Nayyar, 2008, p. 9). If globalization, and especially the revolution in information and communication technology, has influenced the 'ways and means of providing higher education' (ibid., p. 7), neo-liberalism has shaped 'education both in terms of what is taught and what is researched, ... shifting both student interests and university offerings away from broader academic studies and towards narrower vocational programmes' (Duderstadt et al., 2008, p. 275).

Neo-liberalism has also brought in its wake a rampant 'culture of materialism', which has transformed 'a reasonable utilitarianism ... into Narcissist hedonism' (Nayyar, 2008, p. 5), a celebration of individualism and greed, and self-serving ideas based on arrogant power and narrow economic interests. It has disdained knowledge that is antithetical to its core beliefs, and has been hostile to the idea of public good. In these regards, neo-liberalism has effectively incubated the seismic and grave financial and economic crisis that envelopes the world today.

Universities have, in general, been timid in their engagement with and response to neo-liberalism, notwithstanding that it has spawned dubious thinking and policy with respect to the value and social purposes of universities, and has sought to reduce universities to instruments of the economy and business. The pernicious effects on education, knowledge and public reasoning, and especially the arts, humanities and social sciences have been all too evident.

With these features of the history and purpose of universities in the contemporary era, what credence should be given to university rankings? The Shanghai Jiao Tong Institute of Higher Education (SJTIHE) ranking has its genesis in the quest of the Chinese government to create 'world-class universities' as catalysts of economic development and enhancing China's position in the global knowledge economy. As one of the pioneer's of the SJTIHE ranking writes, the concerns were:

What is the definition of a world-class university? ... What are the positions of top Chinese universities in the world higher education system? How can top Chinese universities reduce their gap with world-class universities? In order to answer these questions, I started to benchmark top Chinese universities with world-class universities and eventually to rank the world universities. (Liu, 2009, p. 2)

The benchmarking gave priority to six indicators for which data was available. Differential weights were assigned.

Table 4.1 Shanghai Jiao Tong Ranking: Indicators and weighting

Indicator	Weight(%)
1. Highly cited researchers in broad categories	20
2. Articles published in Nature & Science	20
3. Articles in Science/Social Science Citation Index	20
4. Faculty with Nobel Prizes/Field Medals	20
5. Alumni with Nobel Prizes/Field Medals	10
6. Research performance on 1–5 per staff member	10
Total	100

Source: Adapted from Mohamedbhai, G. (2008).

It is clear that for the SJTIHE a 'world-class university' is a 'research university' that performs well in relation to the six chosen indicators and the manner in which they are weighted.

A second ranking, the Times Higher Education-Quacquarelli Symonds (THE-QS) system, has a slightly different aim, 'to recognise universities as the multi-faceted organisations that they are, to provide a global comparison of their success against the notional mission of remaining or becoming world-class'. Four criteria are considered pivotal to being judged 'world-class': 'research quality', 'teaching quality', 'graduate employability' and 'international outlook'. The THE-QS ranking creates a league table of the world's 'top universities' through: 'academic peer review' (a survey of 6534 academics in 2008); 'employer review' (2339 responses in 2008), 'citations per academic' (using Scopus Elsevier) and academic: student ratios, and the proportions of international academics and students at a university (THE-QS, 2009).

Table 4.2 Times Higher Ranking: Indicators and weighting

Indicator	Weight(%)
1. Academic peer review (email questionnaire)	40
2. Citations per academic	20
3. Academic staff: student ratio	20
4. Proportion of international academic staff	5
5. Proportion of international students	5
6. Employer review (global online survey)	10
Total	100

Source: Adapted from Mohamedbhai, G. (2008).

It is evident that teaching figures alongside research in these indicators.

The Centre for Higher Education (CHE) in Germany's ranking of over 280 universities in Germany 'is exclusively subject specific'. It uses multiple indicators of academic quality as well as the views of some 200,000 students and 15,000 academics. On the basis of its performance in a specific subject a university is located in one of the three categories – the 'top', 'middle' or 'bottom' grouping of universities (Brandenburg, 2009).

With respect to the credence that is to be given to rankings, it is important to critically analyse the purposes and aims that they claim to seek to serve, and the methodologies that they employ. The SJTIHE began its work as an attempt to benchmark Chinese universities as a means of identifying shortcomings and charting a trajectory for their institutional development. It, however, slipped into the creation of a global ranking of universities on the basis of a narrow range of research indicators that are wholly inadequate for measuring performance and quality in relation to the diverse social and educational purposes of universities, and especially the variety of roles they must play in underdeveloped societies. The precise purpose and aims of THE-QS ranking in generating a global league table of universities is opaque. Its discourse is one of 'world esteem', with the 'world-class' university representing the gold standard to which all universities are meant to aspire and by which they should seek to be measured. The criterion of the degree of internationalization of the student body is seemingly to be valued less for the enrichment of a university's academic and institutional culture as much as because international students are a 'prized quarry' as 'universities are free to charge them whatever the market will bear' (Ince, 2007).

Marginson notes that 'in the Times Higher universe, higher education is primarily about reputation for its own sake, about the aristocratic prestige and power of the universities as an end in itself, and also about making money from foreign students'. This seems to 'have been designed to service the market in cross-border degrees, in which the UK and Australian universities are active'. Thus 'it is not about teaching and only marginally about research' (Marginson, 2006a, p. 5; 2007b, pp. 138–139). While the THE-QS claimed that its purpose in ranking was 'to recognise universities as the multi-faceted organisations that they are', it is clear that the criteria that it employs and its dubious use of some of the criteria as proxies for teaching and learning quality violates the idea of universities as 'multi-faceted organisations' that must serve a variety of social and educational purposes. The CHE ranking has no grandiose ambitions such as a global ranking of universities. It seeks to guide 'anybody who wants to take up a course of academic studies, but is uncertain about where' and 'students who would like to change to another university' (CHE, 2009). Its more circumspect aim, its focus on subjects and use of multiple criteria, including the views of academics and students, make it a more useful instrument. The fact that students are permitted to weight the criteria as they choose also means that they are empowered to make choices in accordance with what they seek and value in a university.

On the *methodological* front, the rankings can be critiqued on a number of grounds. The SJTIHE and THE-QS rankings suffer to differing degrees from various weaknesses related to the accuracy, reliability and validity of the data. These include: 'weaknesses in data collection and computation; the arbitrary criteria used in ranking; and the arbitrary weightings and standardization procedures used in combining different data sets into composite indexes' (Marginson, 2008a, p. 7). Such indexes 'undermine validity (as) it is dubious to combine different purposes and the corresponding data using arbitrary weightings. Links between purposes and data are lost. Likewise, it is invalid to mix subjective data on reputation with objective data on resources or research outputs as the Times Higher Education Supplement does' (Marginson, 2007b, p. 139).

While THE-QS claim to make use of 'peer review', its actual technique is less the peer review as undertaken in the academic world as much as a reputational survey. In any event, peer review is not without its problems. While it may be a 'valuable tool, some prejudice may still exist through peer conservatism and institutional reputation favoured by age, size, name and country biases' (Charon and Wauters, 2007). That is to say, older well-known universities in Europe and the United States may be given undue eminence at the expense of newer yet outstanding universities in other parts of the world. Rankings that make use of reputational surveys have been challenged for their halo effects and 'circular character' as 'high reputation generates high ranking generates more high reputation, without any connection to performance' (Marginson, 2008a, p. 7).

The indicators that are used and the weight that is accorded to particular indicators in global rankings privilege specific university activities, domains of knowledge production, specific languages and kinds of research and universities. Thus, the natural and medical sciences and engineering are privileged relative to the arts, humanities and social sciences; articles published in the English language are favoured over those printed in other languages, and journal articles are favoured over book chapters, policy reports and conference proceedings. Moreover, 'comprehensive' universities and generally larger institutions with a wide range of fields, disciplines and faculties and larger numbers of academics and especially researchers are privileged over other universities (Charon and Wauters, 2007). The rankings are therefore self-selecting of those universities whose missions, academic programme offerings, structures and organization strongly match the performance measures that are employed.

Even if credence is given to the performance measures that are used, a recent report has found that the SJTIHE and THE-QC 'rankings are only robust in the identification of the top 15 performers on either side of the Atlantic, but unreliable on the exact ordering of all other institutes' (d'Hombres and Saisana, 2009). When the THE-QS and SJTIHE indicators are combined 'in a single framework, the space of the inference is too wide for about 50 universities of the 88 universities we studied and thus no meaningful rank can be estimated for those universities' (ibid., 2009).

As a consequence of concerns related to the reliability and validity of data, and aware of the pitfalls regarding data and judgements related to learning and teaching, community engagement and other activities of universities, the SJTIHE ranking, to its credit, confines itself to performance measures that are a proxy for research performance. Nonetheless, if the goal is to globally rank universities, the narrow focus on research and the omission of data related to learning and teaching, community engagement and myriad other issues are serious weaknesses (Saisana and D'Hombres, 2008). These issues include equity of student access, opportunity and success; the diversity of students and staff; internationalization and internationalism with respect to students, staff and curriculum; intellectual climate; institutional culture; academic freedom and institutional autonomy; and democratic governance, including student participation. They also extend to the contributions of universities to democratic citizenship and what Nussbaum calls the 'cultivation of humanity' (2006, p. 5). All of these issues, including the visibility of universities in the intellectual and cultural life of societies, and their effectiveness, productivity and efficiency with regard to the employment of public subsidies and financial resources, are hardly peripheral to judgements about the overall quality of universities.

It should be clear that in a range of areas, quantitative indicators alone will not suffice in judgements about quality. Moreover, the use of quantitative indicators such as student applications, entrance grades, staff qualifications, available resources and research outputs as proxies for judgements on the quality of learning and teaching are inadequate and of doubtful value.

The CHE is on sound ground for being sceptical of whole university rankings, composite indexes and league tables. As it states, 'just as universities are not all equally good, so there is no "the" best university'. It is also unlikely that any university will be uniformly outstanding in every discipline and field and every level of academic programme and qualification. Thus, the CHE notes that 'the universities' performance in the individual disciplines, subjects and departments differs far too greatly. Aggregation at the level of whole universities offers no 'useful information as a decision-making aid' (CHE, 2009).

Rankings resonate strongly with both the performative culture of the new public management of recent decades, and the specific national and institutional interests that in conditions of the commercialization and marketization of higher education stand to gain in status, income and power. The SJTIHE and THE-QS rankings are simultaneously the products of the new world of commercialized, marketized and commodified higher education, embody the neo-liberal logic of brazen celebration of power, wealth and prestige and serve as agents of their reproduction. Marginson puts it well: 'discourses of social status are primary in the sustaining of status and are all the more powerful when joined to the force of calculation' (2009, p. 14).

▶ What is at stake?

Insofar as global rankings are concerned, there is much at stake for universities in underdeveloped societies in the global South and for higher education in general.

First, under the umbrella of a hegemonic neo-liberalism, 1950s' modernization theory, which vaunted Western capitalist societies as the symbol of 'development' and proclaimed 'catching up' with the West as the primary task of development, made a triumphant return. With it returned the ideas of Western capitalist societies as the apogee of modernity and the ideal of development. It is entailed that the path to development by 'traditional' societies lies in faithful adherence to the economic and development prescriptions of Northern governments and Northern-dominated multinational institutions such as the World Bank, the International Monetary Fund and World Trade Organisation.

Of course, underdeveloped societies are far from 'traditional' societies, given the changes that imperialism and colonialism have wrought in economic and social structure and conditions. The new ace, however, was supposedly globalization and its purported effervescent quality of generalizing development and creating 'developing' societies in the image of the 'developed'. The previous 'mistake' of the World Bank and other international institutions of disregarding universities in underdeveloped societies as agents of development, which resulted in their serious debilitation, would now, in the epoch of the 'knowledge economy' and 'information society', be rectified and support would be provided for the revitalization of universities.

Wallerstein has argued that twin meanings have tended to be given to development: 'On the one hand...greater internal equality, that is, fundamental social...transformation. On the other hand,...economic growth which involved "catching up" with the leader (i.e. the US)' (1991, p. 115). However, he correctly argues that historical experience shows that 'social transformation and catching up are seriously different objectives. They are not necessarily correlative with each other. They may even be in *contradiction* with each other' (Wallerstein, 1991, pp. 115–116). His conclusion is that 'it should be clear by now that we have to analyze these objectives separately and cannot continue blithely to assume their pairing, which developmentalists...have for the most done for the past 150 years'. The 'rhetoric of development has masked a contradiction that is deep and enduring .... (T)his contradiction is now a glaring one' (ibid., pp. 116–117).

Without detracting from the role of national elites in underdeveloped societies in retarding development and social justice, it must be observed that attempts by countries in the South to develop occur on a terrain of enduring global inequalities, which in many instances have intensified in the epoch of globalization and the hegemony of neo-liberalism. Development, especially of the kind that realizes greater internal equality and social justice, has continued to be elusive. This is so notwithstanding the adherence on the part of many governments in underdeveloped societies to the 'development' prescriptions of Northern governments and multinational institutions and the ubiquitous experts and consultants that traverse 'developing' societies (Chang, 2008).

In the same way that modernization theory depicts Western capitalist societies and institutions as the apex of development and modernity, global university rankings, as the spawn of the modernization paradigm, constitute the 'world-class university', which is essentially North American and European, as the goal of higher education development and the pinnacle of the university hierarchy. One should, of course, not be averse to learning from universities elsewhere and to critically borrow ideas, policies and strategies. The value, however, of a path of uncritical imitation/mimicry of, and 'catching up' with, the so-called top 'research universities' and the pursuit of the status of 'world-class university' for enhancing economic and social development is debatable. In any event, it cannot be blithely assumed that the massive investment that will necessarily be entailed in creating 'world-class' universities will in itself have a profound effect on economic and social development. The creation of such universities may be a necessary condition but is not a sufficient condition for development. Indeed, in many societies in the South the challenge is to create favourable national higher education policy environments and wider economic and social policy environments to facilitate the work and contributions of universities.

Second, Marginson draws attention to Foucault's reference to discourses as 'practices that systematically form the objects of which they speak'. In these terms, 'rankings inculcate the idealized model of institution as a norm to be achieved and generalize the failure to achieve it' (2009, pp. 13–14). Rankings, indeed, 'form the objects of which they speak'. The 'world-class university' has, until recently, not existed as a concept. Nor is it to be imagined as an incontrovertible empirical reality. The 'world-class university' and its status as the gold standard are the descriptive and normative social constructs of the imagination of rankers.

The specific national conditions, realities and development challenges of underdeveloped societies in the South, and the diversity of social and educational purposes and goals that universities in these societies must serve, require national systems of higher education characterized by differentiated and diverse institutions. Of value, then, are institutional differentiation and diversity, rather than homogeneity and isomorphism. It makes little sense for all universities to aspire to a common 'gold' standard, irrespective of economic and social needs, their missions and goals and their capacities and capabilities.

Graham has argued universities should avoid aspiring to 'ideal(s) which they cannot attain'. Otherwise, 'no sense of worth will be forthcoming' and they can have no 'proper self-confidence' (2005, p. 157). It must also be recognized that there are many conceptions and models of the 'university' and that these have changed over time. Thus, the 'name "university" now applies to institutions with widely different functions and characters', and that this means that the 'ideals each can aspire to' will be different (Graham, 2005, pp. 157, 258). Moreover, as Newby argues, 'today's universities are expected to engage in lifelong learning (not just "teaching"), research, knowledge transfer, social inclusion..., local and regional economic development, citizenship training and much more. No university is resourced sufficiently to perform all these functions simultaneously and in equal measure at ever-increasing levels of quality' (2008, pp. 57–58). Institutions, therefore, have to identify, concentrate on and build niche areas of strength that are congruent with their missions and goals, and governments must ensure that institutions display and pursue a diversity of missions. Newby also suggests that 'different activities in universities have different geographical frames of reference' – research tends to be relatively more globally oriented, undergraduate teaching and learning more nationally focused and knowledge transfer and community engagement more regionally and locally focused (ibid., p. 57).

Instead of valuing a horizontal continuum that recognizes the need for universities to have different and diverse missions and which accords respect to universities that pursue various missions, the idea of the 'world-class university' as 'the idealized model of institution' has the perverse effect of privileging a vertical hierarchy. Universities that do not feature in the top 500 of the SJTIHE ranking or the top 200 of the THE-QS ranking are devalued and are, by implication, poor quality, second-rate or failures. In the face of continuing North–South inequalities, the burden of these characterizations, of course, weigh disproportionately on universities in the South.

Third, the performance measures that are used in global rankings privilege publishing in English language journals and in effect privilege the English language. Yet, universities have social responsibilities that relate to their local, regional and national societies. Especially in the arts, humanities and social sciences, prioritizing research and publishing for improvement of ranking and an unadulterated orientation to the global pole can seriously undermine the roles of universities in the intellectual and cultural life of their localities and nations. Today, the competition for and concentration on economic advantage mean that certain kinds of knowledge and research, especially that generated by the natural, medical and business sciences and engineering are privileged. However, as Mkandawire argues, 'attempts to improve Africa's prospects by focusing on scientific advances and the benefits accruing from them have all too often overlooked the important perspectives which the humanities and social sciences afford' and 'it is vital that the social sciences and humanities are granted their rightful place... if Africa's development challenges are to be fully and properly addressed' (2009, p. vii).

Fourth, rankings compromise the value and promise of universities as they 'divert attention from some central purposes of higher education', and 'to accept these ranking systems is to acquiesce at these definitions of higher education and its purposes' (Marginson, 2007b, p. 139). Important as are new knowledge production and the 'scholarship of discovery' (Boyer, 1990), the foundation of the production of high quality graduates that can advance development in the underdeveloped South is high quality learning–teaching. Moreover, community engagement, and specifically service-learning, is also a vital function of universities in the South. Both are 'means for connecting universities and communities with development needs' and 'for higher education staff and students to partner with communities to address development aims and goals' (Stanton, 2008, pp. 3, 2). However, the global rankings are only marginally concerned with learning–teaching and completely ignore the value of community engagement.

Fifth, a dangerous possible consequence of global rankings is related to the contemporary feature of a 'demand overload' on universities, as they are buffeted by the cross-currents of the varied requirements of the state, the market, civil society and institutional constituencies. Not infrequently, the demands on universities are contradictory, irreconcilable and erosive of institutional autonomy, academic freedom and public good ideals. Often, universities, especially in underdeveloped societies, must respond to the differing demands without any significant increase in or with declining public finance, increasing dependence on tuition fees and third stream income, and difficulties in securing and retaining talented academics that are attracted to the higher remuneration packages of the public and private sectors. Rankings and the norm of the 'world class-university' exacerbate the 'demand overload'. They construct ideals which most universities 'cannot attain' and generate public expectations that are unrealistic for most universities in the South. Unchecked, they could reshape and seriously distort the social purposes, goals and priorities of universities. They could also corrode institutional autonomy and academic freedom.

Finally, the extent to which the global rankings have come to be embraced by numerous universities and higher education agencies as knowledge of and on universities and higher education must be a matter of great concern. Instead of bold criticism of the dubious value and ends of rankings and the extremely questionable social science that underpins them, of the indicators that are arbitrarily privileged and the shallow proxies that are utilized as correlates of quality, there is seeming acquiescence. Rather than withering challenges of conceptions of quality that conceive it as timeless and invariant, and attached to a single, ahistorical and universal model of a university, instead of as historically specific and related to the missions and goals of institutions and their educational and social purposes, there is submission to quality as defined by the SJTIHE and THE-QS (Hazelkom, 2008a; 2008b). The validation of rankings as knowledge on universities, notwithstanding their questionable social science underpinnings, is ultimately corrosive of knowledge and science.

▶ The social determinants of rankings

Global rankings and league tables of universities are both rooted in and also an expression of contemporary economic and social conditions and the hegemony of the ideology of neo-liberalism within society and universities. At least four developments have stimulated the rise of global rankings.

The rise of an economy in which knowledge increasingly plays a critical role and is prized for the economic advantage that it can confer on businesses and countries means that new knowledge production and the development and application of knowledge take on great significance. Carnoy contends that a key feature of the global economy is that the accumulation of capital is 'increasingly dependent on knowledge and information applied to production, and this knowledge is increasingly science-based' (1998, p. 2). The implication is that 'if knowledge is the electricity of the new informational international economy, then institutions of higher education are the power sources on which a new development process must rely' (Castells, 1993). Universities, and especially those that have research as a strong and distinctive dimension of their mission, clearly take on great importance in this context. Although universities are increasingly not the sole knowledge-producing and research and development institutions, they remain important sites, especially of fundamental research. Furthermore, they also are the preeminent disseminators of knowledge that cultivate high-level professionals with the capacity to innovate. Rankings and the 'research university', as the embodiment of the 'world-class university' and the new gold standard, reflect the intense competition and pursuit of economic advantage in the 'knowledge economy'.

Second, rankings also both reflect and are an outcome of the rampant marketization and commercialization of higher education. In numerous fields, scientific research has increasingly become a hugely resource-hungry endeavour. Concomitantly, universities themselves, and especially research-intensive universities, have become increasingly organizationally complex and resource-greedy organizations. In the face of declining public subsidies new sources of income, whether through the imposition of tuition fees or the generation of third stream income through contract research, private endowments, donor grants and alumni gifts, have taken on great importance and have intensified competition among universities. It is in this context that internationalization, instead of embodying *internationalism*, has been corroded and reduced to *trans-nationalization*, in which mutual benefit and value for nations are lesser considerations than international students as a valuable source of 'export earnings', income for universities and potential expertise for countries. Rankings, in constituting the 'world-class university' and conferring prestige, simultaneously enhance the competitive power of those universities deemed to be 'world-class' and position them to benefit from the competition for resources and international students. Given continuing North–South inequalities, the attraction of Southern students to Northern 'world-class' universities simultaneously benefits Northern countries, providing them a talented pool from which to replenish scientific expertise and maintain their economic dominance.

It is suggested that the global rankings help to guide governments, businesses and foundations in decision-making on the investment of funds, award of research contracts and the provision of endowments. While they could be a guide in relation to the activities and performance measures that are privileged by global rankings, such rankings are ultimately a poor guide with respect to other important activities of universities. Moreover, they are also of little value regarding a university's performance in specific disciplines and fields, because 'a university may indeed be a leader in the field of research, but the equipment it offers its students may be miserable, or it may be strong in German Studies, but poor in Economics and Business Administration' (CHE, 2009). In short, it is not possible to make judgements on excellence and quality on the basis of the composite indexes that are characteristic of global rankings.

Rankings are also the logical outcomes of the new performative culture that has arisen under neo-liberalism and especially the 'financial and administrative technologies collated in the New Public Management', which conceives of universities 'as firms driven by desires for economic revenues and market share, not by teaching, research and service as ends in themselves' (Marginson, 2009, p. 3) As Marginson goes on to note, the construction 'of higher education as a performative market of competing universities-as-firms' necessitates the 'plausible mapping of the higher education field in the form of a hierarchy of institutional performance, that can be represented as the outcome of market competition.... The ideal model functions as a template against which institutions of higher education are measured and ranked' (ibid., p. 4). The 'world-class university' constituted in accordance with certain preferred criteria and weightings becomes the prize, with performance and rankings depending on how well a university plays the game whose rules have been formulated by the rankers and also how well a university is resourced.

Lastly, as with all social phenomena, rankings are not the products of social structure and conjuncture alone but also of human agency. Inasmuch as globalization and a hegemonic neo-liberalism have provided fertile conditions for the emergence of global rankings of universities and the construct of the 'world-class university' as the gold standard, they are also the offsprings of specific social actors with particular motivations. Burawoy defines politics 'as struggles within a specific arena aimed at specific sets of relations,...struggles that take as their *objective* the quantitative or qualitative change of those relations' (1985, pp. 253–254); and Castells argues that universities are subject to 'the conflicts and contradictions of society and therefore they will tend to express...the ideological struggles present in all societies' (2001, p. 206). In general, higher education has been characterized by the embrace of, accommodation with or acquiescence with the neo-liberal logic. This is in keeping with Castells' contention that 'the more the ideological hegemony of dominant elites is established in society at large, the more conservative ideologies tend to be prominent in universities' (ibid., 2006, p. 6). Rankings, which are far from value-free, technical and neutral instruments, reflect the contemporary higher education terrain and express the state of contemporary struggles in this domain.

▶ The future of rankings

The critique of rankings is not to be assumed to imply that they can be simply ignored or wished away. If a perverse and present burden, the SJTIHE and the THE-QS rankings and others that take the form of reductive composite indexes are likely to shape policy and practice in higher education and universities. It is, however, important to avoid a fatalism that imagines rankings of questionable value are immutable and impervious to the force of critique and social action. Simple assertions of the 'inevitability' of rankings, whether in relation to the 'competitive and market-oriented academic world of the 21st century', 'massification' or other features of contemporary society, are not persuasive (Altbach, 2006, p. 2; see also Liu, 2009, p. 3).

The critique of global university rankings is also not a refusal of critical public scrutiny of universities in the South. Performance indicators and benchmarks, as distinct from rankings, are of much value when carefully conceptualized and designed with clarity of purpose and aims and are respectful of institutional mission and policy goals. They have an important role to play in institutional improvement and development and, through these, in the achievement of national economic and social development priorities and goals. So too do effective monitoring, evaluation and penetrating reviews of universities. None of these important goals, however, are advanced by the THE-QS and SJTIHE global university rankings.

▶ Conclusion

No value can be attached to the SJTIHE and the THE-QS rankings. They are incapable of capturing either the meaning or the diverse qualities of a university or their varied roles in a manner that values and respects their educational and social purposes, missions and goals. They are underpinned by questionable social science, arbitrarily privilege particular indicators and use shallow proxies as correlates of quality.

The challenge for universities in the South is to effectively displace global rankings by alternative instruments that genuinely serve educational and social purposes, contribute to improvement, innovation and development in universities, enhance transparency and critical public scrutiny of universities and facilitate informed choices and judgements on the basis of robust social science and appropriate methodologies.

The global economic crisis provides the opportunity for a new imagination that is freed from the stifling neo-liberal orthodoxy of the past decades. It creates the space for new ideas, and for the recovery of important values related to human development, social justice, freedom, solidarity and internationalism. It also enables us to think about and to act to construct a different kind of world and citizenship, 'a world where markets are servants, not masters' (Mulgan, 2009).

Whether and to what extent this happens depends on whether intellectuals, scholars and universities in the South join hands with other social actors and take on the responsibility of re-thinking and re-making our societies and universities on the basis of other principles, coordinates and logics than the ones that have dominated in recent decades.

The current crisis provides the opportunity to restore to universities their varied social purposes instead of their reduction to instruments of the economy and vocational schools; to recover the vital public good functions of higher education, as opposed to the ideas of higher education as a market, universities as 'firms' and students as 'customers'; and, instead of the destructive logic of global rankings and a universal gold standard, to revalue the diversity of universities and the variety of their missions and goals in relation to the different historical and social conditions and developmental challenges of the South. Higher education 'requires bold visions of internationalism, of alternative globalization, that transcend the edicts of market accountability and narrow commercial calculations and embrace the ethics of social accountability and an expansive humanism that will elevate and empower all...people'. For certain, 'we will have failed the future if we do not vigorously pursue the dreams of university education as an ennobling adventure for individuals, communities, nations, and the world at large, if we do not strive to create universities that produce ideas rather than peddle information, critical rationality rather than consumer rations, and knowledge that has lasting value' (Zeleza, 2005, pp. 54–55).

▶ References

Altbach, P. G. (2006) 'The Dilemmas of Ranking', *International Higher Education*, 42, 2–3.

Bentley, K., Habib, A. and Morrow, S. (2006) *Academic Freedom, Institutional Autonomy, and the Corporatised University in Contemporary South Africa* (Pretoria: Council on Higher Education).

Berdahl, R. M. (2008) 'Developed Universities and the Developing World: Opportunities and Obligations', in Weber, L. E. and Duderstadt, J. J. (eds) *The Globalization of Higher Education* (London: Economica Ltd).

Boulton, G. and Lucas, C. (2008) *What Are Universities For?* (Leuven: League of European Research Universities).

Boyer, E. (1990) *Scholarship Reconsidered: Priorities for the Professoriate* (Princeton: Carnegie Foundation for the Advancement of Teaching, University of Princeton).

Brandenburg, U. (2009) 'Ranking – in a Different (CHE) Way?', http://globalhighered.wordpress.com/2009/01/18/ranking-in-a-different-way/ (Accessed 2 June 2009).

Burawoy, M. (1985) *The Politics of Production: Factory Regimes Under Capitalism and Socialism* (London: Verso).

Carnoy, M. (1998) 'Higher Education in a Global Innovation Economy', Paper presented at a Joint Centre for Higher Education Transformation and Human Sciences Research Council Seminar on Globalisation, Higher Education, High-Level Training, and National Development, Pretoria, 31 July 1998.

Castells, M. (2001) 'Universities as Dynamic Systems of Contradictory Functions', in Müller, J., Cloete, N. and Badat, S. (eds) *Challenges of Globalisation: South African Debates with Manuel Castells* (Cape Town: Maskew Miller Longman).

Castells, M. (1993) 'The University System: Engine of Development in the New World Economy', in Ransom, A. et al. (eds) *Improving Higher Education in Developing Countries* (Washington D.C.: World Bank).

Chang, H. J. (2008) *Bad Samaritans: The Guilty Secrets of Rich Nations and the Threat to Global Prosperity* (London: Random House).

Charon, A. and Wauters, J. P. (2007) 'University Ranking: A New Tool for the Evaluation of Higher Education in Europe', http://ndt.oxfordjournals.org/cgi/content/full/gfm 279v1 (Accessed 6 June 2009).

Council on Higher Education (CHE) (2009) 'Methodology', *CHE University Ranking 2009/10*, http://ranking.zeit.de/che9/CHE_en?module=Show&tmpl=p511_methodik (Accessed 9 June 2009).

Council on Higher Education (CHE) (2006) *A Good Practice Guide and Self-evaluation Instruments for Managing the Quality of Service-Learning* (Pretoria: Council on Higher Education/Joint Education Trust).

d'Hombres, B. and Saisana, M. (2009) 'CRELL: Critiquing Global University Rankings and Their Methodologies', *GlobalHigherEd*, 27 January 2009, http://globalhighered.word press.com/2009/01/27/crell-critiquing-global-university-rankings-and-their-methodologies/ (Accessed 9 June 2009).

Duderstadt, J., Taggart, J. and Weber, L. (2008) 'The Globalization of Higher Education', in Weber, L. E. and Duderstadt,

J. J. (eds) *The Globalization of Higher Education* (London: Economica Ltd).

Du Toit, A. (2000) 'From Autonomy to Accountability: Academic Freedom under Threat in South Africa', *Social Dynamics*, 26, 76–133.

Graham, G. (2005) *The Institution of Intellectual Values: Realism and Idealism in Higher Education* (Exeter: Imprint Academic).

Harvey, D. (2008) *A Short History of Neoliberalism* (London: Oxford University Press).

Hazelkom, E. (2008a) 'Globalization, Internationalization, and Rankings', *International Higher Education*, 53, 8–10.

Hazelkom, E. (2008b) 'Rankings, Diversity, and Excellence: A European Policy Challenge?', *International Higher Education*, 51, 19–21.

Ince, M. (2007) 'Methodology: What the Pick of the Crop Means for the Rest of the Field', *Times Higher Education Supplement*, 9 November 2007. http://www.timeshigher education.co.uk/story.asp?storycode=400069   (Accessed 9 June 2009).

Jonathan, R. (2006) *Academic Freedom, Institutional Autonomy and Public Accountability in Higher Education: A Framework for Analysis of the 'State-Sector' Relationship in a Democratic South Africa* (Pretoria: Council on Higher Education).

Liu, N. C. (2009) 'The Story of Academic Ranking of World Universities', *International Higher Education*, 54, 2–3.

Marginson, S. (2009) 'University Rankings, Government and Social Order: Managing the Field of Higher Education According to the Logic of the Performative Present-As-Future', in Simons, M., Olsen, M. and Peters, M. (eds) *Re-Reading Education Policies: A Handbook Studying the Policy Agenda of the 21st Century* (Rotterdam: Sense Publishers).

Marginson, S. (2008a) 'Globalization, National Development and University Rankings', International Symposium 'University Ranking: Global Trends and Comparative Perspectives', VNU Headquarters, Hanoi, Vietnam, 12–13 November, 2008.

Marginson, S. (2008b) 'Research Rankings, Outcomes Measures and Institutional Classifications: Value Formation in the K-Economy', paper presented at the annual meeting of the Consortium of Higher Education Researchers (CHER), Pavia, 12 September 2008.

Marginson, S. (2008c) 'A Funny Thing Happened on the Way to the K-Economy: The New World Order in Higher Education: Research Rankings, Outcomes Measures and Institutional Classifications', paper presented at IMHE General Conference, Paris, 8–10 September 2008.

Marginson, S. (2007a) 'Global University Rankings' [*presentation version*], paper presented at 32nd Annual Conference of the Association for the Study of Higher Education 7–10 November, Louisville, Kentucky; Symposium, 10 November: 'Comparing Colleges: The Implications of Classification, Ranking and Peer Analysis for Research and Practice'.

Marginson, S. (2007b) 'Global University Rankings: Implications in General and for Australia', *Journal of Higher Education Policy and Management*, 29(2), 131–142.

Marginson, S. (2006a) 'Symposium: Rethinking and Re-imagining Rankings: Multiple Models for World Class Universities'. Association for the Study of Higher Education Annual Meeting International Forum Anaheim, California, 1 November 2006.

Marginson, S. (2006b) 'Global University Rankings: Private and Public Goods', paper presented at 19th Annual Consortium of Higher Education Researchers conference, Kassel, 7–9 September 2006.

Mohamedbhai, G. (2008) 'International Trends in Higher Education – Effects on Higher Education Institutions in the South and in the North: African Perspectives', paper presented at the NUFU Conference, Lilongwe, Malawi, 11–13 January 2009.

Mulgan, G. (2009) 'After Capitalism', *Prospect*, http://www.prospect-magazine.co.uk/article_details.php?id=10680 (Accessed 2 June 2009).

Nayyar, D. (2008) 'Globalization: What Does It Mean for Higher Education', in Weber, L. E. and Duderstadt, J. J. (eds) *The Globalization of Higher Education* (London: Economica Ltd).

Newby, H. (2008) 'The Challenge to European Universities in the Emerging Global Marketplace', in Weber, L. E. and Duderstadt, J. J. (eds) *The Globalization of Higher Education* (London: Economica Ltd).

Nussbaum, M. (2006) *'Education for Democratic Citizenship*, Institute of Social Studies Public Lecture Series 2006, No. 1 (The Hague: Institute of Social Studies).

Saisana, M. and D'Hombres, B. (2008) *Higher Education Rankings: Robustness Issues and Critical Assessment. How Much Confidence Can We Have in Higher Education Rankings?* (Luxembourg: Office for Official Publications of the European Communities).

Sen, A. (1993) *Development as Freedom* (Oxford: Oxford University Press).

Stanton, T. K. (2008) 'Introduction', in Council on Higher Education (ed.) *Service-Learning in the Disciplines: Lessons from the Field* (Pretoria: Council on Higher Education/Joint Education Trust Education Services).

The Task Force on Higher Education and Society (2000) *Higher Education in Developing Countries: Peril and Promise* (Washington: The World Bank).

Times Higher Education-Quacquarelli Symonds (THE-QS) (2009) *World University Rankings*, http://www.topuniversities.com/worlduniversityrankings/ (Accessed 9 June 2009).

Wallerstein, I. (1991) *Unthinking Social Science: The Limits of Nineteenth-Century Paradigms* (Cambridge: Polity Press).

Zeleza, P. T. (2005) 'Transnational Education and African Universities', in Association of African Universities (ed.) *Crossborder Provision and the Future of Higher Education in Africa* (Accra: Association of African Universities).

5 Public–Private Substitution in Higher Education Funding and Kondratiev Cycles: The Impacts on Home and International Students

Vincent Carpentier

▶ Introduction

This chapter provides historical analysis of the position assigned to income from home and international students in the UK, France and the USA taking account of long economic cycles (Kondratiev cycles). The analysis uses historical data sets on the level and structure of the income of universities and the number and characteristics of students since the 1920s. These are interpreted using the theory of systemic regulation which examines the links between economic fluctuations, State action and social change (Fontvieille, 1976; Boccara, 2008). Such a framework offers a way to identify a succession of regimes of higher education which express the articulations (and tensions) between access and funding policies. Those impact on the rise or reduction of inequalities over time (Carpentier, 2006a). The presence of international students is an important, but generally overlooked, aspect of this.

Section 1 explores contemporary form of globalization with its stance on the control of public funding, the impact of economic cycles on the historical fluctuations of public resources devoted to higher education. It draws out the rise of private resources mobilized for higher education since the mid-1970s. Section 2 shows that the impact of these transformations on university resources is different according to whether the rise of private funding (observed in all countries) was used as a substitute for slower growth of public funding or as additional income for universities with rather different transformations of the public/private structure of universities' income in each country. The analysis focuses on fees, the main lever of private resources in universities, and looks at the impact on access and potential inequalities (Section 3) highlighting significance assigned to international students (Section 4).

▶ Globalization, higher education and economic cycles: Approach and methodology

The tensions between access to higher education and funding policies (Carpentier, 2006a) will be analysed through the lens of the theory of systemic regulation, which seeks to provide an explanation of the historical expansion of public expenditure on education in relation to long economic cycles (Carpentier, 2007). Cycles are not deterministic instruments but provide, using the lenses of historical political economy, ways of looking at changes and continuities (Hobsbawm, 1997; Goodson, 2006; Milonakis and Fine, 2009). A cyclical analysis of higher education funding will help to examine how the historical development of education 'reflects, and at times challenges the social, economic, political and intellectual context of its age' (Aldrich, 2002, p. 3). Through this, the dialogue between economic history and history of education (McCulloch, 1998; Sanderson, 2007) is extended to higher education (Silver, 2006; Lowe, 2008).

With regards to higher education, globalization is a multifaceted concept and a complex process (King, 2004; Marginson and van der Wende, 2007). While internationalization is generally used to define increasing links or exchanges between nations, globalization tends to refer to practices adopted across nation states (Held and McGrew, 2002). These global practices have impacted on higher education as 'the economics of globalisation is an increasingly important point of reference in national educational policy making' (Ball, 2008, p. 39).

The 'repositioning of higher education as a global commodity' (Naidoo, 2003, p. 254) impacts on universities' engagement with internationalization (Byram and Dervin, 2008, p. 2). Both need to be placed in historical perspective.

Castells (2000) distinguishes a world economy from a global economy and links the latter with ICT and policies of deregulation. Such policies are associated with the contemporary neoliberal form of economic globalization. Wallerstein (2003) suggests that globalization is not new and that the post 1990s period is a moment of crisis and transformation of the world system which long predates it (2003). The major economic turbulences of 2008–2009 seem to confirm that we are at a turning point with regard to the forms of globalization and deregulation. Long economic cycles offer a perspective on contemporary globalization by locating its specific discourses and practices as a particular form of a movement of internationalization. Two dimensions of the contemporary form of globalization strongly impact on higher education: firstly a constant reference to the knowledge economy – that is the idea of competition increasingly based on knowledge in an open world economy which has been a powerful driver of educational policies, often to the detriment of other rationales (Wolf, 2002). Second, globalization has been associated with a low tax economy and control of public funding endorsed by the 1980s Washington Consensus with its neoliberal emphasis on individualism and market (Serra and Stiglitz, 2008). Tensions between these two agendas are evident within higher education: the expansion of enrolment is seen as a priority for the globalized knowledge economy, but this sits uneasily with pressure for a limitation of state funding despite the fact that historically higher education has expanded through state investment. Tensions are played out in ongoing debates on underfunding. These result from a combination of expanding numbers with inadequate resources which put increasing pressure on universities, staff and students (Olssen and Peters, 2005).

This chapter explores the consequence of these tensions in relation to inequalities as they relate to domestic and overseas students. It will examine how a traditional form of internationalization of higher education (the enrolment of overseas students) interacts or clashes with an emerging form of neoliberal globalization, that is the transformation of university income structure and a search for global private resources. Inequalities emerge out of the dynamic of concern with funding and access. Although this excludes issues of identities and inequalities, 'the importance of recognising how multiple identities and inequalities of 'race', ethnicity, social class and gender (amongst others) affect the way in which people construct, experience and negotiate different educational opportunities and routes' (Archer and Leathwood, 2003, p. 175) is acknowledged. Persistent inequalities within higher education, while related to financial capital, are also articulated to cultural capital and social capital (Bourdieu and Passeron, 1964; Apple, 1982; Reay et al., 2005). Much of the inequality of access to higher education is due to inequality at the compulsory school level (Galindo-Rueda et al., 2004). While this is not explored in depth here, it is argued that in these challenging times funding issues and fees are important aspects of inequalities.

Quantitative analysis in relation to economic cycles is used to illustrate transformations of university funding and access of home and overseas students. However, it is important to stress that numbers offer promises to enhance interpretation but also have important limitations. Quantitative methods are thus used to identify trends and patterns and facilitate contextualization (Carpentier, 2008). Historical data on funding and enrolment at universities in France, the UK and the US since the 1920s (Carpentier, 2004, 2006a, 2006b) are analysed using the method of quantitative history. This method follows principles of national accounting, which provide a stable frame to integrate financial and other relevant data, and allow comparison across time and space (Marczewski, 1961). Funding indicators include the income of universities and its structure (public grants, fees, donations). Non-financial data include the number of home and overseas students. The data on domestic students have been extracted from previous work. In addition, new data on international students have been compiled from statistical reports from the Higher Education Funding Council and its predecessors.[1] For the UK, data are supplied only for universities until 1994. Afterwards, data relating to advanced courses in polytechnics and advanced further education (which became universities after the 1992 Higher Education Act) are included. French and US Data relate to all higher education institutions (public and private).

▶ Public funding of universities and Kondratiev cycles

Figure 5.1 shows there has been an increase in the expenditure per student in all three countries between 1920 to 2006.

There is a higher level of funding per student in the US than in France and the UK. Trends in funding per student have been fairly regular in the US, less regular in France and chaotic in the UK. However, it should be noted that the fast decline of the funding per student in the UK in 1993 was due to the integration of post 1992 institutions (whose funding per student is lower than pre 1992 universities). Nevertheless, it is apparent that such decline was already on its way in the late 1980s

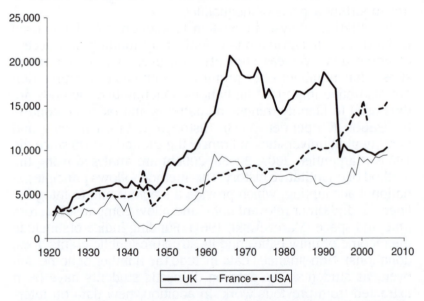

Figure 5.1 University expenditure per student (1990 Geary-Khamis $) 1921–2006

Note: Financial series are expressed in purchasing power parity (PPP) in 1990 Geary-Khamis US $. PPP can be defined as a conversion rate that quantifies the amount of a country's currency necessary to buy in the market of that country the same quantity of goods and services as a dollar in the US. Such a tool is necessary in order to give a comparative estimate of the value of educational expenditure eliminating differences in price level between countries. The PPP indices series are derived from Maddison's calculation of GDP at PPP US $ (Maddison, 1995; 2000) and updated (http://www.ggdc.net/maddison). The GDP at PPP US $ was then divided by the GDP expressed in current $ to obtain the PPP index and applied to the expenditure series.

when the tensions between access and funding policies started becoming visible.

These historical patterns are at the core of contemporary debates on underfunding in France and the UK. In a context of continuous expansion of enrolment, the controversies can be further understood by an examination of the fluctuations in public funding available to universities. Figure 5.2 indicates a strong correspondence between public spending on higher education and long economic cycles (Kondratiev cycles or Long waves) in France, the UK and the USA (Carpentier, 2001, 2006b).

Named after the Russian Economist, Nikolai Kondratiev (1892–1938), four Kondratiev cycles of approximately 50 years have been identified, each showing expansion and depression phases (1790–1820/1820–1848, 1848–1870/1870–1897, 1897–1913/1913–1945, 1945–1973/1973–?) (Loucã and Reijnders, 1999). The graph shows a remarkable correlation: in all the three countries, the growth of public educational resources accelerated during the period of post-war prosperity, only to go into relative decline following the early 1970s' economic downturn

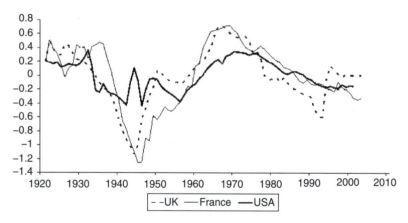

Figure 5.2 Fluctuation of public expenditure on higher education (1990 Geary-Khamis $) (second-order deviation from the regression curve) 1921–2003
Note: A regression curve is the best-fitting curve drawn through a scatter plot of two variables. It is chosen to come as close to the points as possible. A regression curve represents then the shape of the relationship between the variables (here the expenditure and the time) and the long-term trend if the series were regularly distributed. The deviations from the regression curve represent the cyclical fluctuations around the trend. Nine-year moving averages are sliding averages that smooth the data in order to ease the examination of the trend and changes.

precipitated by the oil crisis of 1973. The 2008–2009 crisis may suggest that this downward phase is still going on (Carpentier, 2009). The revival in public expenditure in the early 1990s in the UK is due to the sudden integration of colleges and polytechnics within the university system, but the effect is temporary, as the downward trend continues after this.

While it is difficult to conclude about a clear causal relation, these cyclical fluctuations in public funding of higher education may be connected to development of and crisis in the welfare state. Change in higher education can be understood as part of a wider trend which links the State and the transformation of the socio-economic system. Regulation theories have mapped this (Boyer and Saillard, 2002). The theory of systemic regulation interprets the Kondratiev cycle as an expression of recurrent structural transformations of the capitalist system (Marx, 1894; Fontvieille, 1976; Boccara, 2008). Amongst these transformations, the theory identifies a reversal of the historical relationship between economic cycles and human development around the Second World War. This reversal was revealed by the observation of a transition from a counter-cyclical to a procyclical growth of public spending (Michel and Vallade, 2007). Before 1945, increased levels of public investment in human development took place during long economic downturns (1830s–1850s/1870s–1890s and 1920s–1940s). Such investments (which were seen as unnecessary during the economic upturns) offered opportunities to use an overaccumulated capital to revive productivity levels and provided an escape route out of socio-economic crises. After 1945, a shift occurred as public funding of social development became not only a way out of the crisis but a driver of economic growth. The post-war economic upturn 1945–1973 was driven by the implementation of Keynesian redistributive policies as well as an acceleration of social spendings which contributed to human development necessary to drive productivity levels. This regime hit a crisis in the mid-1970s when stagflation was countered with the adoption of Neoliberalism. Wage austerity as well as the retreat of State funding since the 1970s is a global phenomenon which has affected nearly all social activities. Jessop has interpreted this as a gradual transition from the Keynesian welfare State to a Schumpeterian competition State focusing on innovation and subordinating the social sphere to economic policy (2002).

In the economic crisis of the mid-1970s for the first time a long economic downturn was accompanied by a slowdown in the growth of public funding for the social sphere. During previous crises (1830s, 1870s, 1930s), the dynamic of the economy was revived by the development of a social infrastructure whose logic was not driven by profit. In the 1970s, there were tensions between these two forms of regulation. The neoliberal agenda may be understood as a way to switch back the social infrastructure of human development to a form of capitalist regulation. Neoliberalism may thus be interpreted as interrupting social transformations. But the economy has not really recovered from the downturn of the early 1970s. Instead the overaccumulation of capital was directed towards the financial sphere with catastrophic results, for example the implosion of the financial system in 2008. The 2008–2009 crisis may therefore be seen as the continuation of a long Kondratiev downswing and an opportunity to develop social and ecological innovations towards a more inclusive growth (Carpentier, 2009). Indeed, this framework suggests that the relationship between the social sphere and the economy is historically contingent. It has changed in the past and may be different in the future. The scale of the current economic crisis challenges the post 1970s' discourse of irreversibility of change and may open up an alternative view on the contemporary orthodoxy of limited taxation restricting social progress.

A research programme confirmed such a link between education and Kondratiev cycles, showing that the development of educational systems during downward economic phases like the 1840s, 1870s and the 1930s may have contributed to revived productivity (Fontvieille, 1990; Carry, 1999; Michel, 1999; Diebolt and Fontvieille, 2001; Carpentier, 2003, 2006b). The research also confirmed the Second World War as a period of reversal revealing that funding of public education systems benefited from and indeed contributed to the post 1945 economic upturn before being particularly hurt by constraints on public finances in the 1970s' downturn. This research focused on industrialized countries (France, Germany, the UK and the USA). As such, the comparison does not explain the process in all countries. One should expect a more mixed picture in Africa or Asia. However, other works in Algeria and Senegal have shown that many developing countries experienced similar patterns with increases in public funding from the 1960s followed by drastic public sector reform with the structural adjustment policies of the 1980s (Bouslimani, 2002; Diouf and Fontvielle, 2002). In India, tensions between the demands of the knowledge economy and public funding have emerged (Chattopadhyay, 2007).

Figure 5.2 confirms such a correlation between public funding in higher education and Kondratiev cycles. The sector benefited from the post-war upturn and was particularly exposed to cuts in public funding in the 1970s leading to substantial changes in its income structure as it will be shown below (Carpentier, 2006a). How has the public/private distribution of funding changed and how has it impacted on inequalities?

▶ **Changes in universities' income structure: Are fees drivers of public–private substitution or additional resources?**

Cyclical fluctuations in public resources have impacted on university income differently in France, the UK and the USA and with different consequences for access. The extent to which increased private resources have acted as a substitute for slower growth of public funding or additional income for higher education raises questions about the role fees from home and overseas students play.

Figure 5.3 shows substantial changes in the balance between private and public income for universities since the 1920s.

In the UK, the share of income from public sources grew from 50 per cent to nearly 90 per cent from 1945 to 1973, but contracting to around 50 per cent in the late 1990s (the accounting category 'other income' which does not separate public from private funding has grown substantially – therefore, a more accurate estimation of the share of public income may be closer to 55 per cent). In the USA, much less radical changes occurred with a growth from 38 per cent to 50 per cent between 1945 and 1973 and a post 1970s decline back to 38 per cent. In France, the transformation is much smaller as public funding supplied 96 per cent of university resources in 1960 against 84 per cent at the turn of the century.

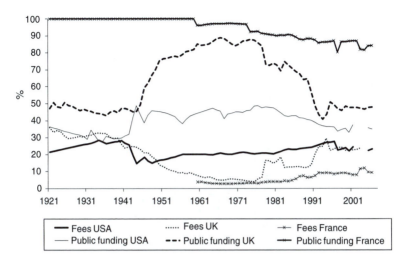

Figure 5.3 Fees and public funding as a share of universities' income: 1921–2006

Table 5.1 shows the post 1970s slowing down of growth of public funding (linked to Kondratiev cycles) was more extensive than the subsequent rise of private resources.

The transformation of the structure of university income that followed meant that although there was some growth in the total available, it was not equivalent to the income that would have been available if the dynamic of public funding had continued (Carpentier, 2006a).

In France, and especially in the UK, private funding (including fees) increased in order to substitute for slower growth of public funding, rather than taking the form of additional resources. The substitution was less important in the USA where total income relied on a greater balance between public and private resources (including drivers like military expenditures and high levels of student debt). This explains the higher spending per student seen in Figure 5.1. One interpretation of persistent underfunding in higher education is that private funding should have been increased further. However, alongside the obvious objection in relation to the commodification of higher education, this raises issues regarding the socially acceptable levels of fees and the volatility of private resources. This is especially pertinent in the current crisis. Another interpretation points at insufficient levels

Table 5.1 Multipliers of public, private and total income of universities (1990 Geary-Khamis $), 1921–2006

	US			UK			France		
	Public	Private	Total	Public	Private	Total	Public	Private	Total
1921–1945	5.51	4.13	4.63	2.35	2.15	2.25	1.22	–	1.22
1945–1973	9.10	8.33	8.66	30.30	4.40	17.19	37.02	1960–73 2.75	38.26
1973–2006	2.67	4.15	3.47	2.48	18.71	4.58	3.54	31.55	4.44

of public funding since the 1970s' crisis (in contrast with previous economic downturns). The main lesson from this is that extra private resources do not necessarily lead to a substantial overall rise in the income of universities. Public–private substitution of resources rather than a substantial increase of funding might be a paradoxical outcome of reforms which seek to introduce private funding (and especially fees) in France and the UK (Belloc, 2003; DfES, 2003).

Various types of private resources are available to universities such as endowments, donations, research contracts and commercial services, but fees remain the main resource with the biggest impact on access. Fees have been at the forefront of a worldwide 'cost sharing' strategy which intends to bring about a 'shift of some of the higher educational per students costs from government and taxpayers to parents and students' (Teixeira et al., 2006). Figure 5.3 shows that the share of fees is traditionally high in the US and low (but increasing) in France. In the UK, from 1962, fees were covered by mandatory grants from Local Education Authorities. Following debates about underfunding in the 1990s, the Dearing Report recommended the introduction of fees with means-tested grants (1997). The 1998 Higher Education Act only partially followed Dearing's recommendation (Watson and Bowden 2007). It introduced upfront fees (£1000) but replaced grants by loans at preferential rates. More recently, the publication of the 2003 White Paper on the Future of Higher Education generated heated debates about the alternative ways in which funding, quality and the widening participation agenda could be connected. Debates focused on the potential impact on access and participation of the proposed top-up fees for home students. The disputed vote on the 2004 Higher Education Act led to the replacement of the £1000 upfront fees by deferred variable fees of up to £3000 (only payable when a graduate earns more than £15,000). A grant of up to £2700 for a family earning up to £20,000 a year was reintroduced. Supporters of the reform invoked the equity issue arguing a predominantly middle-class student body was getting private financial and cultural benefits by working-class taxpayers. They argued that deferred fees and the reintroduction of a grant will allow a continuing expansion of enrolment while resolving the underfunding issue (Barr, 2003). Counterarguments stressed the impact of higher fees on the actual and perceived level of debt on working-class students

(Callender and Jackson, 2005). Variable fees are thought to be a potential source of inequalities between institutions (Brown, 2004).

The first years of implementation of the Higher Education Act of 2004 seem not to have impacted on access but there are still uncertainties. There have been mixed signals. On the one hand, the Brown government in 2008 increased the income threshold for being eligible for a grant from £25,000 to £60,000: this suggests some concerns in terms of access (the maximum threshold has since been reduced to £50,000). On the other hand, there are pressures for lifting the cap on fees. This proposal was made in a rosier economic context with high level of employment and one should note that the impact of the 2008 economic crisis on unemployment, levels of private debt (and increased public debt due to banks bailout) and difficulty in getting loans from banks may change the terms of the debate about fees. At the time of the writing, funding and access policies are clashing more than ever with talks about higher fees, uncertainties about grants, caps on number of students and fewer mentions from politicians of the 50 per cent participation target. A Review of Higher Education Funding and Student Finance is under way. These debates will determine whether extra private funding will act as additional or substitute resources and the extent to which they will impact on access. The history of public–private substitution of funding suggests that an increase in fees, not supported by a rise of public funding, may not change the situation in terms of resources available and could produce more inequalities (Carpentier, 2006a). In the USA, expansion has been sustained because of a greater tradition of offering scholarships than in the UK and an acceptance of far higher levels of student debt (again this may change in the new economic context). In the UK and France, an increase of fees without additional public funding towards student financial support and pedagogy may have a negative impact on access, retention and achievements and severely hit the widening participation agenda.

An exacerbated public/private substitution would bring a situation where the agenda of austerity associated with the neoliberal form of globalization would play against the other agenda of the knowledge economy. However, this does not necessarily have to be the case. The levels of public debt brought about by the bailout of the financial sector in the current crisis could make a case for more money to be spent on productive social activities like higher education. This would mark a return to countercyclical spending as happened during the crises of the 1840s, 1870s and 1930s. However, a rationale for more cuts in higher education as a continuation of the neoliberal austerity of the 1970s could also develop.

Public–private substitution also raises questions about global higher education. Are strategies of internationalization generating additional or substitutive resources? And what are their effects on equity and access?

▶ International students and public–private substitution

Increasing tensions between global agendas related to the knowledge economy and neoliberal austerity have not only impacted on higher education funding and equity within particular countries but have also changed the way universities engage with the process of internationalization. The concern with low taxation explains an increasingly economically driven rationale for the internationalization of higher education based on a search for private resources. This sits alongside more traditional, political and cultural arguments for internationalization. A concept like Borderless Higher Education encompasses diverse manifestations (Bjarnason, 2004) but summarizes well how new and old forms of internationalization are used as forms of income generation for exporting countries and capacity building for importing countries within an expanding global higher education market (Gürüz, 2008). Thus, high income countries create offshore campuses, export degrees physically or by distance learning or welcome international students as ways to generate extra revenue. On the other hand, governments of countries with limited amount of money to invest in public universities import programmes or institutions and send students abroad in order to develop their capacity. Initially, high income countries are the main providers of internationalization and they remain so, but it should be noted that more and more exchanges are taking place between developing countries. In comparing and contrasting international students and domestic students a complex inequality emerges. Williams remarked in the 1980s that 'the overseas student question has given rise to thoughts and speculations which may cause the landscape of British higher education to change out of all recognition by the end of the century' (1984, p. 277). UK overseas students were charged fees a number of decades before this was re-introduced for home students. Thus in 1967, the introduction of differential fees for overseas students paved the way for successive increases and culminated in the decision to introduce full cost fees for non EU overseas students in 1980 (and home rates for EU students). The 2004 Higher Education Act only levied variable fees on home students 40 years later. However, despite the introduction of fees, the number of overseas students grew fourfold from 1981. The steep growth in 1993 is partly due to the integration of new universities.

Figure 5.4 indicates that the dynamic of growth is due to growing enrolment of EU students in the mid-1980s who benefited from the 1980 agreement to charge them the same fees as domestic students. But there has been a sharp acceleration in the number of non EU students since the late 1990s.

Overseas students represented 15 per cent of total enrolment in UK universities in 2007 (17 per cent of full-time and 9 per cent part-time students). Forty-seven per cent of overseas students are female. Thirty-two per cent came from the EU, 41 per cent

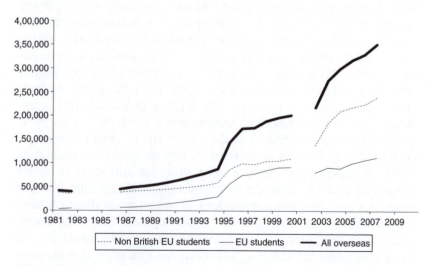

Figure 5.4 Overseas students in UK universities full time and part time 1981–2007

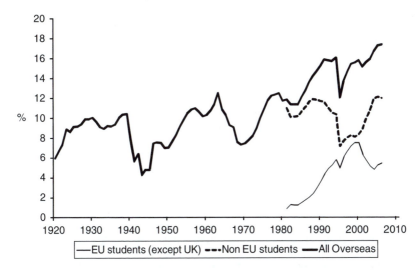

Figure 5.5 International students as a share of all full-time students, UK, 1920–2006

from Asia (including 25 per cent from China) and 9 per cent from Africa (HEFCE, 2007). Seventy-five per cent undertook full-time study and 50 per cent study at undergraduate level.

The historical picture shows that the presence of international students in UK universities was not new (the proportion of overseas students was already 12 per cent in 1981). It was accelerated, rather than initiated, by the globalization process of the 1990s.

Figure 5.5 reveals important fluctuations but signals that the number of overseas students as a share of all full-time students has increased substantially since the 1970s. The graph confirms the EU students' enrolment has risen sharply since the mid-1980s. However, there has been a dramatic increase of the share of non EU overseas students since the 2000s.

Variations depend on a combination of deliberate or constrained choices and strategies from government. Changing cultural, political, social and economic factors have affected institutions and students across time and space. There are too many interrelationships at work here to be able to theorize the full complexity. However, it may be possible to unpack changing patterns of the place of international students since the early 1970s within the higher education system by looking at private/public substitution.

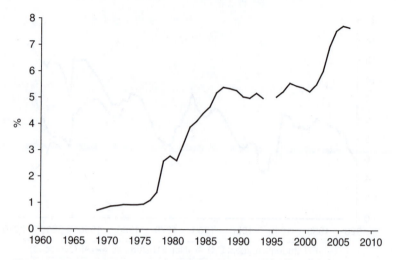

Figure 5.6 Fees from overseas students as a share of universities' income: UK 1968–2006

Figure 5.6 shows dramatic changes in universities' income from fees from overseas students. These are only partially mirrored by increases in enrolment. The share of enrolment by overseas students doubled in this period while their contribution to income grew eightfold.

Such patterns are consistent with the impact of the Kondratiev cycle on the retreat of public funding and pressure to rely on private funding. The graph suggests that in the context of a slowing down of state funding following the crisis of the early 1970s, overseas fees have been used as an instrument to generate extra funding and contribute to the trend for public–private substitution. There are, of course, other factors that could explain such a trend but it is difficult to ignore the fact that only 1 per cent of universities' income was generated by international students' fees in the early 1970s against 8 per cent today. The increase of overseas fees in the 1980s was clearly linked to the context of stagnating public funding (Williams, 1984; Sizer, 1987). The debate at the time revolved around the fact that overseas students were offered a subsidized education by the British State. For some this was problematic, for others an important investment in international relations for the future and a contribution to global justice (Enslin and Hedge, 2008). Since the 1980s, the situation has been reversed and 'institutions are using income

from fee-paying students to upgrade resources and accommodation and to create additional student places' (Baker, 1993,
p. 98). Thus subsidization is going from international to home
students.

The fees charged to international students in UK universities were a forerunner of the public/private substitution of
income. This happened at least a decade before the full impact
of globalization policies and discussion of the importance of
home student's contributions to the cost of their studies. Indeed,
Harris, interestingly, argues that full cost overseas fees 'presaged
over more radical shifts in university politics in the 1980s' (1997,
p. 34). Since the crisis of the mid-1970s, changes in funding
policies have had a strong impact on students. In some cases
reforms led overseas and domestic students to share a common experience of high costs and in others they led to divergent
paths. The public–private interface with regard to overseas students highlights a number of themes concerning the rationale
for changed policy, stability, dependence, pedagogy and social
justice.

The rationale for the particular political economy concerning
the playing out of the balance between home and international
students is in a way quite similar for both sets of students with
regard to balance between fees, financial support and access.
The cost/benefit analysis has been a strong determinant of
policy decisions. This has tended to favour public/private substitution. Such an approach fails to integrate the whole picture.
It tends only to acknowledge factors that can be measured. The
argument for higher fees for overseas students rests on a denun-
ciation of the cost of subsidizing overseas students who get
substantial private benefits without offering social benefits to the
country in which they receive their education, especially if they
return to their home country. A counter argument is made which
highlights economic benefits associated to overseas students.
Fees are gained as well as the spending of overseas students and
indirect resources (fiscal revenue and an increase of GDP if qualified students stay in the UK) (Vickers and Bekhradnia, 2007). It
is clear that this debate is not facilitated by the fact that public and private costs (taxes and fees) as well as private benefits
(wages) are far easier to evaluate than social economic benefits (GDP). Moreover, such calculations tend to put aside cultural
and political benefits which are difficult to measure but indirectly

contribute to society and the economy (not to mention learning for its own sake). Such asymmetry can explain why policies tend to view overseas students' recruitment in monetary terms as part of the public/private substitution strategy rather than incorporating important dimensions like social capital and cultural exchange (the same argument applies for domestic students' fees).

Fees policy is constantly moving and, by shifting priorities of funding strategies at the institutional level, can produce imbalances within the system. Scott states that there could be conflict between strategies and policies towards international and home students (Scott, 1998, p. 109). For example, Bolsman and Miller remarked that as a result of the increase of fees for home students in 2006, 'the differences between home and international student revenue is less marked at the undergraduate level and that the new market for overseas students has shifted to the postgraduate level' (2008, p. 4). This signals different positions and interests from institutions and government in relation to the public/private substitution framework: recurrent changes in fee arrangements (depending on whether money come either from government subsidy or home and overseas fees) affect an institution's approach of the recruitment of full cost overseas students and home students, not necessarily in line with government's intended goal. This illustrates the risk that different and sometimes contradictory political and economic rationales in order to increase or limit the numbers of home and international students could produce instability in the development of the whole higher education system. Ensuring stability would require a holistic approach on the conceptualization of fee policies driven by concerted efforts to align institutions, government and students' perspectives to guarantee a well-funded equitable HE system.

Public–private substitution increases the risk for universities' income to be exposed to a decrease of international students. Watson notes that 'the exposure of UK higher education to its international business is considerable' (2007, p. 30). The crisis in Asia in the late 1990s is a good example of the vulnerability to exchange rate that would lead to students' incapacity to pay for fees. Another example is the development of international competitors for overseas students. This is a pertinent issue in the UK where the average proportion of foreign students to all students is far higher (15 per cent) than in France (8 per cent) or the USA (4 per cent). The long-term slowing down of public funding provoked by public/private income substitution cannot be easily reversed to compensate for potential shorter shocks like the withdrawal of students' fees. The point here is not to limit overseas student numbers but to sustain public funding in order to prevent universities' overreliance on overseas students' fees. This point can be generalized to other private sources of funding (domestic fees, donations, private funding of research) and is particularly relevant in the context of the current economic crisis which may affect student mobility.

Increased overseas fees as a substitute for slower public funding rather than an additional resource raise questions about whether sufficient investment is directed towards the adaptation of the pedagogic environment to diversity (this concern also applies to domestic students). According to Williams, 'in the 1960s and 1970s the anxiety was almost entirely financial: there was little concern about the academic or political implications of large numbers of overseas students' (1987, p. 16). The question of the learning experience is central within a more diverse community of students and some authors suggest that 'internationalisation has been driven largely by the marketisation discourse which has not been followed by the development of new pedagogical practices' (De Vita and Case, 2003, p. 384). Harris argued a decade ago that 'unless universities take seriously the implications of having overseas students, which include organizational and staff development issues as well as the proper adaptation of teaching methods and techniques, there is serious potential for things to go wrong' (1995, p. 77). Although efforts have recently been made to address this issue, there is still much to be done. While pedagogic innovations do not only rely on resources, fees should not be operating as substitution for public money if quality is to be maintained and diversity embraced. There are considerable risks in not meeting the pedagogic needs of international students. They may question the value for money of the offered programme and move to other countries. As Stiasny points out, 'international students have, simply, much more choice' (2008, p. 35).

Grants for home students and international scholarships for overseas students are instruments to promote social mobility at home and abroad. Such financial support is crucial in addressing 'the enormous challenge confronting higher education (which is) how to make international opportunities available to all equitably' (Altbach et al., 2009, p. 32). If overseas fees are mobilized as a substitution for slowing down public funding, there is an issue about the government's offer of international scholarships raising problems in terms of global social justice. It is worth noting that there was a temporary reduction of the number of overseas students following the two significant increases of fees in 1967 (for one year) and 1980 (for three consecutive years). The fact that numbers increased again afterwards may suggest that the impact of fees is not big on access. However, one can argue that a fee rise may change the social composition of the overseas student body (figures are difficult to find) and increase global inequalities. According to a recent report, 'over 70 per cent of (overseas) students were paying fees and living costs from their own or their families' resources, except for research postgraduates, the majority of whom were funded by scholarships from other sources' (Council for International Education, 2004, p. 53).

It is difficult to find information about the number and value of scholarship for international students offered by government and other national scholarships (from the country of origin or the host country) as well as universities (which are developing rapidly in a context of institutional competition). The following therefore does not claim to offer a full picture.

The Commonwealth Scholarship and Fellowship Plans are funded by the Department for International Development and the Foreign and Commonwealth Office. The Commonwealth Shared Scholarship Scheme is funded jointly by the Department for International Development and participating universities in the UK. The schemes support mainly postgraduate, although 50 per cent of overseas students are undergraduate. The number of awards nearly doubled over the last decade but this was mainly due to distance learning awards which share of total awards grew from a quarter to half from 2003 to 2007. From 1998 to 2007, the expenditure in real terms for commonwealth awards increased from 10 per cent. As a result the expenditure per awards nearly halved from 13, 362 to 7649 (this represents 0.5 per cent of all overseas students). Around 60 per cent and 30 per cent of these scholarships are offered to students from sub-Saharan Africa and 30 per cent from South Asia (Commonwealth Scholarships, 1997–2008).

Other scholarships are available like the British Chevening Scholarships funded by the Foreign and Commonwealth Office. Around 1000 postgraduate scholarships and 200 fellowships are offered each year. The Overseas Research Students Awards Scheme (ORSAS) is funded by the Department for Innovation, Universities and Skills for postgraduate non EU students. ORSAS funding pays the difference between the international and domestic student tuition fees and funds 600 students a year. HEFCE is to phase out funding from 2009–2010, when the grant will be reduced by a third, with a 50 per cent cut the next year and no funding from 2011 (http://www.orsas.ac.uk/england).

Thus only a few government scholarships are offered and most of them at postgraduate levels. No centralized data are available on scholarships from UK higher education institutions (which are increasingly important) and from students' country of origin. It is therefore difficult to know exactly how the student support system manages to promote international social justice and social mobility within the context of high fees. What is clear is that financial support has not matched the growth of fees and enrolment.

The main lesson from this discussion is that overseas fees (as well as home fees and arguably the other private resources of higher education) should be seen as additional resources and not substitutes. The continuation of the public/private substitution of funding may produce huge problems as more financial commitment demanded from overseas students would not be matched by sufficient public resources to increase funding per student (for both domestic and overseas students and not a transfer of resources between the two), to maintain a quality and diverse pedagogy with additional financial support for all students.

▶ Conclusion

The political economy of higher education is constantly evolving and points to the dangers inherent in considering the present as permanent. The historical lens points to the combination of cultural, political, economic and financial motivations behind the expansion of numbers of overseas students. There have been tensions in the past between different, and sometimes contradictory, driving forces. However, the risk is that financial motivation tends to dominate the agenda to a point where the expansion of the higher education system in the direction of inclusion may suffer. This is especially important today as the recent financial crisis will probably alter the whole spectrum and debates about higher education.

Analysed in terms of the Kondratiev cycle, international students appear as forerunners of the greater financial contribution demanded of students after the 1970s' economic crisis. This was part of the trend to substitute private funding for slowing down public resources rather than bringing additional income into higher education. This substitution failed to resolve the problems of underfunding and posed new equity issues. It is possible that the current economic crisis may test public–private substitution to the limit putting education institutions at the mercy of volatile private sources of funding.

The current crisis needs to be put in the context of increasing inequalities (Atkinson and Piketty, 2007). Private debts have in a sense masked the reality of inequalities brought by neoliberal controls on public spending. While higher education acts as a shield from unemployment, it may be the case that uncertainty and growing unemployment will deter more and more potential students from paying higher fees (even deferred). Some US banks have refused to offer student loans. Private resources from donations and businesses may also decrease. Recent events have shown us that private resources are more volatile and without substantial increase in public funding there is a risk of a return to a restricted expansion of higher education. Beyond the obvious impact on inequalities, such a move would mean that the global (neoliberal) agenda of public austerity has compromised the other agenda (and discourse) of the knowledge economy.

As globalization accelerated, Scott asks whether there is a conflict between massification of higher education and internationalization of universities (Scott, 1998, p. 121). To avoid this, it is crucial to consider both home and overseas students' fees as an additional income rather than substitute for public resources: the acceleration of public funding is crucial in order to generate an increase of funding per student (which was the stated goal of most reforms initially) to ensure fair access (through scholarships and grants) and improvement of quality for all students. The lens of economic cycles signals that previous economic downturns were overcome by countercyclical spending on human development and that higher education was part of that process. Only in the 1970s did this not occur, deepening the recession. The crisis offers the opportunity to return to a more balanced structure of funding for higher education and develop new mechanisms which could guarantee public funding independent from additional private funding. The provision of sufficient resources to develop a strong and inclusive higher education system contributing to social cohesion and national and global economy will require adequate public investment not private substitution.

▶ Note

1. University Grants Committee (1966–1979) *Statistics of Education, Vol. 6, University statistics*, Universities' Statistical Records, Vol. 3, London; University Grants Committee (1980–1988) *University statistics, Vol. 1, Students and Staff, Universities'* Statistical Records, London; University Funding Council (1980–1988) *University statistics, Vol. 3, Finance*, Universities' Statistical Records, London; University Funding Council (1989–1994) *University statistics, Vol. 1, Students and Staff*, Universities' Statistical Records, London; University Funding Council (1989–1994) *University statistics, Vol. 3, Finance*, Universities' Statistical Records, London; Higher Education Statistics Agency (1995–current) *Resources for Higher Education Institutions*, Higher Education Statistics Agency Limited, Cheltenham; Higher Education Statistics Agency (1995–current) *Students in Higher Education Institutions*, Higher Education Statistics Agency Limited, Cheltenham.

▶ References

Aldrich, R. (2002) *A Century of Education* (London: Routledge Falmer).

Altbach, P. G., Reisberg, L. and Rumbley, L. E. (2009) *Trends in Global Higher Education: Tracking an Academic Revolution: A Report Prepared for the UNESCO 2009 World Conference on Higher Education* (Paris: UNESCO).

Apple, M. (1982) *Cultural and Economic Reproduction in Education* (London: Routledge and Kegan Paul).

Archer, L. and Leathwood, C. (2003) 'Identities, Inequalities and Higher Education', in Archer, L., Hutchings, M., and Ross, A. (eds) *Higher Education and Social Class: Issues of exclusion and inclusion* (London: Routledge Falmer).

Atkinson, A. B. and Piketty, T. (2007) *Top Incomes over the Twentieth Century: A Contrast between European and English-Speaking Countries* (Oxford: Oxford University Press).

Baker, I. (1993) 'Lessons from the Introduction of Fees for Overseas Students', *Journal of Higher Education Policy and Management*, 15(1), 95–98.

Ball, S. (2008) *The Education Debate* (Bristol: Polity Press).

Barr, N. (2003), 'Financing Higher Education: Lessons from the UK Debate', *The Political Quarterly*, 74(3), 371–381.

Belloc, B. (2003) 'Incentives and Accountability Instruments of Change', *Higher Education Management and Policy*, 1(1), 23–40.

Bjarnason, S. (2004) 'Borderless Higher Education', in King, R. (ed.) *The University in the Global Age* (Houndsmills: Palgrave Macmillan).

Boccara, P. (2008) *Transformations et Crise du Capitalisme Mondialisé: Quelle Alternative?* (Pantin: Le Temps des Cerises).

Bolsmann, C. and Miller, H. (2008) 'International Student Recruitment to Universities in England: Discourse, Rationales and Globalisation', *Globalisation Societies and Education*, 6(1), 75–88.

Bourdieu, P. and Passeron, J. C. (1964) *Les héritiers, les étudiants et la culture* (Paris: Editions de Minuit).

Bouslimani, A. (2002) 'La régulation systémique à l'épreuve de la problématique éducation-développement: vers l'élaboration de la notion de système social d'accumulation', *Economies et Sociétés*, Série F(40), 475–500.

Boyer, R. and Saillard, Y. (2002) *Regulation Theory: The State of the Art* (London: Routledge).

Brown, R. (2004) 'The Future Structure of the Sector: What Price Diversity?', *Perspectives*, 8(4), 93–99.

Byram, M. and Dervin, F. (2008) *Students, Staff and Academic Mobility in Higher Education* (Newcastle: Cambridge Scholars Publishing).

Callender, C. and Jackson, J. (2005) 'Does the Fear of Debt Deter Students from Higher Education?', *Journal of Social Policy*, 34(4), 509–540.

Carpentier, V. (2001) *Système éducatif et performances économiques au Royaume-Uni: 19ème et 20ème siècles* (Paris: L'Harmattan).

Carpentier, V. (2003) 'Public Expenditure on Education and Economic Growth in the UK, 1833–2000', *History of Education*, 32(1), 1–15.

Carpentier, V. (2004) *Historical Statistics on the Funding and Development of the UK University System, 1920–2002*, UK Data Archive. Online at www.data-archive.ac.uk (accessed March 2010).

Carpentier, V. (2006a) 'Funding in Higher Education and Economic Growth in France and the United Kingdom, 1921–2003', *Higher Education Management and Policy*, 18(3), 1–26.

Carpentier, V. (2006b) 'Public Expenditure on Education and Economic Growth in the USA in the Nineteenth and Twentieth Centuries in Comparative Perspective', *Paedagogica Historica*, 42(6), 683–706.

Carpentier, V. (2007) 'Educational Policymaking: Economic and Historical Perspectives', in Crook, D. and McCulloch, G. (eds) *History, Politics and Policy Making in Education* (London: Bedford Ways Papers).

Carpentier, V. (2008) 'Quantitative Sources for the History of Education', *History of Education*, 37(5), 701–720.

Carpentier, V. (2009) 'Viewpoint: The Credit Crunch and Education: An Historical Perspective from the Kondratiev Cycle', *London Review of Education*, 7(2), 193–196.

Carry, A. (1999) 'Le compte satellite rétrospectif de l'éducation en France:1820–1996', *Economies et Sociétés*, Série AF(25), 1–281.

Castells, M. (2000) *The Rise of the Network Society*, 2nd ed. (New York: Blackwell Publishers).

Chattopadhyay, S. (2007) 'Exploring Alternative Sources of Financing Higher Education', *Economic and Political Weekly*, 20 October, 4251–4259.

Commonwealth Scholarships (1997–2008) *Commonwealth Scholarship Commission in the United Kingdom, Annual Report to the Secretary of State for International Development*.

Council for International Education (2004) *Broadening Our Horizons: International Students in Uk Universities and Colleges* (London: United Kingdom Council for Overseas Students' Affairs: The Council for International Education).

Dearing, R. (1997) *The National Committee of Inquiry into Higher Education: Higher Education in the Learning Society* (Norwich: Her Majesty's Stationary Office).

De Vita, G. and Case, P. (2003) 'Rethinking the Internationalisation Agenda in UK Higher Education', *Journal of Further and Higher Education*, 27(4), 383–398.

Diebolt, C. and Fontvieille, L. (2001) 'Dynamic Forces in Educational Development: A Long-Run Comparative View of France and Germany in the 19th and 20th Centuries', *Compare*, 31(3), 295–309.

Diouf, W. and Fontvielle, L. (2002) 'Développement de l'éducation, croissance économique et contrainte démographique dans les pays d'Afrique au Sud du Sahara', *Economies et Sociétés*, 40(3–4), 589–605.

Department for Education and Skills (DfES) (2003) *The Future of Higher Education, White Paper*, Department for Education and Skills, January.

Enslin, P. and Hedge, N. (2008) 'International Students, Export Earnings and the Demands of Global Justice', *Ethics and Education*, 3(2), 107–119.

Fontvieille, L. (1976) 'Evolution et croissance de l'Etat français 1815–1969', *Economies et Sociétés*, Série AF(13), 1657–2149.

Fontvieille, L. (1990) 'Education, Growth and Long Cycles: The Case of France in the 19th and 20th Centuries', in Tortella, G. (ed.) *Education and Economic Development since the Industrial Revolution* (Valencia: Generalitat Valenciana).

Freeman, C. and Louçã, F. (2001) *As Time Goes By, From the Industrial Revolutions to the Information Revolution* (Oxford: Oxford University Press).

Galindo-Rueda, F., Marcenaro-Gutierrez, O. and Vignoles, A. (2004) 'The Widening Socio-Economic Gap in UK Higher Education', *National Institute Economic Review*, 190, 75–88.

Goodson, I. (2006) 'Long Waves of Educational Reform', in Goodson, I. (ed.) *Learning, Curriculum and Life Politics: The Selected Works of Ivor F. Goodson* (Abingdon: Routledge).

Gürüz, K. (2008) *Higher Education and International Student Mobility in the Global Knowledge Economy* (Albany, NY: State University of New York Press).

Harris, R. (1995) 'Overseas Students in the United Kingdom University System', *Higher Education*, 29(1), 77–92.

Harris, R. (1997) 'Overseas Students in the UK', in McNamara, D. and Harris, R. (eds) *Overseas Students in Higher Education: Issues in Teaching and Learning* (London: Routledge).

Held, D. and McGrew, A. (2002) *The Global Transformation Reader*, 2nd ed. (Cambridge: Polity).

Hobsbawm, E. J. (1997) *On History* (London: Abacus).

Jessop, B. (2002) *The Future of the Capitalist State* (Cambridge: Polity Press).

King, R. (2004) *The University in the Global Age* (Houndsmills: Palgrave Macmillan).

Loucã, F. and Reijnders, J. (1999) *The Foundations of Long Wave Theory* (Cheltenham: Edward Elgar Publishing).

Lowe, R. (2008) *The History of Higher Education (Series: Major Themes in Education, 5 Volumes)* (London: Routlegde).

Maddison, A. (1995) *Monitoring the World Economy 1820–1992* (Paris: Organisation for Economic Co-Operation and Development).

Maddison, A. (2000) *The World Economy: A Millenial Perspective* (Paris: Organisation for Economic Co-Operation and Development).

Marczewski, J. (1961) 'Histoire quantitative, buts et méthodes', *Cahiers de l'Institut de Sciences Economiques Appliquées*, Série A.F. 15, 3–54.

Marginson, S. and van der Wende, M. (2007) 'Globalisation and Higher Education', *Organisation for Economic Co-Operation and Development* (Education Working Paper No. 8).

Marx, K. (1894[1970]) *Capital, Volume 3* (London: Laurence and Wishart).

McCulloch, G. (1998) 'Education and Economic Performance', *History of Education*, 27(3), 202–206.

Michel, S. (1999) *Education et croissance économique en longue période* (Paris: L'Harmattan).

Michel, S. and Vallade, D. (2007) 'Une Analyse de long terme des dépenses sociales', *Revue de la régulation*, 1, 1–32.

Milonakis, D. and Fine, B. (2009) *From Political Economy to Economics: Method, the Social and the Historical in the Evolution of Economic Theory* (London: Routledge).

Naidoo, R. (2003) 'Repositioning Higher Education as a Global Commodity: Opportunities and Challenges for Future Sociology of Education Work', *British Journal of Sociology of Education*, 24(2), 249–259.

Olssen, M. and Peters, M. A. (2005) 'Neoliberalism, Higher Education and the Knowledge Economy: From the Free Market to Knowledge Capitalism', *Journal of Education Policy*, 20(3), 313–345.

Reay, D., David, M. and Ball, S. (2005) *Degrees of Choice: Class, Race, Gender and Higher Education* (Stoke-on-Trent: Trentham Books).

Sanderson, M. (2007) 'Educational and Economic History: The Good Neighbours', *History of Education*, 36(4–5), 429–445.

Scott, P. (ed.) (1998) *The Globalization of Higher Education* (Buckingham: Society for Research into Higher Education and Open University Press).

Serra, N. and Stiglitz, J. (2008) *The Washington Consensus Reconsidered: Towards a New Global Governance* (Oxford: Oxford University Press).

Silver, H. (2006) 'Things Change but Names Remain the Same: Higher Education Historiography 1975–2000', *History of Education*, 35(1), 121–140.

Sizer, J. (1987) 'The Impacts of Financial Reductions on British Universities: 1981–84', *Higher Education*, 16(5), 557–580.

Stiasny, M. (2008) *Mobility Matters: 40 Years of International Students* (London: United Kingdom Council for Overseas Students' Affairs: The Council for International Education).

Teixeira, J., Johnstone, B., Rosa, M. J. and Vossensteyn, H. (2006) *Cost-sharing and Accessibility in Higher Education: A Fairer Deal?* (Dordrecht: Springer).

Vickers, P. and Bekhradnia, B. (2007) *The Economic Costs and Benefits of International Students* (Oxford: Higher Education Policy Institute).

Wallerstein, I. (2003) 'Globalization or the Age of Transition? A Long-Term View of the Trajectory of the World-System', in Kohler, G. and Chaves, E. J. (eds) *Globalization: Critical Perspectives* (New York: Nova Science Publishers).

Watson, D. (2007) *Managing Civic and Community Engagement* (Buckingham: Open University Press).

Watson, D. and Bowden, R. (2007) 'The Fate of the Dearing Recommendations: Policy and Performance in UK HE, 1997–2007', in Watson, D. and Amoah, M. (eds) *The Dearing Report: Ten Years On* (London: Bedford Way Papers).

Williams, G. (1987) 'The International Market for Overseas Students in the English-Speaking World', *European Journal of Education*, 22(1), 15–25.

Williams, P. (1984) 'Britain's Full-Cost Policy for Overseas Students', *Comparative Education Review*, 28(2), 258–278.

Wolf, A. (2002) *Does Education Matter? Myths About Education and Economic Growth* (London: Penguin Books).

6 The Inter-Relationship of Employment, Marriage and Higher Education among Pakistani Students in the UK

Diana Leonard and Maryam Rab

We discovered a shared interest in international education and gender when Maryam Rab was studying in London. This developed when Diana Leonard was attached to the university in Rawalpindi where Maryam is the Registrar. We spent time together as friends and decided to conduct an exploratory study looking at Pakistan-domiciled postgraduate students who had studied in the UK and returned home, the use these students made of their postgraduate qualifications and some of the other effects studying abroad had had on their lives. We follow Rizvi's suggestion (2005, p. 81) that 'use' is a better concept than 'outcome' when exploring graduate destinations and career trajectories, because it stresses an active process of cultural production.

Although modest this project is useful because we have so little knowledge about what happens to foreign students who study in the UK once they graduate and return home. There have been occasional follow-up studies, mainly by funders (Unterhalter and Maxey, 1995; ACU, 2003), but as far as national statistics and government policy are concerned, they disappear when they 'return abroad',[1] though there is some consideration of those who remain in the West in migration studies and in studies of postcolonial identity. We hoped that working together as a Pakistani and a British researcher would help us 'see' material which each of us would normally take for granted; that joint research might help to counter the continued prioritizing of Western national concerns in much work on international students (Madge et al., 2009); and that concentrating on one country would work against the tendency to homogenize 'international' students. We were especially keen to do research on Pakistan since this country, and Islam generally, are often singled out as being especially hard to understand and stigmatized as 'Other' in current Anglo popular culture (Luke, this volume).

However, our group of informants is not only small but also unfortunately not typical. After we had undertaken the fieldwork, we obtained a special set of data on Pakistan-domiciled students in the UK in 2004–2005 from the Higher Education Statistics Agency (HESA). This showed that while nearly two-thirds of Pakistanis in the UK are studying at Masters and Doctoral level, as are our informants,[2] the majority attend post 1992 ('new') universities in London.[3] Those we interviewed, on the other hand, had almost all (6/7) attended elite (Russell Group) institutions. Our informants are also unrepresentative in that we spoke to more women than men, whereas 87 per cent of Pakistanis studying at postgraduate level in the UK are men; and our informants studied 'untypical' subjects: business studies, clinical psychology, human rights, international development and law, while most Pakistanis in the UK study business studies, computer science and engineering and technology.[4] Hence we can only generalize cautiously from our data.

We interviewed seven people who were conveniently located and willing to spend time exploring their experiences with us. They provided a starting point to consider areas that make the nature of inequalities in global higher education particularly complex. The one to two hour long semi-structured interview/ conversations we had with them took place in Islamabad, Rawalpindi and Lahore in 2006.[5] Our respondents comprised three men (two married) and four women (one married). Five had gained a Masters degree in the UK, one an LLB and the other a PhD.

Our study covered how individuals chose particular universities and the nature of marketing, students' previous experience of travel and living abroad, their treatment by the administration, international office and teaching staff in the UK university, the relevance of their course curriculum to Pakistan, racism and attitudes to Islam they experienced and their relations with British Pakistanis. In this chapter, we shall focus on issues of employment and family, and draw on feminist dual systems theory to suggest how labour market and family work are both patriarchally structured and supported by the education systems in both Western and postcolonial situations.

▶ Intersecting economic systems and supporting education systems

The interconnections of the divisions of labour and associated power relations in two economic systems – the European marriage and family system and the emergent capitalism of the eighteenth and nineteenth centuries – were explored by several authors in the 1970s and 1980s (Hartmann, 1979; Delphy, 1984; Davidoff and Hall, 1987; Delphy and Leonard, 1992). Until the eighteenth century, most production for the market in the agricultural and artisanal sectors in Europe took place in household units, headed by older men. This production used the unpaid labour of wives and children and also younger unmarried brothers and sisters and apprentices; and household heads protected and maintained these family members. These units were later supported by emerging enterprises and the wage labour market, when it in turn was structured around men as the primary wage-earners: the 'breadwinners' – with of course clear socio-economic divisions between them and 'their' families (Delphy and Leonard, 1992).

Over time, family production of goods for the market declined, though many wives continued to support their husband's specific employment or to help reproduce his labour power and to generate extra income for the household by taking outside paid jobs. But most of the labour of wives and daughters became used primarily for producing a comfortable home environment, emotional care and specialist child-rearing. Some men's dependents might however be 'conspicuously leisured' as a mark of their husband/fathers' status.

Histories of the rise and fall of colonialism introduce a third economic system: the material advantages which accrued to the colonizers during the period of occupation, and how the material relations left in place at 'independence' ensured a continuing, mutual but unequal, economic dependence between the two parties (Wallerstein, 1976). Raw materials from the former territories had to be exchanged for manufactured goods from the 'developed' societies (Hayter, 1981), and in addition the socioeconomic and gender divisions of the colonial period, which were the product of the imposition of patriarchal colonialism and patriarchal capitalism onto an extended but also strongly patriarchal indigenous extended family system, were continued if not exacerbated by the postcolonial settlement (Boserup, 1970; Mies, 1986; Tinker, 1990).

A related analysis suggests a causal connection between the various economic systems and the education systems developed to support them (Carnoy, 1982). There were different forms of education provided for the children of the elite, the middle and the working classes in the nineteenth and twentieth centuries in Western countries, and these maintained the gender and class divisions of both the home and the public sphere. The formal and informal curricula and the pedagogy provided in Public, grammar and elementary schools aimed to develop appropriate upper, middle and working class skills and associated masculine and feminine behaviours and sensibilities. But the education of girls was generally in a poor second place because it did not increase their marriageability and would benefit their husband's family rather than their family of origin. Similarly, the schooling promoted in colonial situations was from the start part of the 'colonizing apparatus' that re-shaped a territory's economy, power and culture (Mudimbe, 1994; quoted in Connell, 2009, p. 9), and produced appropriate (male and female) colonial subject identities.

In the nineteenth and much of the twentieth centuries, most vocational training in the West and its colonies excluded girls and women, since they were to become wives and not breadwinners; and they were later admitted only under limited, constraining circumstances. Similarly, universities were only for upper and then middle class men, later extended to some able boys from poorer families and middle class girls. Only recently have larger numbers of working class girls gone to university in Britain (Dyhouse, 1995; Leathwood and Read, 2009) and substantial numbers from former colonies enrolled in postcolonial universities or joined those in the metropole.

So, for example, in the modest higher education system left in the Indian sub-continent by Britain in 1947, there were few universities in the part that became Pakistan,[6] and according to the 2008 report from the Ministry of Education of Pakistan 'only 3.7% of the 18 to 23 age cohort participates in higher education. Even though enrolment in both public and private institutions is increasing rapidly, at approximately 30% per year, the gross enrolment ratio does not compare well with other developing countries' and women continue to be under-represented (Ministry of Education, 2008, p. 18). Since 2002, a Higher Education Commission (HEC) has been actively developing indigenous Pakistani HEIs, including establishing several women's universities. However, both the HEC and the World Bank (2006) recognize that the country is going to depend on overseas training for many of its university and other professional staff for some years to come.

As a result, various Western countries, and in the case of Pakistan especially the UK, now benefit from a situation where fees are paid by South Asian students and their government to study abroad in a technically advanced English-speaking country, and British universities have come to depend heavily on such international students for their financial viability (Gürüz, 2008). Moreover, many external powers, including DFID and USAID, contribute large amounts of educational aid, including higher educational support, to Pakistan because of its current strategic importance. They hope thereby to raise the socio-economic status of the country, to 'stabilize' pro-Western governments, to counter Islamic fundamentalism and so to reduce possible attacks on the West.

This brief outline shows the continuing interconnections of structures of dominance and advantage in private and public production, international relations and in and between educational systems. We cannot of course cover the complex interconnections and historical transformations of each sector here, though we would stress that inequalities in one economic system are not always perfectly aligned with those in another: changes in one may well be in conflict with others (Walby, 1997). But the framework is helpful in understanding the situation of all overseas students in UK universities, and the continuing differences in the experiences of men and women from different countries.

▶ Some postgraduate students from Pakistan

The people we interviewed all came from middle or upper middle class backgrounds. Three fathers were army officers, two were in the civil service, one was a chartered accountant and business trader and one owned a private secondary school. Only one informant made any mention of an occupation for a mother – teaching English at a university. The other mothers were all

> at home, basically a housewife. But she is much more than that I think. **Interview 7**

Our respondents had all been to English-medium (single sex) secondary schools (the elite) and, as might be expected (Rahman, 2004; Qureshi and Rarieya, 2007), most had done UK O and A levels. All bar one had a Masters degree (the fourth year of an honours degree or a 1- or 2-year course in Pakistan) from good universities. The exception gained her masters in the USA.

But despite these advantaged backgrounds, everyone we spoke to said they had found it difficult or extremely difficult to finance their studies in the UK. Three of our informants had scholarships (two women and one man) and said they could not have gone to the UK without. One was a well-endowed university's own award; another a Foreign and Commonwealth Office Chevening award; the third an award from a Pakistani benefactor for a woman student. The first two gave good support with living expenses in addition to the fees, but the third only covered fees. This student expected to get employment in the UK to pay for her food, accommodation and travel, alongside some savings and help from her family.

In all the three cases, the informants represented it as serendipitous that they had heard about, applied for and got their award. As will be seen from subsequent discussions, these seemingly well-rehearsed tales show the importance of contacts in accessing resources in Pakistan, potential students' limited knowledge of the UK higher education system and a general lack of guidance in making choices.

> It was actually all a big coincidence, but little bit of luck. This particular university... is pretty new and I happened

to visit their Lahore office because I knew someone there. And they mentioned a particular scholarship...just for one female each year to go to London to do a Masters at this college. **Interview 5**

In four cases, the fathers/families paid the fees and much of the living expenses. This was a considerable struggle for most, especially since families in Pakistan are large by UK standards: our informants had a median of three other siblings. For girls it was especially difficult to get family funding because preference is given to boys' education. One father had paid what the interviewee estimated was the £30,000–£35,000 cost of his law qualification. Another, who had been working in his father's business for several years, had his fees paid but had to meet the costs of his accommodation, food and leisure. Meeting the costs could involve sale of investments and sometimes loans from uncles.

For the two women whose fees were paid by their families, the situation was rather different. As one described it, their families had 'bailed them out' – supported their education abroad to extricate them (and the family) from difficult social situations.

One, whose parents married her 'very young', at 19, had her education interrupted by moving to live abroad with her husband, but when the marriage did not work, the family raised the money for her to go to the USA to complete her bachelors and do a Masters. There was then a second arranged marriage, which also was not happy, and by 'force of will' she came to the UK to do a doctorate, while her husband was living elsewhere.

The other young woman had got into medical school in Pakistan, but wanted to be a veterinarian. Her parents would not allow this because of the sex ratio in class (four women to a hundred men), so she did a BSc, but then could not study the specialist area she wanted at Masters level. So she switched and did 'a practical degree', a Masters in Public Administration, instead. Even after this she 'could not find a decent job'. So she started teaching maths and science in schools and worked in the administration at a local university. There 'various people who had their own PhDs from abroad' encouraged her to study and showed her 'that you do not have to be conventional and can live beyond what is considered the norm'.

During that time, my parents continuously tried ... not introducing, but people coming over and seeing me for their sons or whatever. And that never sort of worked out. It was about seven years this happened; and one year I applied to England for the heck of it and got into the University of X. And I was just fascinated. And then the next year I was really, really upset and I used to go into depression, you know, sort of become very, very violent as well as aggressive at times. So they got really tired and they said 'she needs a break'. Somehow they managed this. Money they were supposed to be saving up for [my] marriage. They gave it to me and I do not know how. I mean, I know how. I used to walk everywhere, because I needed to save money, but I ended up in London. **Interview 6**

Thus in Pakistan, as in the UK (Reay et al., 2005), professional middle class families use their family and other connections and their cultural knowledge and economic capital to secure and reproduce their advantaged positions. In Pakistan, this is done partly through using the fee-paying sectors of their national education system, and supplementing these with a distant, not always well-understood and super expensive, postcolonial higher education system at postgraduate level. Access to the latter may involve an application for grants which form part of official international aid.

▶ Employment

Although family production continues in many parts of rural Pakistan, both family production and production in the capitalist labour market, which dominates in the cities, are highly sex segregated and more male dominated than in the West. Most of the service sector and semi-skilled jobs for women in the West are done by men in Pakistan, and it is even harder for women to get into senior posts and professional positions. This affects the significance and place of education in men and women's lives.

We found that two of the three men we interviewed were over 25 when they went to the UK, and all were established in jobs in Pakistan. The oldest had been in the police for more than 10 years, including a spell in a UN peace-keeping force. Another had been the chief administrative officer in his father's school; and the youngest, 'from a legal background', 'had planned to go into law since the 7th grade'. He had done an internship with a senior judge and then joined a leading law firm in his home town – which he told us about at length and with great pride.

But the situation of the women was significantly different. Most were in their early twenties when they were in the UK, which is 'marriageable age' for women in Pakistan, so that was a conflict. But in addition, women's youth meant they lacked labour market experience when they wanted to study in the UK, which had various effects. For instance, one was not eligible for a Chevening scholarship, which requires 2 years employment experience, 'because I had never worked in my life'; while the woman who had a scholarship which only covered her tuition fees and who had relied on getting a job in London had a hard time finding anything.[7]

> I was [eventually] a sales assistant in [a domestic goods chain]. Which was an interesting experience! Because you [a middle class woman] do not do work like that in Pakistan! When I was told to mop the floor, that was a little disheartening initially...I had tears in my eyes. Is this what I came here for? But then, when I saw my manager do it the next day, I realized [it was] not a big deal and everyone does it. But initially it was strange. Even getting a part-time job was really difficult. I did not think it would be. I am a bachelor student and a scholarship student [I thought I would have] no problems. [But] I got there in September and I [only] got the job in February. **Interview 5**

Men not only managed to get work more easily, it was also better paid work which they saw as relevant to their area of interest or as giving useful general business experience. One said he earned £200 a week (£100 wage and £100 in commission in 2002) in a call centre for one of the UK energy companies

> it was a very good organization to work with. That experience is also really very nice. That has really helped me working here in Pakistan.... they are very professional...I did not come back and work in a call centre here, but, you know, that professional attitude of coming in on time, mobile

should be out of sight. Here...you would see very, very senior people using their mobiles in meetings...no lateness, three lateness you would be fired.... **Interview 2**

Another man wrote a report for a voluntary organization while studying, using his past work experience, and this led him to consider looking for work with them in the future.

Among the women, the doctoral student did pick up bits of research work – designing questionnaires and interviewing – in universities which contacts told her needed someone who spoke Urdu. While another 'stayed back a bit' and worked with her supervisor as his assistant for 4 months while waiting to defend her dissertation. She then remained in contact with him – to mutual benefit – on her return. But two of the women did not seek work while in the UK, one because

> you have to be very aggressive to get work with the Pakistani passport...now that the European Union is opened and [there is fear of a] Pakistani...being terrorist. **Interview 6**

However, the main difference between men and women in the effects of their prior experience – or lack – was in their employment capacity when they returned to Pakistan. The woman who had 'never worked in her life' found that

> no one is prepared to employ you. Everyone has a favourite or a reference. I was going through the newspapers and...I think my first job was in March. So three months and maybe a hundred applications. No reply. No call even. I got only two calls and they said 'Oh. No experience.' That was it. Minimum of one year, that's what they say. So, was a shock. I was ready to work without pay [to get experience]...**Interview 1**

The one who had gained a PhD in the UK spent a year making some efforts to get a university teaching job in Pakistan but all she was offered was temporary, part-time work with poor pay. She rejected this, even though people said 'That is how it's done here'. That is, you have to do that for a while and work up. And the woman who chose a UK Masters degree in a different field from her Pakistani Masters could not get work or funding for further study for 2 years. When asked 'So what jobs have you tried for?' she said:

> Mostly on education and development.... Everything – research, teaching, co-ordination, administration in NGOs... And then the earthquake hit at that time [2005]. So it was a lot on rehabilitation. I applied any and everywhere I could. But of course I knew no one in the organization and when it did work out, for example [with an agency] in Islamabad, they could not afford to pay me a lot and I [would] need to live in another city...independently. And I could not afford to live off that, no matter how hard I worked [with part-time teaching as well].... [I have the] advantage of being a girl and not having to provide for anyone, and can live at home, and therefore able to take time finding a job or initially do voluntary work...But I can't move to another town without a good salary as it must be a respectable location, and secure, and it's an issue for the family – so [I'm] constrained... **Interview 6**

The only woman who got a job immediately on return had taught O level and undergraduate economics for a year at the college where she had completed her own degree,[8] and she did business studies in the UK. On her return, she 'walked into an office' and was offered work as a marketing manager. She took this for 4 months while she applied for something more interesting and better paid.

This difference between men and women's experiences prior to study in Britain, their access to employment for additional spending money while studying, and the over all place of study abroad in their lives is generally not noticed in Western studies of international students because it is assumed that such students are like 'home' students. That is to say, that they will come directly from school if they are doing undergraduate studies, or from Masters degrees which directly followed their first degree if they are doing doctoral studies: that they are young. Also that whether or not they marry in the future is optional, but if they do, marriage will take place after the student years;[9] whereas marriage is socially required for both women and men in Pakistan. However it should take place at different normative ages for the two sexes; and the timing of both marriage and study abroad is more in men's (or perhaps more accurately, in men's families') control than in women's.

▶ Family and social life

It would be hard to overstate the importance of the family in Pakistani life, nor the associated pressures to marry and have children. There is not the same focus on the individually chosen emotional relationship with the spouse as in the Western marriage and family system, but usually on parental involvement in the choice of a spouse and on strong bonds of attachment with a wider family group. There is also a well-known stress on honour and not doing anything which could bring you and your parents or the wider family – your brothers and sisters and their in-laws, and your aunts and uncles and cousins – into disrepute.

All the men we spoke to openly expressed how much they missed their (extended) family and particular people within it (their mother or father or son or a brother) when they were in the UK. The three men we spoke to, who were already in arranged marriages when they went to the UK, said little spontaneously about their wives (and we did not follow this up). One who had two children by the time he was in the UK and whose wife was pregnant with another said he found it 'really tough being alone' but also

> You take something, you leave something. So I had to do my course. I was there. Being alone at times, I really enjoyed being myself, while I missed my family. I really did not have time [to be homesick] ... The time I have, I go to sleep. You know, there you really had to think and ... at times ... I [lived] very close [to college], so you know you can do the walk there, So I really enjoyed that moment. Ya, especially the few sunny days, the very few!, ... I totally enjoyed those ones believe me. **Interview 3**

Another made no mention of his wife coming to the UK and overall talked more about his brother-in-law's job than his wife. But he made much of having promised his mother he definitely would return to Pakistan if he studied abroad. He called home every second day and the person he mentioned talking to was his mother, who was living in the same building as his wife.[10] He returned to continue living jointly with his parents; and while he enjoyed going clubbing in the UK, and described himself as 'quite liberal' in his views, in Pakistan he and his wife accept that they 'have to follow the house [i.e. his parents'] rules'.

The single man gave the impression of kicking up his heels while abroad,[11] but he too did not find it difficult to reintegrate because 'it was just returning to normal life'. He had in any case visited Pakistan no less than four times during the year he was 'away', for a week or 10 days at a time. He also phoned regularly, and if he did not, his parents 'tracked him down' with his mobile. He used his relatives in England, and unmarried Pakistani women students, to take care of him:

> **What about your relatives, did you see much of them, were they helpful to you?**
> They were helpful to me a lot, especially the relatives in Manchester. I mean after a month or so you definitely needed a break. You wanted to go back to your culture and you wanted your food.... So the relatives I would go to in Manchester, I would always go for my food. Or for that matter anybody in London. When I would go, I would say, I am coming for food. Just cook that particular dish for me!
> **Interview 4**

None of the men found much difficulty reintegrating when they returned: one suggested it helped that he came back when it was his brother's wedding – 'so everyone was there for ten days' – and also because his 'friends were still around' in his home city.

Women, by contrast, did not have the same connections and all of them said they were homesick while in the UK, some acutely: 'It never goes away.'[12] However, one went to 'a girls' college' on her father's insistence, and she praised it, saying she 'found a home' there: '[It] embraced me.' For others, in London,

> I felt I was on my own. If I didn't go back [to my room] for two days, no one would notice...I wouldn't want to go through that again. Being alone scares me.... Coming back was not that big a problem [though] initially the control of my time and space by the family was difficult. 'You've come

back now. You can't be out late. Or out with boys.' It hit me initially.... I found lots of relationships were not the same as when I left. My sisters' perception of me [had changed]: 'so fussy', 'so particular'...I kept saying 'I want to go back' for the first three months. Now I'm settled in. Looked after and cooked for...I'd like to go back for shopping!...My parents are conservative about relations with boys. Over the years they have loosened up, but I can't have male friends over. In London they wanted me to go out with, you know be looked after by, boys I knew from my old college. Back here, the same people are not acceptable. A little confusing! It's not their fault: it's the culture; and I'm of marriageable age. So have to careful. **Interview 5**

In Pakistan the young women were not required to do direct domestic labour: shopping, cooking and cleaning are mainly done by servants. But they were expected to remain at the affective centre of the household, to manage its affairs, to support children and anyone sick and to visit relatives. This leaves them little free time:

I do not have a social life [at home in Pakistan]...I really do not have a social life. I came back in September and my friend who got married [the following] January, she left for Dubai, to UAE. And my married friends are very busy with their lives and they are also very sort of dependent on their husbands, the ones who do live in the city. They do not move alone .... They do not have time. Their husband wants them to stay home.... The family life is the centre of life here and there is no such thing as [women's] friendship. I am more friends with male friends now, because they are more independent – if they are single that is...thankfully my sister-in-laws are not very conservative...the elder one is...a very very decent person. The younger one...at the end of the day, in her heart, she is still a very conservative person...I think I can see it more so because I know it is in me as well. But since I have been allowed to live a life...So I have more of a prospective. **Interview 6**

The single man (aged 23) said (with a grin) that having studied abroad had made him a more marriageable bachelor, though his mother wanted him to be more settled and to be earning more before he married. Meantime he played sport. However, for unmarried women the situation was mixed. One (aged 23) said that

> Having a degree form abroad has improved my prospects. It's really funny. [She imitated her mother on the phone.] 'My daughter's back from London.' 'Oh **really**!'

But she later commented that:

> I hate this arranged marriage thing. But every few weeks – you have to go through with it. [I've] got one at 5 o'clock today. [laughed] I feel like a cow! And you know how it goes: Can you cook? You drive! You swim! She's too fast, she won't fit in!! **Interview 5**

Another woman (aged 28) felt that being away for the year when she was 22–23, and working hard on and being successful in her career since, had hindered her marriage prospects, to the extent that she was no longer concerned if a man was Muslim and that she would consider marriage to a Western man.

> Mother is becoming desperate! She used to call me in [England] and say 'I hope you are not thinking of settling down.' But now she says 'No problem. Just get married!' Because suddenly she's realized that the day I touch thirty, she won't be able to make me get married. And frankly, very few proposals are coming to the family in the traditional fashion. I can't believe going abroad was the **only** reason and may be I came from a family where I was raised by a military man to speak up too much. [She also suggested she hadn't nurtured some possible relationships sufficiently, putting her job first.] ... [Also there] is a very strange phenomena going on. People have moved from the west back here and they are bringing their young daughters. They have a lot of money and they want their daughters to get married among the Muslims in Pakistan ... after 9/11. So [when men] have option of a 26-year-old Pakistani with less money and a 19-year-old, beautiful, more money, they opt for that ... frankly

I [know] about seven or eight girls from UK study or Harvard, they [have] all got married through love marriages. They married their colleague or something, but no arranged marriages. It is a closed chapter on that. Or they fake their ages... **Interview 1**

The one who was in her second marriage but living apart from her husband said she was very attached to her family, and especially her mother, so she had wanted to come back to her country as, 'My heart is happiest here.' However, her mother had disapproved of her having other romantic relationships as an adolescent, and now in adulthood she 'felt shackled.'

So you have a clear sense that this is home despite the extensive experience you have had abroad?
Right. Right Right... [But she was worried she might just be 'kicked out'.] I think for a person like me it is going to be pretty hard... people can put immense emotional pressure on – that I have been enduring for a number of years. Because you are living in a dichotomy, a dichotomy that you do not believe in, and you think it is wrong, and you can only voice it: you can keep saying that this is not the way I would want it. But you know that you could end up hurting people who are so close to your heart. That if it is [a] choice between hurting, continuously hurting, yourself and not hurting other people that you caremore about, then you end up doing that. **Interview 7**

▶ **Future plans**

Only the men informants had long-term plans, and then only up to a point. One who had been back for 4 years was thinking of doing a PhD in the UK in a year's time – if he could get a Higher Education Commission grant. He had wanted to be an economist before he went to the UK for his Masters, but when he returned to Pakistan he moved back into his father's business until this closed. Then he took up what he called a 'bureaucratic' ICT management job with a government agency. He had his doctoral topic ready and had started working on journal papers from his Masters dissertation. Long-term he 'wanted to work as economist, probably in the public sphere'.

The man who had been back longest had decided on his return to change field to Human Rights. But, he said

> I gave myself a year [in the old job]... Try to think Pakistani if you can! I mean, I am not saying [its totally different in] another part of the world, but in UK and Europe you may still think 'I am going to do that', and you will have opportunity to do that. In Pakistan, you say 'I am going to do that', but you never know whether you will do it or not. But I was quite lucky, because I remember – I mean, just few months down the road, I found [a UN agency] looking for somebody [with my] profile... There were a lot of people after it... at the end I was lucky. I got the position and... started working and learning simultaneously. [He did a part-time law degree.]
> **Interview 3**

He had been promoted within the agency but says he is 'a restless soul' and will move on, perhaps within the same organization, but abroad. Or he may look for a job and move to the UK – but he will get the job first.

The third man had been back less than a year when we spoke but he stressed that he found he was treated differently, taken more seriously, on return.

Do you think it changed your sense of identity?

The... degree itself... I mean living abroad also makes the difference, but it was the [qualification] itself. Because... people start taking you seriously with a foreign degree. In Pakistan, unfortunately, the set up is that no matter how good or fantastic or wonderful a [professional] you are, it is only after a foreign qualification from any university that people start taking you seriously.... So now I consider myself, you know, much superior to what I was before when... practising.... I am more known now... than I was before. And generally the title 'barrister' itself, it is quite reputed one.... So people love it here in Pakistan....

I mean there is a strange sort of jealousy in the legal circle against people foreign qualified... unfortunately for most of the people who are based in Pakistan they...cannot spend that [amount of money].... There is an element of grouping involved as well. So just to counter that grouping, we have done a bit of grouping ourselves [forming an elite informal club]. **Interview 4**

He says his dream is later to go to Harvard and specialize in corporate consultancy, and he may later go into politics.

It is probably no accident that the women we managed to interview were single (apart from the one with her husband abroad) and most had been back in Pakistan only a short time. They had not yet been drawn back fully into their families and so had freedom to meet us.

The woman with a scholarship had been back a year. After her first job, where she 'did not find marketing very appealing', she answered an advertisement and moved to a recruitment company which finds local partners for overseas businesses. She says this post (in Human Relations) is still not very relevant to her degree. She wants to be in international finance and would hope to start her own recruitment agency 'five years from now'.

What were your plans after your degree?
I just thought a foreign degree would add a lot of value to my resume. That didn't happen...Anyone who is aware of Y university doesn't really give it much value. If I had LSE on my CV...or Manchester Business School... But it does make a difference actually having been to the UK rather than having a UK external degree.... [In her present company] We recruit on an ongoing basis and there is this particular way of people who have been abroad: how they carry themselves, their body language. Even if it is a bad university. **Interview 5**

The woman looking for a job in a development NGO or a PhD grant for 2 years did some distance-learning courses; while the one with a doctorate had started her own clinic and got a job with foreign aid institution, but she was not happy and, through contacts, moved to a reasonably senior post in university administration. The woman who had graduated from Oxbridge had been in Pakistan for 6 years and was finally flying high, even though initially she did not even get called for interviews.

Fortunately I met, came across at a conference, [a UN] representative here, and he asked...and was surprised and upset
at the system. He said, 'you come to my office tomorrow,
bring your credentials, and I'll try you for ten days. Give you
a task. You'll work with me.' And I worked with him for a
year plus as his assistant.... I was writing legal reports for
him. He used to dictate to me, and give me more theoretical
work which he had forgotten. More like a mentor. That was
my break. **Interview 1**

Then she applied to an American Foundation and was given
accelerated promotion to be a Programme Officer, which would
normally need 5 years experience. When the Foundation pulled
out of work in Pakistan, she was approached by a US government agency to manage a training unit, and then to run their
whole national portfolio.

▶ Conclusion

This account has looked at the experiences of some Pakistani
postgraduate students in the UK in the light of interconnecting
systems of family, labour market and international relations. It
has tried to show how their individual situations are part of the
long-standing and complex but close relationship between education and the reproduction of the advantaged positions and
dominance of upper and middle class men and postcolonial
nations.

We have shown how family households make different
demands on sons' and daughters' labour and time, and invest
differentially in their education. Fathers are the heads of households and the main decision-makers, and if an individual father
(or husband) favours women having (a degree of) emancipation,
they can allow/ facilitate this. They may be given encouragement in this by their wife and other extended family members,
but it is equally possible that relatives will try to dissuade them
from allowing their daughter, or son, study abroad.

Men from middle ranking families will however usually be
helped to access better paid, more prestigious jobs in either
family businesses or the labour market in Pakistan, with higher
salaries 'to support their families' (i.e. which maintain their

dominant position in the household). This may well involve a period of education abroad, but for them the timing of this is relatively open – apart from being contingent on family finances – and they can return to the jobs they already hold as stepping off points when they graduate.

Women, on the other hand, are faced with difficult choices since their marriageability declines with age. They can either undertake their studies in their twenties and possibly miss the marital boat, or marry first and then have their husbands and in-laws controlling if, when and where they can undertake further study or have employment. Although there were no instances in our small sample, we know from experience that there is a third possibility: doing postgraduate studies abroad while accompanying one's husband on his studies or on business. But this is risky: it may not happen, and requires studying when and wherever he is located, possibly leaving small children behind in Pakistan. Alternatively, women may wait to study until they are older and have a post where an employer or the HEC will pay overseas fees and hold their job open till their return. But this requires they remain single.[13]

Given Western governments' commitment to increasing the diversity of home students in higher education ('widening access', that is, using it to engineer greater equity), and given the role they see HE as having in development generally (including improving the national skills base and efficiency, and specifically supporting good relations between the student's country of domicile and the West in the future), one would hope they will move on from their current stress on what international students contribute to Western economies.

This would include more monitoring of the socio-economic backgrounds of foreign students to ensure that grants are not just creamed off by the indigenous elite and their contacts. (For good practice see for instance the Ford Foundation International Fellowships Programme, Volkman et al., 2009.) It would also involve a greater recognition of the financial strain imposed by the current high fees, and an encouragement to individual universities not just to recruit and enrol foreign postgraduates, but also to offer them more support. This could include not only more bursaries but also more employment within the university itself (as in the American system), together with better advice and help. This applies particular to women students who will have had little prior experience of negotiating such things on their own.

Much educational aid at all levels today (primary, secondary and tertiary) may have as one of its declared aims the improvement of the situation of women in poor countries, and especially in poor Muslim countries. But good intentions and some scholarships are not enough. We also need more continuing pastoral care and for Western lecturers to be better informed about students' backgrounds and to give some practical help.

For example, HEIs could provide more protective environments and appropriate accommodation so that fathers can be persuaded to let their daughters out from under their wings. They could recognize that in many cultures women are more socially and geographically controlled at home than their brothers and not used to being apart from family support and guidance, hence they may suffer pronounced separation anxiety/homesickness and can benefit from social support. Departments could give better (gender sensitive) careers guidance, including the advisability of women getting some work experience before their period of study, and help with relevant paid or unpaid work placements in the UK (since here too the labour market is sex segregated and women generally earn lower wages). Universities and individual departments might also actively improve their connections in students' countries of origin (e.g. through continuing contacts with former students and work with the HEI's own and the British Council's alumni associations) to help women in particular get their first 'break' into employment after they graduate and return.

Without such changes, international higher education (and the distribution of 'development aid' in the form of scholarships) will continue to actively support rather than to counter the reproduction of male dominance in the family, local social stratification systems and existing imbalances between the education systems of the West and former colonial countries.

▶ Notes

1. The government department with responsibility for universities, the Department for Business, Innovation and Skills (BIS) has recently (December 2009) asked the International

Graduate Insight Group (i-graduate) to look at the geographic and occupational destinations of non-EU graduates from UK HEIs, with a view to including this group within the annual Destinations of Leavers from Higher Education (DLHE) surveys conducted by HESA.

2. In 2004/05, there were 2765 Pakistani undergraduates, and 4150 (3290 taught and 860 research degree) postgraduates at UK universities.

3. UK universities with more than a hundred Pakistan-domiciled students in 2004–2005 were: Middlesex (306 students), London Metropolitan (250), East London (135), Greenwich (114) and South Bank universities (106) in London; and in the North of England, Manchester (168), Bradford (125) and Sunderland (104).

4. A quarter of the men study business and administrative studies, a quarter computer science and a third quarter engineering and technology, with one in ten law. The 13 per cent of women are also mainly in business and administrative studies and the rest in education, computer studies and social, economic and political studies at Masters level. Some study biological sciences at doctoral level.

5. We met with these individuals in the foyers of five star hotels in each city and at the home of Maryam Rab's relatives, these being appropriate venues for women for such encounters. The interviews were recorded and then transcribed and analysed thematically.

6. Strictly West Pakistan. East Pakistan split away and became Bangladesh in 1971.

7. We did not ask systematically about employment in the UK, but it was one of the topics which emerged in a qualitative study which would probably have been overlooked in a survey – as was the fact that employment was a source of some of the best friendships our informants made in the UK.

8. It is common practice in Pakistan for universities and individual teachers to keep on their former students as teaching assistants, full or part-time, for a few years precisely to give them some experience.

9. The extent to which this does apply to the home students, and the significance of the timing of marriage and future responsibilities of British men and women graduates is

    raised by some of the work on the different significance of student debt.

10. Married sons and their families often have flats in the house of their parents.

11. Diana Leonard's age and both the interviewers being women probably militated against men talking openly about their social activities in the UK. If we were to develop this work, we would employ a younger, male interviewer to run some focus groups to discuss this.

12. Two returned as soon as they could and one of them completed her dissertation in Pakistan, which was disadvantageous.

13. A strength of the extended family system is that such women can live as members of a household if they wish and are likely to have many nieces and nephews if they like contact with children.

▶ References

Association of Commonwealth Universities (ACU) (2003) *Directory of Commonwealth Scholars and Fellows 1960–2002* (London: Association of Commonwealth Universities).

Arnot, M. (2002) *Reproducing Gender?: Essays on Educational Theory and Feminist Politics* (Abingdon: RoutledgeFalmer).

Boserup, E. (1986) *Woman's Role in Economic Development* (Aldershot: Gower).

Carnoy, M. (1982) 'Education, Economy and the State', in M. Apple (ed.) *Cultural and Economic Reproduction in Education* (London: Routledge & Kegan Paul).

Connell, R. (2009) Plenary Address to the Gender and Education Association 7th International Conference, 25–27 March, Institute of Education, University of London.

Davidoff, L. and Hall, C. (1987) *Family Fortunes: Men and Women of the English Middle Class 1780–1860* (London: Hutchinson).

Delphy, C. (1984) *Close to Home: A Materialist Analysis of Women's Oppression* (London: Hutchinson).

Delphy, C. and Leonard, D. (1992) *Familiar Exploitation: A New Analysis of Marriage in Contemporary Western Societies* (Cambridge: Polity Press).

Dyhouse, Carol (1995) *No Distinction of Sex?: Women in British Universities, 1870–1939* (London: UCL Press).

Gürüz, K. (2008) *Higher Education and International Student Mobility in the Global Knowledge Economy* (Albany, NY: State University of New York Press).

Hartmann, H. (1979). 'Capitalism, Patriarchy and Job Segregation by Sex', in Z. R. Eisenstein (ed.) *Capitalist Patriarchy and the Case for Socialist Feminism* (New York: Monthly Review Press).

Hayter, H. (1981) *The Creation of World Poverty* (London: Pluto).

Leathwood, C. and Read, B. (2009) *Gender and the Changing Face of Higher Education: A Feminised Future?* (Maidenhead, McGraw-Hill/ Open University Press).

Madge, C., Raghuram, P. and Noxolo, P. (2009) 'Engaged Pedagogy and Responsibility: A Postcolonial Analysis of International Students', *Geoforum*, 40, 34–45.

Mies, M. (1986) *Patriarchy and Accumulation on a World Scale: Women in the International Division of Labour* (London: Zed Press).

Ministry of Education (2008) *National Report on the Development of Education* (Islamabad: Ministry of Education).

Mudimbe, V. Y. (1994) *The Idea of Africa* (Bloomington: Indiana University Press).

Purvis, J. (1991) *A History of Women's Education in England* (Milton Keynes: Open University Press).

Qureshi, R. and Rarieya, J. F. A. (2007) *Gender and Education in Pakistan* (Karachi: Oxford University Press).

Rahman, T. (2004) *Denizens of Alien Worlds: A Study of Education, Inequality and Polarization in Pakistan* (Karachi: Oxford University Press).

Reay, D., David, M. E., Ball, S. (2005) *Degrees of Choice: Social Class, Race And Gender in Higher Education* (Stoke on Trent: Trentham).

Rizvi, F. (2005). 'Rethinking "Brain Drain" in the Era of Globalisation', *Asia Pacific Journal of Education* (25)2, 175–192.

Tinker, I. (1990) *Persistent Inequalities: Women and World Development* (Oxford: Oxford University Press).

Unterhalter, E. and Maxey, K. (1995) *Educating South Africans in Britain and Ireland: A Review of Thirty Years of Sponsorship by the Africa Educational Trust* (London: Research on Education in South Africa, Institute of Education, University of London).

Volkman, T. A., Dassin, J. and Zurbuchen, M. S. (eds) (2009) *Origins, Journeys and Returns: Social Justice in International Higher Education* (Brooklyn: Social Science Research Council).

Walby, S. (1997) *Gender Transformations* (London: Routledge).

Wallerstein, I. (1976) *World Systems Analysis: Theory and Methodology* (Beverly Hills: Sage Publications).

World Bank (2006) *Higher Education Policy Note: Pakistan: An Assessment of the Medium-Term Development Framework* (New York: World Bank).

7 Globalization Perspectives and Cultural Exclusion in Mexican Higher Education

Juan Carlos Barrón-Pastor

In 1991, the Mexican census labelled groups appearing at the bottom of statistical tables on inequalities as 'illiterate' or 'non-educated' (INEGI, 1990). At that time, I was studying at the National Autonomous University of Mexico (UNAM). Concerned about poverty, I decided to move from my urban middle-class environment to 'teach' and 'help' poor people who, 'because of their ignorance', 'came low' in these statistical rankings. With time and experience, I realized that the people I intended to teach were not ignorant. They were not the remnants of an ancient, lost civilization. The more I interacted with them, the more I realized the culture they lived was complex, rich, developed, beautiful and ethical. Today, Mexican academic centres have generated extensive information about indigenous peoples; indeed, it seems we know more about them than they know about themselves. However, one thing has not changed: they remain at the bottom of statistical tables on inequalities. Powerful discourses position indigenous peoples as needing 'help' to develop capabilities. Allegedly, by developing these, they can fit into the 'modern' world doing the ugly jobs that 'civilization' needs (and no one wants to do), while sometimes wearing the colourful clothes we find so attractive.

This chapter was written during 2008's 'Black Autumn' of global financial capitalism. Ban Ki-Moon, United Nations Secretary General, listed crises that will unfold when this chapter is published: a financial crisis, a food crisis, an energy crisis, collapse of trade negotiations, wars emergencies and climate change (UN, 2008). Throughout 2008, the Millennium Development Goals and the poor of the planet have appeared to be at the bottom of any list of priorities. We seem far away from the agenda set by the 2004 Human Development Report, in which the United Nations Development Programme concluded that indigenous peoples are more 'prone' to poverty than those considered non-indigenous (UNDP, 2004). A very long distance separates the current moment from the Zapatista uprising, which took place in southern Mexico in 1994. This reinstated indigenous peoples on the Mexican political agenda, inspired social movements worldwide and questioned the role capitalist globalization assigned to indigenous peoples. These achievements now seem far away.

This pessimistic panorama has prompted my concern to explore some connections and contrasts between perspectives on globalization and education through an analysis of efforts to widen indigenous participation in Mexican higher education. Indigenous knowledge and participation in higher education, although currently considered marginal, is anticipated to gain importance in coming years (De Sousa, 2007). Some commentators suggest the future could bring a more multi-polar world with increased opportunities to challenge the current dominance of the G8 countries (Jalife-Rahme, 2007). Consequently, the experiences of 'peripheral' countries (Tendler, 2002) like Mexico, which have some experience of attempting to diminish the reproduction of inequalities in higher education, may become highly relevant.

The theoretical resources used for this chapter link discussions of globalization discourses with approaches to understanding education and inequality. Spring (2008) categorizes four discourses understanding globalization in different forms. Globalization can be understood in terms of a world culture, a culturalist perspective, a postcolonial perspective or a world systems perspective. These can be associated with three approaches to indigenous peoples in Mexico: Liberal Humanist Theory (LHT), Critical Race Theory (CRT) and anti-systemic theory. In the third part of the chapter, 'programmes' or 'initiatives' which promote the participation of indigenous peoples in higher education in Mexico are discussed: Affirmative Action programmes, Intercultural Universities and the nongovernment Land University (UNITIERRA). All intend to diminish the inequalities of indigenous peoples. But the alignment of each with a particular perspective on globalization raises questions about how far each can successfully challenge inequality. Before engaging this discussion, some background analysis on Mexico is needed.

▶ A (not very favourable) snapshot of Mexico

Mexican society is widely considered to be emblematic of inequality. In 2006, Mexico ranked tenth in the world in terms of Gross National Income but was ranked 80th in terms of its income per capita (World Bank, 2007). Mexico has one and a half times higher inequality rates than a typical OECD country, and is by far the most unequal country of the OECD (OECD, 2008). Even though recent studies suggest that inequalities fell significantly between 1996 and 2005 (López-Acevedo, 2006), this data has to be treated with care, since in the last 15 years around 25 million Mexicans have emigrated from the country (INEGI, 2005). Before the recent financial collapse, a Mexican journalist estimated that between 2006 and 2008, 19 million people may have had insufficient income for food (González-Amador, 2008), because of the rise in food prices and the contraction of the labour market. In terms of education, while 42 per cent of Mexico City inhabitants of university age are studying, only 13 per cent of Mexicans have a university degree (INEGI, 2005). Nationally, while 23 per cent of the population under 24 years are in higher education (WDE, 2007) 29 per cent of indigenous people have had no formal schooling, 75 per cent of them have not gone beyond elementary school and only 3 per cent have reached higher education (INEE, 2007).

Inequalities in Mexico are the result of complex historical processes. The colonial caste system imposed by Spanish conquerors distinguished between *criollos* for 'pure European' descendants, *mestizos* for mixed and *indígenas* for aboriginals. These divisions can still be found in Mexican society, shaping social, cultural, economic and political norms (Bonfil, 1987). In the 2006 election, *criollo* discourses interpreted the indigenous 'question' as a 'problem of poverty', while *mestizo* discourses viewed it as a 'problem of poverty and discrimination' (Barrón-Pastor, 2006). During the elections, political assertions by indigenous candidates were generally overlooked, although these dealt with key questions concerning political representation, social exclusion, respect for their knowledge, capacity to administer resources and territories, migration and juridical demands to recognize rights.

There is no agreement about the size of the indigenous population in Mexico. Simplifying cultural diversity in terms of language is problematic, but it gives some indication of scale. It is estimated that around 13.3 million persons speak at least one of the 62 original languages that still survive in Mexico (PUMC-UNAM, 2008). These 62 linguistic systems and their diverse populations are overseen by one legal framework for 'indigenous peoples'. Ninety per cent of the registered speakers of indigenous languages live in 12 States; thus, it is common to associate them with these States, but it is important to note that registered speakers of indigenous languages live in 2330 of 2348 Mexican counties and 88 per cent of them live in areas considered to have 'high' or 'very high' exclusion levels (INEGI, 2005).

As in many parts of the world, indigenous peoples in Mexico are at the bottom of the socio-economic scale (Serrano et al., 2002). Many programmes exist to promote inclusion and access for indigenous peoples into higher education, some supported by global organizations with diverse and sometimes contradictory agendas. Indigenous peoples in Mexico point out that they do not want to be considered the objects of these policies but rather to be treated as actors capable of making decisions on issues that concern them, especially in education (Montemayor, 2000). This was a key clause of the agreements reached by the Mexican government with the Zapatistas and other indigenous organizations in 1996 (San Andrés Accords, 1996). Despite this, in 2001, the Mexican government imposed a legal framework for indigenous peoples, which ignored those agreements. This forms the basis for Mexican government policies, including those related to education (CDI-UNDP, 2006). This legal framework is widely considered in breach of the 169 International Agreement of the International Labour Organization of the United Nations (ILO-UN, 1991), which Mexico also signed (López-Bárcenas, 2002). Thus, although current frameworks ignore the only agreement reached with the Zapatistas, a number of authors consider policies to increase participation of indigenous students in higher education as responses to demands made by the Zapatistas (Coronado and Hodges, 2004). A large number of programmes for indigenous peoples have been developed by government and higher education institutions. This reverses the tendency of the twentieth century when policies for indigenous peoples were 'colour-blind'. Many authors have criticized colour-blind politics as perpetuating the historical treatment of indigenous peoples as different and 'problematic' (Bonfil, 1987; Montemayor, 2000; García Canclini, 2006). Progressive colour 'consciousness' instead of race neutrality has been advocated (Holmes, 2007), together with interaction and participation (Barrón-Pastor, 2008, 2010). Academic research reveals that indigenous students aspire to a better quality of life and to overcome exclusion, but without renouncing their identities (Flores-Crespo and Barrón-Pastor, 2005; Barrón-Pastor, 2008). This is already happening in many intercultural programmes and institutions (Flores-Crespo, 2007; Barrón-Pastor, 2008); however, the role for indigenous students in these programmes often seems to be a passive one (Castellanos, 2005; Llánes Ortíz, 2008).

Two main schemes designed for indigenous students in higher education are Affirmative Action programmes and Intercultural Universities. Affirmative Action programmes are result-oriented procedures 'utilized to insure that non-whites and women are not disadvantaged in efforts to secure employment' [in this case through education] (Combs and Gruhl, 1986, p. 1). Their success is commonly presented in terms of increments of quotas of 'minorities' (Curry, 1997); however, increasing quotas of minorities do not necessarily mean diminishing racism and other forms of exclusion in schools (Barrón-Pastor, 2008). Intercultural Universities aim to promote the creation of professionals committed to the development of indigenous peoples, to revaluate indigenous knowledge and 'to favour a synthesis process [of this knowledge] to scientific advances (...as well as taking advantage of difference to bring together complementary and shared knowledge with other subjects and other development dimensions' (REDUI, 2008 my translation). Affirmative Action

and Intercultural Universities have given visibility to indigenous peoples in higher education Institutions (Flores-Crespo
and Barrón-Pastor, 2005) but they have failed to diminish
inequalities or promote social mobility (CDI-UNDP, 2006).

If policies for indigenous peoples in Mexican higher education
have not emerged from dialogue with indigenous representative
groups, what are their origins? Some explanation is apparent
from considering particular perspectives on globalization.

▶ **Globalization and the inter-cultural dimension
of inequalities in education**

Spring (2008) has distinguished four perspectives on globalization in writing on education. Firstly, there is a view of 'world
culture', which comes from the assumption of 'the existence of
a world culture that contains western ideals of mass schooling,
which serves as a model for national school systems [and the
premise that] all cultures are slowly integrating into a global
culture' (Spring, 2008, p. 334). Secondly, this view is comple-
mented by a 'culturalist' approach, which 'emphasises cultural
variations and the borrowing and lending of educational ideas
within a global context' (Spring, 2008, p. 334). Thirdly, Spring
identifies a 'postcolonial' view which perceives globalization 'as
an effort to impose particular economic and political agendas on
the global society that benefit wealthy and rich nations' (Spring,
2008, p. 334). Fourthly, Spring identifies a 'world system' perspective in which the globe is perceived as integrated but with
two major unequal zones, where 'the goal of the core is to legit-
imise its power by inculcating its values into periphery nations'
(Spring, 2008, p. 334).

A 'world culture' perspective is evident in the work of UNDP
on indigenous peoples. The 2004 Human Development Report
of the United Nations Development Programme (UNDP, 2004)
shows that around the world indigenous peoples suffer exclusion and survive at the bottom of the scale of human development indicators. They are presented as more prone to poverty
than non-indigenous persons (UNDP, 2004). Using the Human
Development Index as a tool to demonstrate the discrimination or disadvantage of some culturally identified 'minorities',
the report presents indigenous cultures as 'vulnerable' and

encourages decisive action to address this. Education policies are stressed to help 'make progress' (UNDP, 2004, p. 265). The report emphasizes the importance of educational practices and policies equipping students with skills for the global workplace which would allow them to move to higher positions in the Human Development Index. But this approach suggests that indigenous peoples have specific characteristics that must be transformed in order to overcome poverty. The argument put forward by the report is that cultural diversity issues have to be well managed because they can 'become one of the greatest sources of instability between the states and within them' (UNDP, 2004, p. 2). Despite the polite text, indigenous people come to be associated with dangerous extremists. This reveals a tendency to stereotype and misrepresent other cultures as evil, threatening or something to be afraid of doing little to redress cultural inequalities (Barrón-Pastor, 2010).

The Report is an example of how authors who work with a version of liberal humanism interpret indigenous peoples. They are depicted as prone to poverty and thus potentially untrustworthy unless they develop certain capabilities. This analysis exhibits a deep distrust of 'culture'. Sen (2006), for example, argues that the exaltation of certain aspects of culture reproduces practices that may impoverish the life of individuals. He views cultural identity as a potential source of violence and brutality that needs to be subordinated to 'reason' (Sen, 1999a), through which one may choose among identities (Sen, 1999b, 2006).

Sen explores cultural diversity in relation to concepts of reasoning (Sen, 1999b, 2006). He rejects the notion that rationality is 'Western', suggesting such claims have roots in the history of colonialism and invites us to go beyond the 'limited horizons of the colonized mind and its fixations with the west' (Sen, 2006, p. 88), arguing that the colonization process is over. Despite its atrocities, it is now just a shameful past (Sen, 2006, pp. 84–88). This implies that indigenous groups have a deficit that entitles them to special treatment from governments and international organizations, and as the HDR-UNDP 2004 advocates, specific, well-targeted policies will be able to fix what is wrong with them (UNDP, 2004).

Such policies entail negotiation and choice between global and 'local knowledge' (UNDP, 2004, p. 97), and this approach exemplifies what Spring calls 'culturalist' approaches. For Sen

(2006, p. 39), there is no discovering of cultural identities but rational processes of choosing and acquiring them. If cultural identities were discovered, he argues, life would be conceived as mere destiny. Sen's idea of multiple identities suggests humans choose among certain identities. This explains 'cultural exchanges' where people decide what to keep, what to take and what to abandon in a kind of cultural marketplace. The subject thus becomes separated from identity and the asymmetric relations between hegemonic and marginal cultures are overlooked. Some cultural identities are anchored to poverty, powerlessness and deprivation, while others draw on symbols of freedom, consumerism and abundance. Cultural diversity is not free from forms of power and domination.

Writers who draw on critical race theory point to major problems with this approach (Delgado and Stefansic, 2001; Esseed and Goldberg, 2002). When these authors write about 'race', they discuss a social rather than a biological relationship and do not refer to skin colours, but to a 'system of socially constructed and enforced categories that are constantly recreated and modified through human interaction' (Gillborn, 2008, p. 3). While they may oversimplify 'whites' and 'blacks', they argue they do this to be able to work with the relationship between hegemonic and minority groups. 'Race inequality should be placed centre-stage as a fundamental axis of oppression' (Gillborn, 2008, p. 1). Thus racism is the rule not the exception in patterns of exclusion in education, and '*racial inequalities are effectively locked-in as a permanent feature of the system*' (Gillborn, 2008, p. 68; underlined in the original).

From this perspective intrinsic characteristics of 'minoritized' groups are less important in explaining inequalities than the oppression of a racist system designed to keep some up and others down permanently. But to maintain those dynamics, certain exceptions are allowed to create an illusion of racial mobility. Elites utilize opinion, discourse and legislation to practice the exclusion, marginalization and problematization of minorities. This meets with struggle, opposition and tension from those casts as minorities (Van Dijk, 1998). Inequalities tend to be reinforced, so that certain groups persistently fail in accessing higher social positions (Gillborn, 2008). Reversing the current inequalities would require an exponential increase in the participation of 'minoritized' groups. Authors who draw on critical race theory present cultures and peoples in dichotomous and adversarial positions. This does little to help minoritized groups transform these harmful dynamics. This is a problem when societies are seeking freedom for everybody and need radical change, paths of reconciliation and rapprochement, rather than more social unrest and polarization.

▶ Mexican higher education for indigenous peoples: Affirmative action and intercultural universities

What Spring calls 'world culture' and 'culturalist' globalization are evident in Mexico in 'initiatives' linked to *criollo* discourses which interpret the indigenous 'question' as a 'problem of poverty', which needs the development of specialized skills for the global workplace to overcome the lack of infrastructure and access to education. Mexican higher education policies of affirmative action stress an approach through the establishment of a legal framework that ignores what indigenous voices have said.

One of the main problems with affirmative action is defining the users of the programmes. The Mexican Constitution refers to all Mexicans as persons, but an indigenous 'person' is not mentioned, thus they only legally exist as a 'group'. This group has racial characteristics, its 'own' territorial, social, cultural, economic and political institutions, and has to be conscious of being indigenous (Mexican Constitution, 2nd article, reformed August 2001). To define and qualify for 'quotas', the indigenous must claim identification. By contrast, to be Mexican, a person just needs to be born in the territory or acquire the nationality. Affirmative Action programmes use three criteria to select users: one must speak an indigenous language, identify himself/herself as belonging to an indigenous group or have one person of his/her household speaking an indigenous language (Flores-Crespo, 2007). In practice, this identification as a form of 'positive segregation' is highly problematic because conservative groups within the universities attack Affirmative Action programmes by questioning the 'real' identity of Affirmative Action users, and accuse Affirmative Action programmes of privileging a minority as there are many students with similar economic conditions and racial characteristics that cannot prove they meet the legal criteria to be considered indigenous (Flores-Crespo and Barrón-Pastor, 2005).

Intercultural Universities exhibit what Spring calls the 'culturalist perspective'. Intercultural Universities promote 'exchange of knowledges' (*intercambio de saberes*), constructing databases, producing information, generating research, promoting new knowledge, publishing relevant literature and building up national and international networks (REDUI, 2008). These institutions are inspired by the UNESCO Universal Declaration on Cultural Diversity, which states that 'as a source of exchange, innovation and creativity, cultural diversity is as necessary for humankind as biodiversity is for nature' (UNESCO, 2001). The UN has promoted research teams with prestigious institutions such as the National Autonomous University of Mexico (UNAM), which are in the process of creating 'culturally pertinent indicators' based on indigenous peoples' rights and demands arising from social movements (UN-UNAM, 2008).

While there are elements of cultural exchange here reminiscent of Sen's marketplace of identities, postcolonial initiatives are also evident because of the engagement with resistance and negotiation. But very complex processes of reproduction and transformation are entailed. In Intercultural Universities, many actors struggle daily to overcome exclusion but also bring their own agendas, interests and demands to this process, which highlights problems of representation and cooperation (Tromp, 2007; Avila and Mateos, 2008). In the context of Intercultural Universities, it is impossible to forget the historical inequalities associated with European imperialism. International, national, local and indigenous actors coincide in these institutions, but do not always seek equal dialogue or participation. Here, unlike the segregation 'in a positive way' associated with Affirmative Action, there is a predominance of *mestizo* actors (Tromp, 2007; Avila and Mateos, 2008; Baronnet, 2008; Llánes Ortiz, 2008). Many intend to appropriate 'the best of two worlds' but in seeking to reconcile their 'shameful' indigenous past with aspirations of 'western modernity' many tensions emerge (Bartra, 2001).

A number of studies describe how indigenous rights advocates were ignored in the process of constructing these institutions (Tromp, 2007; Baronnet, 2008; Llánes Ortiz, 2008). Interviews I conducted in 2008 with indigenous students attending Intercultural Universities confirmed data reported by

Michael Corbett (2007). Students commented that standardized curricula, programmatic pedagogies, prescribed texts and tests reinforce the idea that education is about learning something that someone, somewhere else, has decided is important. These practices do not appear relevant for these students. Rather they appear designed to make them leave their territories.

Indigenous students in Affirmative Action programmes and the Intercultural Universities expressed major concerns about the push to migrate. Professional jobs are not available in indigenous communities. Although almost all had expected to return to their communities, pressures to leave were particularly stressful. Thus although these institutions and programmes were created to enhance access to professional occupations, most students interviewed did not have a serious expectation of getting a job. Thus, postcolonial and culturalist trends in the current phase of globalization have only ambiguous benefits for many indigenous students in Affirmative Action programmes and the Intercultural Universities.

A different way of interpreting globalization and developing a response through higher education is associated with the work of Immanuel Wallerstein. Over many years he has asserted that the modern world system is in terminal crisis and that the period of transition to another system will be more violent than the last years of the twentieth century (Wallerstein, 1996). While the liberal illusion of diminishing inequalities through gradual reforms will end (Wallerstein, 1995), small inputs, which he calls 'anti-systemic movements', will be very important for the transformation of the world system into something else (Wallerstein, 1999).

In Mexico, many anti-systemic collative actions aim to form social movements. These seek not to reform, but to construct a different, better system. In terms of higher education, anti-systemic movements challenge the assessment that indigenous peoples are 'destined' to be at the bottom of any league table of inequalities. They express a permanent aspiration for human freedom, but do not view this as based on property in land. They question ideals of progress promised by modernity. They suggest indigenous peoples are at the bottom of indices of human development or other statistical tables not because they are incapable of improving their positions, but because they are particular targets in a war conducted by global capitalism against humanity. Taking account of the world system, they refuse to be the periphery but also refuse to aspire to be the centre.

Indigenous peoples have a leading role in anti-systemic social movements and 'have become vocal opponents of globalization and agentic members of a community seeking change in the world-system' (Teixeira and Smith, 2008, p. 45). Their influence has been decisive in the construction of a number of autonomous projects, including higher education experiments such as UNITIERRA. These initiatives stand in contrast to policies of the Mexican government which seems to assume that indigenous peoples have only local perspectives and are only capable of making local decisions.

UNITIERRA was formed by a coalition of civil organizations, associated with the mass social movement 'Popular Assembly of the Peoples of Oaxaca' (APPO), which emerged in Oaxaca in 2006. Its main goal is to contribute to the formation of competent persons to serve Oaxaca's communities. It seeks to learn from the world, more than about it, and particularly to learn what is needed within the current reality of Oaxaca. The approach to learning is to build capacity to learn, and to learn by oneself what one decides with others is appropriate (Esteva, 2006). Gustavo Esteva, a community leader and one of the coordinators of the project, says that since its formation in 2001, UNITIERRA has worked in more than 400 communities. Currently it is working with more than 500 people in Oaxaca on different programmes for a range of levels using a particular version of action research. In an interview Esteva stressed that UNITIERRA 'students' learn foremost how to stay in their communities and regions and lead a dignified life: 'UNITIERRA is for those who wish to stay and prosper in Oaxaca'.

UNITIERRA is a 'university' that has no teachers, no classrooms, no curriculum and no campus. The work is mainly inspired by the de-schooling ideas of Ivan Illich. It also draws on the philosophy and action of wise indigenous persons, such as Floriberto Díaz, who stated that indigenous education spins around three axes: Land, Work and People (Cardoso, 2008). Those engaged with UNITIERRA define themselves as learning/studying/reflecting/acting autonomous communities, within a non-structural organization managed by a committee that conveys the practice and experience of Communal Assemblies (UNITIERRA, 2008). These institutions have their own research programmes targeting the creation of 'green' technologies, the systematization of their knowledge, the construction of virtual networks and libraries, the promotion of arts and creativity, the production of education processes respecting their forms of organization, the connection of students with their communities through work and the exploration of contemporary possibilities for indigenous philosophies where land ownership is sometimes linguistically impossible to express.

To define areas of apprenticeship, UNITIERRA explores with communities both the kind of knowledge or skills not currently available to them and the kind of learning they want for their young people. The organization of learning is in the hands of the person who learns. It does not depend on a system of control and grading by teachers or tutors, nor is it based on the efforts of those who teach. It is based on the interest, initiative and determination of the person who learns. According to Esteva, it is not easy for people to take education into their own hands, even though 'students' in UNITIERRA learn faster than expected. Learning is achieved in practice through observation and practice. These activities are realized with the support of a tutor, and the individual who carries out a set of activities. In the process both learn how to share knowledge. UNITIERRA organizes specialized lecture circles, seminars, conferences and workshops, as abstract information and theoretical knowledge are also considered necessary, to facilitate the acquisition of such information and knowledge useful in professional practice.

► Conclusion

It is uncertain what impact this new global crisis will have on inequalities, and particularly on the role indigenous peoples will play in higher education. However, whether the current crisis may ultimately serve capitalism, which historically administers 'crisis' and 'bubbles' to concentrate wealth and create new profit cycles (Freytas, 2008), or if it will be 'the end of the world as we know it' (Wallerstein, 1999); crisis times can be the occasion to think again and learn from current efforts to diminish more effectively the reproduction of cultural inequalities in higher education.

Spring's (2008) classification of perspectives on globalization helps to analyse the perceptions of actors concerned with the reduction of inequalities and exclusion of indigenous peoples in Mexican higher education. Affirmative Action and Intercultural Universities both intend to address issues of poverty and lack of access to education for indigenous peoples. These efforts are valuable, but do not entirely correspond to indigenous peoples' demands or perspectives. UNITIERRA is a good example of an organization strengthening non-ethnocentric inputs when considering indigenous knowledge. Instead of focusing in quotas or fair demands, and without labelling knowledge as indigenous or non-indigenous, UNITIERRA have listened and incorporated what some indigenous groups are seeking to create: autonomous organizations based on communities which aim to respect the life inherent in everything, and sharing life experiences through innovative education practices without schooling. Their efforts are resulting in new affordable 'green' technologies, in systematizing trustworthy knowledge and in enriching cultural diversity and humankind.

Understanding the dynamic of cultural inequalities in Mexico helps to illuminate global inequalities. It thus seems advisable to rethink the role assigned to indigenous peoples in international development, to go beyond hegemonic epistemologies and to better tune our ears and listen carefully without prejudice to what indigenous voices have to say on designing another world.

▶ References

Avila-Pardo, A. and Mateos Cortés, L. (2008) 'Configuración de Actores y Discursos Híbridos en la Creación de la Universidad Veracruzana Intercultural', *Travaux et Recherches dans les Amériques du Centre (TRACE)*, 53, 64–82.

Baronnet, B. (2008) 'La Escuela Normal Indígena Intercultural Bilingüe "Jacinto Canek". Movilización étnica y autonomía negada en Chiapas', *Travaux et Recherches dans les Amériques du Centre (TRACE)*, 53, 100–118.

Barrón-Pastor, J. C. (2006) *Constructing Problems and Solutions for Indigenous Peoples: A Critical Discourse Analysis About Identity and Cultural Violence in Mexican Main Political Platforms*, MRes Dissertation, University of East Anglia, available at: http://juanchobarron.googlepages.com (accessed 27/02/09).

Barrón-Pastor, J. C. (2008) '¿Promoviendo Relaciones Interculturales? Racismo y acción afirmativa en México para indígenas en educación superior', *Travaux et Recherches dans les Ameriques du Centre (TRACE)*, 53, 22–35.

Barrón-Pastor, J. C. (2010) 'Uprooting Fear of Cultural Diversity: Becoming Participative Together', in Robinson-Pant, A., Cox, S., Dyer, C. and Schweisfurth, M. (eds) *Children as Decision Makers in Education* (London: Continuum).

Bartra, R. (2001) *Anatomía del Mexicano* (Mexico:Plaza/Janés).

Blanco, J. (2007) 'Educación, Miseria y Desigualdad', in La Jornada, 13 February 2007, available at: http://www.jornada. unam.mx/2007/02/13/index.php?section=opinion& article=022a1pol (accessed 27/02/09).

Bonfil, G. (1987) *México Profundo. Una civilización negada* (Mexico City: Grijalbo).

Cardoso R. (2008) *Floriberto Dìaz, Escrito, Comunalidad energía viva del pensamiento mixe; ayuujktsënää'yën, ayuujkwenmää'ny, ayuujkmëjkäjtën*, available at: http:// www.nacionmulticultural.unam.mx/Portal/Izquierdo/ PUBLICACIONES/publi-a/publi-a-espa.pdf (accessed 27/ 02/09).

Carrillo, C. (2006) *Pluriverso: Un ensayo sobre el conocimiento indígena contemporáneo* (Mexico: Mexico Multicultural Nation University Programme at the National Autonomous University of Mexico (PUMC-UNAM)).

Castellanos, R. (2005) *Memoria de Experiencias (2001–2005) Programa de Apoyo a estudiantes indígenas en instituciones de educación superior* (Mexico: Programa de Apoyo a Estudiantes Indígenas en Instituciones de Educación Superior (ANUIES-FF)).

CDI-UNDP (2006) *Informe sobre Desarrollo Humano de los Pueblos Indígenas 2006*, available at: http://www.cdi.gob.mx/ index.php?id_seccion=1916 (accessed 27/02/09).

Combs, M. and Gruhl, J. (eds) (1986) *Affirmative Action. Theory, Analysis and Prospects* (Jefferson: McFarland).

Corbett, M. (2007) *Learning to Leave: The Irony of Schooling in a Coastal Community* (Winnipeg: Fernwood).

Coronado, G. and Hodges, B. (2004) *El hipertexto Multicultural en México Posmoderno. Paradojas e incertidumbres*, Centro de

Investigaciones y Estudios Superiores en Antropología Social (CIESAS) (Mexico City: Porrua).

Curry, G. (ed.) (1997) *The Affirmative Action Debate* (London: Addison-Wesley).

De Sousa Santos, B. (ed.) (2007) *Another Knowledge is Possible: Beyond Northern Epistemologies* (London: Verso).

De Sousa Santos, B., Arriscado Nunes, J. and Meneses, M. P. (2007) 'Introduction: Opening the Canon of Knowledge and Recognition of Difference', in De Sousa Santos, B. (ed.) *Another Knowledge is Possible: Beyond Northern Epistemologies* (London: Verso).

Delgado, R. and Stefancic, J. (2001) *Critical Race Theory: An Introduction* (New York: New York University Press).

Didou, S. and Remedi, R. (2004) *Pathways to Higher Education: Una evaluación de la experiencia en México* (Mexico City: Mimeo).

El México Nación Multicultural de la Universidad de Programa (2008) *Sistema de Información de los Pueblos Indígenas de América: México*. http://www.nacionmulticultural.unam.mx/Portal/Izquierdo/SIPIA/pueblos/mexico.html (accessed 27/02/09).

Essed, P. and Goldberg, D. T. (eds) (2002) *Critical Race Theories* (London: Blackwell).

Esteva, G. (2006) 'Universidad de la Tierra (Unitierra): The Freedom to Learn', in Fasheh, M. and Pimparé, S. (eds) *Emerging and Re-emerging Learning Communities: Old Wisdoms and New Initiatives from Around the World* (Paris: UNESCO).

Flores-Crespo, P. (2007) 'Ethnicity, Identity and Educational Achievement in Mexico', *International Journal of Educational Development*, 27(3), 331–339.

Flores-Crespo, P. and Barrón-Pastor, J. C. (2005) *El Programa de Apoyo a Estudiantes Indígenas en Instituciones de Educación Superior. ¿Nivelador académico o promotor de la interculturalidad?*, Biblioteca de educación superior, serie investigaciones (Mexico: Programa de Apoyo a Estudiantes Indígenas en Instituciones de Educación Superior (ANUIES)).

Freytas, M. (2008) 'La Crisis Global y el Mito del «Final de la Era del Dólar', available at: http://www.voltairenet.org/article158235.html (accessed 27/02/09).

García Canclini, N. (2006) *Diferentes, Desiguales y Desconectados. Mapas de la interculturalidad* (Barcelona: Gedisa).

Gillborn, D. (2008) *Racism and Education: Coincidence or Conspiracy* (London: Routledge).

González-Amador, R. (2008) 'Aumentó este Sexenio la Pobreza Extrema', in *La Jornada*, 31 August 2008, available at: http://www.jornada.unam.mx/2008/08/31/index.php?section=politica&article=008n1pol (accessed 27/02/09).

Holmes, D. (2007) *Affirmative Reaction: Kennedy, Nixon, King and the Evolution of Color-blind Rhetoric, Rhetoric Review 2007*, 26(1), pp. 25–41.

Instituto Nacional de Estadistica y Geografia (INEGI) (1990) *XI Censo general de Población y Vivienda 1990*, available at: http://www.inegi.org.mx/sistemas/biblioteca/detalle.aspx?c=16659&upc=0&s=est&tg=136&f=2&pf=Pob (accessed 15/04/10).

Instituto Nacional de Estadistica y Geografia (INEGI) (2005) *Conteo de Población y Vivienda 2005*, available at: http://www.inegi.gob.mx/est/contenidos/espanol/rutinas/ept.asp?t=medu07&c=3274 (accessed 27/02/09).

International Labour Organisation-UN (ILO-UN) (1991) *Convention (169) Concerning Indigenous and Tribal Peoples in Independent Countries*, available at: http://www.unhchr.ch/html/menu3/b/62.htm (accessed 27/02/09).

Inter-Agency Network for Education in Emergencies (INEE) (2007) *La Educación para Poblaciones en Contextos Vulnerables: Informe 2007, Capítulo 2 El caso de las primarias indígenas*, available at: http://www.inee.edu.mx/images/stories/documentos_pdf/Publicaciones/Libros_Informes_Capitulos/Informe2007/informe2007_cap2.pdf (accessed 27/02/09).

Jalife-Rahme, A. (2007) *Hacia la Desglobalización* (Mexico: Jorale).

Kymlicka, W. (1995) Multicultural Citizenship (Oxford: Oxford University Press).

Lenkersdorf, C. (1996) *Los Hombres Verdaderos. Voces y testimonios tojolabales* (Mexico: Siglo XXI).

Lenkersdorf, C. (2008) *Aprender a Escuchar: Enseñanzas maya-tojolabales* (Mexico: Plaza y Valdes).

León-Portilla, M. (1997) *Pueblos Originarios y Globalización* (México: Colegio Nacional).

Llánes Ortíz, G. (2008) 'Interculturalización Fallida: Desarrollismo, neoindigenismo y Universidad intercultural en Yucatán, Mexico', in *Travaux et Recherches dans les Amériques du Centre (TRACE)*, June, 53, 49–63.

López-Acevedo, G. (2006) *Mexico: Two Decades of the Evolution of Education and Inequality*, World Bank Policy Research Working Paper 3919, May 2006, available at: http://www-wds.worldbank.org/external/default/WDSContentServer/WDSP/IB/2006/05/11/000016406_20060511120731/Rendered/PDF/wps3919.pdf (accessed 27/05/09).

López-Bárcenas, F. (2002) *Legislación y Derechos Indígenas en México* (Mexico: Red-es, Ce-Acatl).

Martínez, L. (2005) *Inmigración y Diversidad Cultural en México* (Mexico: UNAM).

Montemayor, C. (2000) *Los Pueblos Indios de México Hoy* (Mexico City: Planeta).

Morfin, O. (2006) 'Hiding the Politically Obvious: A Critical Race Theory Preview of Diversity as Racial Neutrality', *Educational Policy*, January/February 2006, 20(1), 249–270.

Organisation for Economic Co-Operation and Development (OECD) (2008) *Growing Unequal? Income Distribution and Poverty in OECD Countries*, The Mexico note is available at: http://www.oecd.org/dataoecd/45/38/41527666.pdf (accessed 27/05/09).

Programa México Nación Multicultural de la Universidad Nacional Autónoma de México (PUMC-UNAM) (2008) *Sistema de Información de los Pueblos Indígenas de América: México*. http://www.nacionmulticultural.unam.mx/Portal/Izquierdo/SIPIA/pueblos/mexico.html (accessed 27/02/09).

Red de Universidades Interculturales (REDUI) (2008) *¿Qué es la Universidad Intercultural?* Red de Universidades Interculturales, available at: http://www.redui.org.mx/cont_esp.php?id_article=14&id_rubrique=2 (accessed 27/02/09).

San Andrés Accords (1996) 'An English Translation of the Agreements', available at: http://flag.blackened.net/revolt/mexico/ezln/san_andres.html (accessed 27/02/09).

Sen, A. (1999a) *Development as Freedom* (Oxford: Oxford University Press).

Sen, A. (1999b) *Reason before Identity* (Oxford: Oxford University Press).

Sen, A. (2006) *Identity and Violence: The Illusion of Destiny* (New York: Norton).

Serrano, E., Ambríz, A., and Fernández, P. (eds) (2002) *Indicadores Socioeconómicos de los Pueblos Indígenas* (Mexico: INI, CONAPO).

Spring, J. (2008) 'Research on Globalisation and Education', *Review of Educational Research*, 78(2), 330–363.

Teixeira, S. and Smith, K. (2008) 'Core and Periphery Relations: A Case Study of the Maya', *Journal of World-System Research*, 14(1), 14–49.

Tendler, J. (2002) 'The Fear of Education', Background paper for *Inequality and the State in Latin America and the Caribbean* (Paris: Organisation for Economic Co-Operation and Development), available at: http://www.oecd.org/dataoecd/43/40/2489865.pdf (accessed 27/02/09).

Tromp, R. (2007) *Higher Intercultural Education in Mexico: A Case Study of the Process of Creation of the Indigenous Intercultural University of Michoacán* (MA Dissertation, University of East Anglia).

UN (2008) A Call for Global Leadership: Ban Ki-Moon's address to the General Assembly (New Yoark: United Nations), 23 September, available at: http://www.un.org/News/ossg/hilites/hilites_arch_view.asp?HighID=1168 (accessed 11/12/09).

United Nations Development Programme Human Development Report (UNDP) (2004) *Cultural Liberty in Today's Diverse World*, available at: http://hdr.undp.org/en/reports/global/hdr2004/ (accessed 27/05/09).

UNESCO (2001) *UNESCO Universal Declaration on Cultural Diversity* (Paris: UNESCO), available at: http://unesdoc.unesco.org/images/0012/001271/127160m.pdf (accessed 27/02/09).

Universidad de la Tierra (2008) Available at: http://unitierra.blogspot.com/ (accessed 27/05/09).

Van Dijk, T. (1998) *Ideology. A Multidisciplinary Approach* (London: Sage).

Van Dijk, T. (2005) *Racism and Discourse in Spain and Latin America* (Amsterdam: John Benjamin).

Wallerstein, I. (1995) *After Liberalism* (New York: New Press).

Wallerstein, I. (1996) *The Age of Transition: Trajectory of the World-System, 1945–2025* (London: Zed Press).

Wallerstein, I. (1999) *The End of the World As We Know It: Social Science for the Twenty-First Century* (Minnesota: University of Minnesota Press).

World Bank (2007) *Gobernabilidad Democrática en México, Más allá de la Captura del Estado y la polarización Social* (Washington: World Bank), available at: http://siteresources.worldbank.org/INTMEXICOINSPANISH/Resources/igr-espanol.pdf (accessed 27/02/09).

World Data on Education (WDE) (2007) *World Data on Education 2006/2007 6th edition* (Madrid: Organización de Estados Iberoamericanos para la Educación, la Ciencia y la Cultura), available at: http://www.oei.es/pdfs/Mexico_datos2006.pdf (accessed 27/05/09).

Part 3
Struggling for Equality

8 Pedagogy for Rich Human Being-ness in Global Times

Melanie Walker

▶ Global hard times and higher education

In contemporary times higher education has risen to the top of national policy agendas for its key part in producing highly skilled graduates to promote and service knowledge economies. In the UK, for example, in 1998, the Department for Trade and Industry published its *Competitiveness White Paper* outlining the government's approach to economic growth through stimulating a high skills knowledge economy. The emphasis was on 'a global marketplace' in which 'knowledge, skills and creativity' would provide the UK with its 'competitive economic edge' and constitute the 'distinctive assets of a knowledge-driven economy' (DTI, 1998, p. 6). In line with this, the UK White Paper on Higher Education (2003, p. 64) stated that the overriding policy priority was to ensure the expansion of 'an appropriate type and quality' of higher education 'to meet the demands of employers and the needs of the economy and students'.

What has developed is a downgrading of the intrinsic goods of learning and democratic citizenship. Instead the key higher education policy discourse has been that of market fundamentalism – the doctrine that market exchange is an ethic in itself and a guide for all human action (Harvey, 2005). This is underpinned by human capital theory, which views education as an instrumental, investment to improve productivity and the level and distribution of individual earnings. According to these ideas, if a university education makes someone a better producer, able to both earn more and contribute more to national income, then higher education has been deemed to be successful. The assumption has been that economic growth and human development mean the same thing. Any discourse of 'global citizenship' in universities is then much more about competitive edge, market niches, and lucrative recruitment than about global obligations and understanding.

A decade on this economic rationality and commodification of knowledge looks increasingly hollow as economies accelerate downhill (*The Economist* 17 January 2009), and in the UK economic meltdown looks set to outperform all other European countries in the extent and depth of its financial collapse. The rich and powerful may no longer 'have all the best tunes' (Holford, 2008, p. 25). We find ourselves in a time of intense global financial and economic crisis; the focus on human capital outcomes and marketization of higher education has neither equipped society to avoid such an outcome, nor has it removed continuing inequalities, nor contained human greed, and nor resolved devastating conflict such as that most recently in Gaza in early 2009. The emphasis on human capital appears increasingly dysfunctional at a time when jobs are being shed in the banking and finance sectors, and in professions dependent on the financial and property sector so that graduates may well struggle to find employment after university as supply outstrips demand. Even before this last economic crisis struck, it was becoming clear that higher education opportunities were becoming harder to cash in as the number of graduates has risen; opportunity based on education, jobs, and rewards is splitting apart (Brown, 2003). Prior to this grave global slowdown, Turner (2007) was already reporting the rise of graduates overqualified for their jobs so that one in three graduates are in a job that does not require a degree. He cited research from the London School of Economics, conducted by Frances Green and Yu Tzu, suggesting that the career ambitions of growing numbers of young people will never be fulfilled.

If human capital and economic growth have failed to provide both for economic and human security, then serious questions ought now to be raised about the appropriateness and sustainability of this as a continuing higher policy direction; we need rather to rebalance higher education goals in the direction of a much more expansive public good, and the formation of graduates as rich human beings. As many scholarly commentators remind us, everywhere universities as educational institutions have the potential to pursue or bring about both reproductive and transformative goals; teaching and learning always appear in a political context. Social and economic structures constrain what is possible and what is regarded as legitimate and worthwhile. In global times of inequalities and economic recession universities might still promote knowledge and learning for narrow self-interest above all. On the other hand, they could foster other-oriented imaginative and ethical human beings, so that whatever future pathways their graduates might choose, one can hope that their university education has been one which enables them to choose well for self, other, and society (Booth et al., 2009). Higher education is located within society and social change; changes in higher education might influence society as much as society in turn shapes higher education. For example, higher education institutions might become 'as-if' places – 'places where the long term goals of social change are lived inside the institution as if they were already the norms for society' (Bivens, 2009, p. 3).

Against the dominant and arguably failing neo-liberal discourse, recent hopeful moves led by the Global University Network for Innovation (GUNI, 2008), have included an explicit attention through university education processes and outcomes to human development which involves more than producing human capital. Human development can be understood as 'creating an environment in which people can develop their full potential and lead productive, creative lives in accord with their needs and interests' (UNDP, 2009, in Taylor, 2008, p. xxiv). The goal of human development is understood to be 'freedom' to exercise genuine choices and to participate in decision-making that effects people's lives. It is reinforced by human rights which help 'to secure the well-being and dignity of all people, building self respect and the respect of others'. To take up human and social development is also to orient universities to global concerns and obligations to human well-being, and not just economic growth at any cost.

My particular interest in this chapter is with the articulation of the core research and teaching functions of universities in relation to richly critical student learning experiences and agency formation, and how such teaching and learning cultures of analysis, enquiry, and argumentation around ideas and complex problems ought to contribute in some way to society and the social good. In particular how might human development and rights take educational and pedagogical form in relation to research and teaching functions. At issue is that without both a critical function and a research function, and strategies to link these through teaching and learning and a culture of enquiry which is genuinely *educational*, we might argue that the university loses both its own capacity for self-critique and its ability to provide students with the capabilities to contribute to democratic changes in social and political life (Aronowitz, 2000). In a recent plenary address, Brighouse (2007) made the important question explicit. We need, he argued, a new normative account of higher education, one which asks 'Whose interests is higher education serving?', and of course, to what end are knowledge and skills being acquired?

The most important question is surely then that of Luke (2006, p. 5) when he asks 'What pedagogies are for human being?', and Barnett's (2007, p. 153) educative call for a student 'to stand differently in the world'.

▶ Research and teaching: Technique or transformation

In addressing these issues and questions, I draw on interview data from a research project in which I explored the research/teaching nexus in one research-intensive English university.[1] The universality of the research and teaching functions in universities suggests a much wider relevance beyond the local and national context of the study; how they are connected through pedagogy in the formation of persons then has wide resonance and says something significant about what universities do and are for. The aim in the project was to expand the mainstream literature on the research/teaching nexus (for example, Brew, 2006, Jenkins et al., 2003) by embedding it in debates about the normative purposes of higher education. Both the research and teaching elements in the nexus ought then to inflect towards a more equal and more just student experience on the one hand, and an engagement with what

Habermas (1989) calls the 'moral urgencies' of society on the other. The overarching research question in the project was to ask how engagement with research ought to foster students' intelligent action, social responsibility, and agency to choose and plan a good life (Walker, 2008). In particular, the project drew conceptually on the capability approach (Sen, 1992, 1999; Nussbaum, 2000) to expand pedagogical debates about the research/teaching nexus in new directions. The conceptual framework was brought into conversation with empirical subjects using qualitative data from interviews with 9 lecturers and 21 students in three departments (History, Politics, and Animal and Plant Sciences) at one research-intensive university in the north of England.

I want now to elaborate somewhat by raising the question of how the research/teaching nexus ought to be understood as a challenge to universities in the world and the interests they serve. In her recent book, Brew (2006) goes some way towards addressing the broader purposes of higher education insofar as she considers the relationship between research and teaching as integral to developing a 'new' higher education grounded in a pluralistic and 'inclusive' approach to understanding the research–teaching relationship. Such a higher education, argues Brew, would be enquiry-based and essential for unpredictable futures and tackling 'some of the world's big problems' (2006, p. xiv), such as world poverty. But Brew relies heavily on an enquiry-based education to do this, as if enquiry in and of itself will generate such commitments and concerns. Yet the risk is that a philosophy of critical enquiry might as easily be one which promotes individualism and market values, as the values and attitudes of numerous highly educated graduates remind us. To be fair, Brew does acknowledge that teaching includes inculcating attitudes of mind such as 'showing concern and respect'. She supports 'inclusive scholarly knowledge-building communities' of students and academics in partnership 'in the challenging process of coming to understand the world through systematic investigation and collaborative decision-making in the light of evidence' (2006, pp. 3–4). These are laudable aims for higher education. However, they do not take us far enough if we do not at the same time articulate a broader set of normative purposes about what coming to understand the world is for, whose interests such understanding ought to serve, and what this means in the face of neoliberal drivers.

Skills of enquiry could as easily lead to technicist and instrumental forms of higher education and change under contemporary conditions of market fundamentalism in an unequal globalized knowledge economy. Thus in current concerns with the link between research and teaching, research competencies are seen to enhance not the capability to be educated, but employability in a knowledge economy by developing higher order competencies (Simons, 2006). As Simons (2006) explains, in the European context, the starting point for policy is not the older Humboldtian perspective of the edifying potential of academic enquiry, but the economic demands of society. Research is reframed as yet another teaching 'method'. But to reframe education through research in this way as a set of competencies to be achieved is, argues Simons, to diminish scholarship and the pursuit or duty of truth. A persuasive example of the potential capture and technical narrowing of the value of the research/teaching nexus for student learning achievements is that of the current importance given to students' 'communication skills' (communication as a research skill). To become better communicators is seen to empower students to take control of their futures. Cameron explains:

> But what is called 'empowerment' in the discourse [...] has little to do with liberating people from existing constraints on their agency and freedom. In many cases it has more to do with teaching them to discipline themselves so that they can operate more easily within those constraints: become more flexible, more team-oriented, better at resolving the conflicts and controlling the emotions that disrupt business as usual. (2000, p. 179)

Rather, what are needed she argues, are forensic or rhetorical skills – the ability to argue, to challenge, and to persuade. As Simons (2006, p. 43) asks, is there still 'an academic duty or a normative orientation in research that allows for a reflection upon "education through research" that is different from the reflection inaugurated by the needs of the knowledge society and the operationalisation of research as a "teaching method?"'.

Papestephanou and Angeli (2007) further explicate the problem. They point to two different discourses that shape critical thinking, a goal which features prominently in lists of desirable research competences or skills. On the one hand, there is the skills paradigm (found in discourses and practices of key skills, generic skills, transferable skills, and graduate attributes) embedded, they argue, in Habermasian purposive rationality, technicism, and instrumentality, which is relevant to being 'a customer and consumer of services and goods, and not to the active participant in the possible transformation of the public sphere' (2007, p. 609). The idea is to optimize outcomes, in the case of UK higher education, human capital outcomes but this end would not be open to critique. What counts is 'effectiveness, outcomes and performance' (2007, p. 607). Ends and meaningfulness are not questioned, nor goals revised; in this way higher education, and its fundamental claim to foster critical thinking, is captured by the neoliberal project, while ironically seeming still to serve its own values and purposes to develop 'higher order thinking'.

A pedagogy of technique is only weakly framed in equality and commitments to social and human development. It would be characterized by strong commitments to student learning, weaker commitments to underpinning values or orientations to justice. Students would be recognized as having agency in their learning but other than agency for human capital there is no clear guidance of how to evaluate or value this agency, or whether it would encompass agency as democratic citizens. It sits comfortably with a conception of equity underpinning a 'pedagogy of consequence' that prepares students to perform an economic role (Unterhalter, 2008). Brew's pedagogical approach, while laudable in its deep concern for teaching and learning, typifies the absence of a transformative discourse in much of the work on the research/teaching nexus. While it is not inherently a problem that employers want graduates with the skills to undertake research, we need to understand this critically and understand why this has rapidly risen up the agenda as a policy concern in the UK.

Might greater clarity of how we understand justice be of some help in thinking about how to develop and evaluate learning and pedagogies? Rawls (2001) argues that as human beings we have a capacity for justice and we have a capacity for a conception of

the good and to revise and change this if we have good reason to do so. Justice provides us with a principled basis for
settling policy agreements, for educational arrangements, and
for the design of higher education. It is to concepts of justice
(not enquiry) that we ought to turn in settling disputes or decid-
ing on moral (pedagogical) action, a point Unterhalter (2008)
makes about 'connected pedagogies' – that they are oriented
to understanding how we ought to act. Social and educational
problems arise from the gap between educational reality (for
example, problem-based or enquiry learning in which ends are
not problematized) and the demands of justice. A prestigious
MBA programme could have deep problem solving demands,
plenty of discussion, and skills development and yet have educated the professionals who have presided over the current
financial and business implosion.

Thus Strike (1989) argues that while critical thinking is a
democratic virtue, egalitarian justice demands more than the
ability to reason well. It also requires the ability for dialogic
listening, for fair interpretation of the perspectives of others,
for respectful disagreement, and for successful participation in
the complexities of democratic decision-making. We could also
add the significance of 'ontological security' (Brooks and Everett,
2008), that is, having the confidence to make life and life planning decisions that might run counter to dominant trends to
be a particular kind of 'enterprising student' or 'responsible
person'. It further points to the importance of work in fostering well-being so that work and employment enlarge people's
opportunities for human security in a fast changing, high risk
economy. Thus the importance of real freedoms to achieve lifetime projects for a decent life and decent job in society requires
a delicate balance between economic objectives, social aims,
and social progress. As Salais (2004, p. 283) writes, 'Work
is changing, demanding flexibility and autonomy; its practice
raises the issue of effective freedoms and contradicts the logic
of subordination'. Educating for employment is not inherently
problematic; what is problematic is the narrow way in which
this is understood and how such narrow conceptualizations
translate into impoverished or 'thin' skills-based and training
pedagogies.

Strike (1989) helps us to understand the significant difference
between versions of pedagogies, including those grounded in

the research/teaching nexus: the difference is between a thin conception of equity which turns on being trained for a job, and a thick conception of equity that prepares students to understand the world in which they live (while also being educated for employment). This latter underpinning of equity requires that students develop their capacity for communicative rationality and autonomous decision-meaning, their capacity for citizenship (and justice), and their capacity for meaningful activity in association with others. It may also demand particular attention to the structure of disciplines (like history, politics, and biology) as providing unique spaces for developing rational discourse grounded in and adjudicated by the standards and argument forms of those disciplinary traditions (Strike, 1989).

An alternative approach demands a concept in which education is not only for economic growth, but also for democratic community and contributions to more justice in society and the world. For example, Papestephanou and Angeli also argue that 'there is a surplus of critical thinking that cannot be canalized in the skill talk' (2007, p. 618). They employ Habermas's concept of communicative rationality, which is oriented to human potential and actions for mutual understanding, formative dialogue, self-analysis, and transformation of ends so that 'that goals are not there simply to be achieved or approximated, but first and foremost to be checked in introspection, but more appropriately in deliberation' (2007, p. 609). Critical thinking is then morally pertinent (2007, p. 609). A communicative rationality view of critical thinking argues that, 'a critical thinker cannot just be one who carries out an action successfully, but chiefly one who considers and, when necessary, questions the appropriateness or moral relevance of the action' (Papestephanou and Angeli, 2007, p. 608).

More interesting then is Barnett's (2005b, p. 94) argument that not only is research challenged by an uncertain and 'supercomplex' world, but teaching too needs to be oriented to 'the production of human capacities – qualities and dispositions'. Teaching needs to take 'an ontological turn' from knowledge to being, in which teachers take account of students 'as human beings as distinct from knowing beings' so that students have the possibility opened up to 'come into a new mode of being' (Barnett, 2007, p. 1). Ontology, he suggests, trumps but does not displace epistemology. *Both* knowing *and* being ought to be taken into account in university teaching. A world of uncertainty and change, as Barnett argues, poses curriculum challenges not just of knowing and of right action but also crucially challenges us as beings in the world. How do I understand myself? How do I orient myself? How do I stand in relation to the world? What do I become as a human being as a consequence of what I experience as a learner?

▶ Pedagogy for becoming and being richly human: Theorizing and practice

I now turn to an empirical investigation of these ideas and student learning in the disciplines of history, politics, and biology (Walker, 2008). The research/teaching nexus which was the focus of investigation was found to include: a lecturer who is him or herself producing original knowledge through research in their discipline, and whose curriculum and pedagogy is shaped by their own research activity, what counts as knowledge for them, how knowledge is produced in their discipline, and what research skills are needed to do research in their discipline. Students encountered research in different ways: a curriculum based on the lecturer's own area of expertise, transmission of research knowledge in lectures, reading papers written by the lecturer, going to a seminar given by their lecturer, enquiry-learning of research skills, and undertaking their own research project, sometimes in the lecturer's field of expertise, sometimes in a related area. Such encounters with research were shaped by the level of learning, whether in the first, second, or third year of an undergraduate degree. In all the interviews the emphasis tended to be on final year experiences where direct engagement with research was more developed than in the first or second year. In all three disciplines lecturers understood research to be deeply educative. Knowledge is partial, uncertain, revisable, and open to contestation, and this is important in so far as they expect and hope that their students will develop critical faculties and learn to interrogate knowledge and ideas.

To understand the formation of graduates, I drew on the generative lens of Amartya Sen's (1992, 1999) 'capability', that is a conception that a person is able through her education to develop a reasoned understanding of her own valued beings and doings through a university education which is 'the practice of freedom' (Freire, 1970). Capabilities for Sen comprise the real and actual opportunities, that is, substantive freedoms that people have to do and be what they value being and doing. This is a powerful argument for pedagogies through which an individual can explore her own conception of what it is she has reason to value. If an important normative goal were to be capability expansion, then higher education would be a part of expanding both the capability to be educated but also in turn the capability to make valued choices in other spheres of life. Thus Sen argues that, 'the ability to exercise freedom may, to a considerable extent, be directly dependent on the education we have received, and thus the development of the educational sector may have a foundational connection with the capability-based approach' (2003, p. 12). Capabilities cannot be narrowed to skills or internal capacities; this would shift the focus to individual success or failure, whereas the capability approach directs us to the social arrangements, for example pedagogical conditions or normative purposes of universities that enable or diminish student capability formation.

Valuable beings and doings, or functionings, are constitutive of human well-being; a capability is a *potential* functioning. Functionings might include taking part in discussions with peers, thinking critically about society, being knowledgeable, having an ethical disposition, having good friendships, being able to understand a plurality of perspectives on an issue, and so on. Educational development in such terms means the widening of human capability and achievements to be able to choose a good life of well-being, from among various alternatives. Choosing from among genuine alternatives is itself 'a valuable feature of a person's life' (Sen, 2003, p. 8). The focus is on what matters to people, on the important things in each person's life that they can actually do and be, formulating, choosing, and pursuing their own goals. Various capabilities might constitute an individual's capability set and such valuable capabilities might be formed through research pedagogies (for example, the capability of critical thinking, or the capability of imagination, or the capability of voice).

Moreover, Sen is concerned with both the intrinsic and instrumental dimensions to education. Having education is then a valuable achievement in itself; but it also helps graduates to do many other things that are also valuable such as getting a meaningful job; it enhances freedom to achieve a range of valued functionings that may follow from earning an income. Sen (2003) does not reject human capital outright; indeed he sees synergies insofar as human capital and the capability approach are both concerned with the role, agency, and abilities of human beings. But a focus on economic growth, Sen argues, does not tell us why economic growth is important or what wealth is for. Thus education ought not to focus only on human capital and the 'usefulness' of human beings to the exclusion of valuable non-economic ends and more expansive understandings of what is valuable in human lives.

With regard to students' capability formation to choose a life that is good for them, research/teaching pedagogies in this project generated in students a strong awareness of how research in the subject was undertaken, the dynamic nature of the knowledge generated, and the kinds of skills required; what they had learned and achieved and how this had expanded their choices and opportunities whether in relation to economic opportunities, personal fulfilment, and the likelihood of lifelong learning, or their role as critical educated citizens. I found evidence of: 'thick' practical reasoning (that is being able to reason about and choose a 'good' life), critical awareness of knowledge, alternative perspectives and society, and notions of human solidarity, developed individually and intersubjectively, and supported by good teaching which fosters confidence, voice, participation, and achievement. We might describe these, using Sen's language, as 'functional capabilities' which support a pedagogical process of becoming and being. While these capabilities are not developed to the same depth and degree or look the same for each student in each of the three disciplines, they nonetheless did emerge in some way as valuable for each of the students. There was evidence of both 'epistemological knowing', which involves students' critical engagement with knowledge and knowing, and 'ontological being', which involves reflexive reasoning about the self and the 'becoming and being' self in the world. The first is crucial for the second, but the second arguably stands prior to epistemology (Barnett, 2007) – we are human beings before we are students or learners, but as human beings can be transformed by knowing and knowledge.

Key to such pedagogy is the idea of becoming more fully human. For Freire (1970) we humanize ourselves when we engage in critical, dialogical praxis. We dehumanize ourselves and others when we actively prevent this. Knowledge and knowing are never complete and both arise from dialogue, human practice, and engagement with the messy realities of life (and human development). Lecturers in this pedagogical mode are critical and reflective intellectuals, having a questioning frame of mind, and open to learning from their students and from other lecturers. In all cases therefore these were also pedagogies which were shaped by pedagogic rights (Bernstein, 2000) without which students cannot develop fully the capabilities to live well in a democracy (Walker, 2006). The absence of rights points us to the work needed to change prevailing institutional and policy circumstances. Moreover, to say that pedagogic rights are also human rights is to say that educational institutions that fail to promote or protect those rights in any practical way are defective.

Bernstein (2000) proposes three multi-dimensional integrated rights to link education and democracy, underpinned by assumptions of ethical obligations beyond self-interest to defend or promote the pedagogic rights of others. The rights are: 'enhancement' involving critical understanding and seeing new possibilities which is the key to the formation of confidence and agency. The second right is 'inclusion' the right to be included socially, intellectually, culturally, and personally, which is fundamental to 'communitas'. The third is 'participation' in shaping and transforming political outcomes ('civic practice'). These rights would be integral to relations of pedagogical intersubjectivity characterized by human dignity and the realization of each person's full potential in acquiring knowledge. The capabilities 'identified and privileged in the formulation of the rights in question' (Sen, 2004, p. 321) would have to be expanded through research/teaching pedagogies to secure these rights.

In this project there was evidence in the best teaching of attention (probably implicit rather as an explicit feature of a pedagogical philosophy) that students were being supported in developing and sustaining their individual confidence and participating with others in knowledge formation and critique. To take just one example, Peter Otto a history lecturer explained that:

> It is difficult to find one's own voice. I mean that's the most difficult thing...What I do in classes, let's say I'm playing the devil's advocate and I might just change position, I can always support the weaker student initially, even if I think, until the weaker student is confident him or herself and that way you'll always be on the side of the weaker one or of the minority. And that gives people some confidence and I'm using a trick which I find quite useful, I always make experts, say you get your own special area, you prepare something and especially the weaker ones and I use that in second year teaching as well and they work fine where they are experts and then you call on them and say 'They are experts' and since they know more about it than their colleagues, even the quiet ones tend to dare to speak and have an opinion. But what I must not do, not doing is sort of telling in front of classmates, 'That's completely wrong or rubbish or whatever'. (Interview 26/04/07)

Students in his class developed at least a modest sense of their civic agency. The importance of the right of 'civic practice' is explained in this way:

> I'm not telling them what they should be, Left or Right, I mean I have my preferences but that's not my task and as a teacher it's not my job and I shouldn't say, 'This is the right perspective on the world'. What I rather try to teach them is 'Look, it's difficult and sometimes there are contradictions which can't easily be solved and you have to make a decision, but you have to make a decision based on choices and each decision has moral implications and you have to know that and you can't just say the way I live is the best way to live and it's the only way to live and therefore it's a great way to live and I'm not responsible for the consequences.

The formation of civic agency, even if modest that this enables, is captured by his student Paula when she says, 'I don't think I've changed in any dramatic sense, but it's made me just more aware of the way I look at the world....I think it is something that could, you know, if you choose the right thing, I don't know, maybe make a difference'.

Students' ability to reflect critically on their lives and their futures is grounded in research pedagogies which enable access to knowledge, an understanding of knowledge as provisional and contested, and a coming to know which includes engaging with a plurality of views among their own peers in classes. This is a complex capability. For their part, students identified having come to critical understandings through exposure to different points of view, their fellow students, and to academic texts. There is evidence that these young people are asking questions, not taking arguments at face value, showing respect for the views of others, and in the case of history and politics in particular, thinking imaginatively about lives very different from their own. Here is one illustrative example taken from final year politics in which Patricia discusses her acquisition of knowledge and learning capability, her developing confidence and participation (pedagogic rights), and being educated through the research pedagogy of her dissertation exploring the Rwandan genocide:

> I think with politics almost everything is revisable.... so much of it is different people's theories and it is different analysis, so I think, you're never really going to have a set perfect definition of anything within politics, it's all quite fluid and it's all going to change quite a lot, but it is quite important to have all these different theories because then it helps each person to develop it a bit further. Because you've got all these different things that you can look at in different ways, that you can understand things.... before, I thought I knew what I knew and I'd just argue the point, whereas you do find that you'll be sitting in a group situation and you'll find different points of view coming in and you can understand partly what people are saying and that then shapes my argument that I'm going to give in response.... I don't want to go into anything even related to politics once I've finished university, so it almost seems a bit like, 'Well will it [her dissertation study] ever be valuable to me?' but then I think you can never discount knowledge, I think it's never going to be something that you will never come across again, but I think particularly because my dissertation does look at human nature and actions which are in some ways quite inexplicable. Well I

think it will be quite valuable to me in that I just have a better understanding firstly of world events and what's happened, but also why things have happened. (Interview 19/03/2007)

Patricia's comments show how critical and imaginative knowing is crucial to being. This core capability supports a process of thick practical reasoning, of subjecting goals and values to reasoned scrutiny, and questioning those same goals and values as one identifies and chooses what one values being and doing. This is constitutive of becoming a strong evaluator, who can consider what he/she is becoming as a person, that is their ontological being.

Paula, a final year history student, describes some of her valued functionings:

…it made me more aware of looking at my own viewpoint and the way I look at news stories and things like that and the assumptions I make, because I come from a very white middle-class background, I come from a town that's, you know, there's not racial tension because there are only white people really and things like that, so it's very easy to make assumptions or hold views that you never have to test because you are only surrounded by sort of the same kind of people as you and I think maybe that's part of coming to uni as well, but this course has made me reassess and think about my own prejudices and my own stereotypes and stuff. I think this has given me more confidence in a certain kind of debate. Debate was always quite big at my school, but everyone held the same opinion…. That said, I have no idea what I want to do….so, it could be difficult matching my ideals against the reality of the world, I'm not sure…. I think the way it's made me reassess my prejudices because that's very much, I mean, your judgements and your prejudices make you, very much characterise the way you deal with the world and deal with people, read things, interpret things, things like that and by having to look at that and challenge, those being challenged. (Interview 02/04/2007)

Taylor (1985) adds an explicit ethical dimension to such choosing by conceptualizing human beings as self-interpreting, 'strong evaluators' able to evaluate some ethical values or ideals or goods to be more important than others. To develop students' capability as strong evaluators is to develop them as subjects able to reflect on and to be able to re-examine their valued ends, when challenged to do so. They reflect on what is of more or less ethical significance in the narrative interpretation of their lives. We see this in Stella, another history student who explained:

> When you find that you're really good at hockey or whatever, that suddenly changes everything, that you then factor hockey in your life, for the rest of your life because you enjoy it so much and although I can't do degree, after degree, after degree, I can certainly continue to engage with the [southern African] region and that is important to me. It's been an awakening to what I'm interested in. (Interview 21/02/2007)

Similar evidence can be found across the whole data set. There are hopeful stories of identity formation, which point to being human as a rich and complex thing, and to human flourishing and well-being. Not all of the students whose voices are represented in the project are the same: they included middle- and working-class students, men and women students, and minority ethnic students. Disciplinary knowledge was being mediated by lecturers committed both to epistemology and ontology, to teaching and to student learning, and to facilitating pedagogical intersubjectivity, which enables rather than disables student's voices and confidence. What the student voices show is that what it means to be educated though research is something more complex than the acquisition of discrete research skills for employability.

Such transformative pedagogies can expand student identities and challenge research-intensive universities' marketized approaches to graduate skills and attributes. Conceptualizing research-enhanced pedagogies, student identity formation, and teaching in the language of capability and pedagogic rights not only counters dominant human capital language, but also provides a framework for reimagining the research/teaching nexus as human being-ness in university teaching and learning. Quality in student learning would require integrating learning the subject and developing reflexive judgement about what makes life good for that person, that is their well-being and agency. We might then argue that pedagogies ought to be evaluated in terms of whether the substantive freedoms that students have are expanded so that they are able to become and to be onto-logically secure, having the capabilities to make well-reasoned, critical, and reflective choices in an uncertain world about what makes life good for them.

▶ Conclusion

All of the students interviewed for this project were concerned that a university education both develop them personally and equip them for economic opportunities they had reason to value. Nearly all showed concern with how they might contribute to society through the kind of work opportunities they chose. For students in history this was most striking, for others it was less clear, but overall these students demonstrated a general other-orientedness encouraged and developed through the dis-ciplinary pedagogies base of the three areas investigated. How-ever this cannot be assumed to be also a global concern. Apart from history, global concerns or 'global citizenship' (claimed as a key goal at the case study university) were thin and weak or not evident at all. Attending to this gap may be easier to do in current times of recession in which the have-nots of the countries and of the world may come banging at the gates of privilege and the notion of the 'global' university might be recast to include global obligations and educate 'narrative imagina-tions' (Nussbaum, 1997). There is the broader moral point, that students having the advantage of higher education owe obliga-tions to others and to other globally in a world of deepening gulfs between those inside mainstream economies and those on the margins or outside.

When markets are shrinking, commitments to student devel-opment and to society, grounded in responsible teaching and truthful enquiry may then come to the fore. The time seems overdue for a rebalancing of the goals of university education away from an unfettered marketization in which profitability concerns constrain genuinely educational purposes. Univer-sities must again become key locations for pedagogies and teaching which, in philosopher Martha Nussbaum's concep-tualization, 'cultivate humanity', rather than producing eco-nomically useful but obtuse 'machines'. We ought, she argues, to be developing capabilities of practical reason and moral imagination for addressing the urgencies of contemporary times. University education, Nussbaum (2006, p. 15) argues, should be construed not merely as producing technical skills but also, and more importantly, 'as a general empowerment of the person through information, critical thinking and imagination'. There is also room for optimism in what Habermas (1989) describes as a 'promissory note' for universities as a space for the 'lifeworld' to flourish against the colonizing effects of 'system' (money and power). For Habermas universities have not departed the horizon of the lifeworld or left behind the moral–political liabilities of the age. In the unfinished project of modernity, he argues, we can mobilize the resource of reason in reaching for autonomy, justice, and democracy. It allows us to ask – indeed we ought to ask – what a university pedagogy that reaches for the goals of communicative reason and social justice would look like, what form of academic professionalism is required of us as university teachers, and what kind of public policy is needed to support such goals.

▶ Note

1. The project 'Ontology, identity formation, and lifelong learning outcomes: theorizing the relationship between discipline-based research and teaching' was funded in 2006–2007 by a research grant from the Higher Education Academy. The HEA's financial support is gratefully acknowledged.

▶ References

Aronowitz, S. (2000) *The Knowledge Factory: Dismantling the Corporate University and Creating True Higher Learning* (Boston: Beacon Press).

Barnett, R. (2000) *Realizing the University in an Age of Supercomplexity* (Buckingham: Society for Research into Higher Education/Open University Press).

Barnett, R. (2005b) 'Recapturing the Universal in the University', *Educational Philosophy and Theory*, 37(6), 785–797.

Barnett, R. (2007) *A Will to Learn. Being a Student in an Age of Uncertainty* (Maidenhead: Society for Research into Higher Education /Open University Press).

Bernstein, B. (2000) *Pedagogy, Symbolic Control and Identity* (London: Routledge).

Bivens, F. (2009) 'Visioning a Human Rights Based Approach to Higher Education', *GUNI Newsletter*, 39(26), 2–4.

Booth, A., McLean, M. and Walker, M. (2009) 'Self, Others and Society: A Case Study of University Integrative Learning', *Studies in Higher Education*, 34(8), 929–939.

Brew, A. (2006) *Research and Teaching: Beyond the Divide* (New York: Palgrave).

Brighouse, H. (2007) 'The Globalization of Higher Education and a Professional Ethics for Academics'. Plenary lecture presented at the conference 'Learning Together-Reshaping Higher Education in a Global Age', London, 22–24 July.

Brooks, R. and Everett, G. (2008) 'The Prevalence of "Life Planning": Evidence from UK Graduates', *British Journal of Sociology of Education*, 29(3), 325–338.

Brown, P. (2003) 'The Opportunity Trap: Education and Employment in a Global Economy', *European Educational Research Journal*, 2(1), 141–179.

Cameron, D. (2000) *Good To Talk? Living and Working in a Communication Culture* (London: Sage).

Department of Trade and Industry (DTI) (1998) *Our Competitive Future: Building the Knowledge-Driven Economy* (London: The Stationery Office).

Department for Education and Skills (2003) *The Future of Higher Education* (London: The Stationary Office, Cm 5735).

Freire, P. (1970) *Pedagogy of the Oppressed* (New York: Seabury Press).

Global University Network for Innovation (GUNI) (2008) *Higher Education in the World* (New York: Palgrave MacMillan).

Habermas, J. (1989) 'The Idea of the University: Learning Processes', in Habermas, J. (ed.) trans. S. Weber Nicholson *The New Conservatism: Cultural Criticism and the Historians* (Cambridge: Polity Press).

Harvey, D. (2005) *A Brief History of Neoliberalism* (Oxford: Oxford University Press).

Holford, J. (2008) 'There is a Wider Purpose for Universities than Serving the Economy', *Times Higher Education*, 13 November 2008, 24–25.

Jenkins, A., Breen, R., Lindsay, R. and Brew, A. (2003) *Re-Shaping Teaching in Higher Education: Linking Teaching and Research*

(London: RoutledgeFalmer /Staff and Educational Development Association).

Luke, A. (2006) 'Editorial Introduction: Why Pedagogies?', *Pedagogies: An International Journal*, 1(1), 1–6.

Nussbaum, M. (1997) *Cultivating Humanity. A Classical Defence of Reform in Liberal Education* (Cambridge, MA: Harvard University Press).

Nussbaum, M. (2000) *Women and Human Development* (Cambridge: Cambridge University Press).

Nussbaum, M. (2006) 'Education and Democratic Citizenship: Capabilities and Quality Education', *Journal of Human Development*, 7(3), 385–396.

Papestephenou, M. and Angeli, C. (2007) 'Critical Thinking Beyond Skill', *Educational Philosophy and Theory*, 39(6), 604–621.

Rawls, J. (2001) *Justice as Fairness. A Restatement* (Cambridge, MA: The Belknap Press).

Salais, R. (2004) 'Incorporating the Capability Approach into Social and Employment Policies', in Salais, R. and Villeneuve, R. (eds) *Europe and the Politics of Capabilities* (Cambridge: Cambridge University Press).

Sen, A. (1992) *Inequality Re-Examined* (Oxford: Oxford University Press).

Sen, A. (1999) *Development as Freedom* (New York: A. Knopf).

Sen, A. (2003) 'Human Capital and Human Capability', in Fukudo-Parr, S. and Kumar, A. K. (eds) *Readings in Human Development* (New Delhi, Oxford and New York: Oxford University Press).

Sen, A. (2004) 'Elements of a Theory of Human Rights', *Philosophy and Public Affairs*, 32(4), 315–356.

Simons, M. (2006) ' "Education through Research" at European Universities: Notes on the Orientation of Academic Research', *Journal of Philosophy of Education*, 40(1), 31–50.

Strike, K. (1989) *Liberal Justice and the Marxist Critique of Education* (New York and London: Routledge).

Taylor, C. (1985) *Human Agency and Language*, Philosophical Papers 1 (Cambridge: Cambridge University Press).

Taylor, P. (2008) 'Introduction', in Global University Network for Innovation (ed.) *Higher Education in the World* (New York: Palgrave MacMillan).

Turner, B. (2007) 'Rise in Graduates Over-qualified for their Jobs', *Financial Times*, 24/25 November, p. 3.

UNDP (2009) *Human Development Reports.* Available at http://www.undp.org (accessed 15/01/10).

Unterhalter, E. (2008) 'Considering Equality and Equity in Higher Education Pedagogies'. Paper presented at the Higher Education Colloquium, University of Nottingham, 21 May 2008.

Walker, M. (2006) *Higher Education Pedagogies* (Maidenhead: SRHE/Open University Press).

Walker, M. (2008) *Ontology, Identity Formation and Lifelong Learning Outcomes: Theorising the Relationship Between Discipline-Based Research and Teaching* (York: Higher Education Academy).

9 Tackling Inequality Through Quality: A Comparative Case Study Using Bernsteinian Concepts

Andrea Abbas and Monica McLean

Education is central to the knowledge base of society, groups and individuals. Yet, education [...] is a public institution, central to the production and reproduction of distributive injustices. Biases in the form, content, access and opportunities of education have consequences not only for the economy; these biases can reach down to drain the very springs of affirmation, motivation and imagination. In this way such biases can become, and often are, an economic and cultural threat to democracy. Education can have a crucial role in creating tomorrow's optimism in the context of today's pessimism. But if it is to do this then we must have an analysis of the social biases in education. These biases lie deep within the very structure of the educational system's processes of transmission and acquisition and their social assumptions. (Bernstein, 2000, p. xix)

▶ Introduction

Our broad interest is in understanding how judgements about the quality of 'teaching and learning'[1] in higher education affect and are affected by inequalities in society. In an ever-expanding and increasingly international higher education system, globally there are efforts to standardize the quality of university teaching and learning (OECD, 2008). Yet globally focused education systems are hierarchical and perpetuate inequalities by focusing on public rankings that rely on indicators which penalize universities of lower social status and those in poorer countries that have fewer resources and more students from less advantaged backgrounds than in higher status universities and rich countries.

The findings of a small-scale, UK-based study of sociology lecturers presented here challenge orthodox judgements about pedagogic quality. The lens of Basil Bernstein's ideas about how knowledge is distributed differentially in educational institutions according to hierarchies in society is employed and allows us to use the example of the UK to argue that most sociology lecturers are eager for their students to learn the specialized and potentially transformative discourse of sociology, despite such goals being harder to achieve in universities which appear lower down league tables.

▶ Context of the study

The political and policy context of this study is a globally expanded higher education, which aspires both to market competitiveness and to increased social inclusion. Monitoring the quality of teaching and learning is seen as central to achieving these goals (Lemaitre, 2002; Rhoades and Sporn, 2002; Saarinen, 2005). In many countries the form and focus of quality systems are linked to increasing government control, declining state resources and internal pseudo markets, all aligned to meet a perceived need to compete in a global market. While national and international socio-economic and political processes influence specific configurations of quality systems and some are more sensitive to social inequalities (Bottery, 2000; McCarthy and Dimitriadis, 2000; Vidovich, 2004), there are widespread doubts that current systems justify optimism that they contribute to both competitiveness and equality (Brennan and Shah, 2000a, 2000b; van Damme, 2001; Vidovich and Slee, 2001; Billing, 2004; Jones, 2004; Vidovich, 2004; Aelterman, 2006).

Generally, the push to widen participation in higher education is implicated in a different role for the state as it moves away from providing welfare to citizens towards facilitating take-up of opportunities for which the individual is responsible (Beck, 1992; Ainley, 2004). Yet in the UK there is clear evidence of limits to the benefits of higher education for those who are economically and socially disadvantaged (Forsyth and Furlong, 2000, 2003; Morley, 2003; Furlong and Cartmel, 2005; Voight, 2007). Within a stratified system, students from lower socio-economic backgrounds – likely to be 'first generation' university students – tend to enrol in the less prestigious and less well-resourced universities (Forsyth and Furlong, 2000; Archer et al., 2003; Bowl, 2003; HESA, 2005; Reay et al., 2005; Archer, 2007). Whatever university they attend, the costs are greater for poorer students: they are more likely to take on employment to finance their studies and to have personal or financial problems (Furlong and Forsyth, 2000; Archer and Leathwood, 2003; Hutchings, 2003; Moreau and Leathwood, 2006); they are less satisfied with their university experience and are more likely to 'drop-out' (Bekhradnia et al., 2006; Vignoles and Feinstein, 2009). When they leave university compared to their middle-class peers, they are disadvantaged in the labour market and in postgraduate education and training (Furlong and Cartmel, 2005; Brookes, 2006).

Compounding disadvantage, rankings are based on institutional status and wealth (for example, entry qualifications and staff–student ratio). The reflection and exacerbation of inequality play out in international league tables: of the world's top 15 universities in the THE-QS table, 11 are US and 4 UK universities; in the top 100 universities, all of the few not in the US or UK, are in other European countries, Australia, Canada, Japan and Singapore; in the top 200 only the University of Cape Town and the National Autonomous University of Mexico fall outside these countries (THE-QS, 2009). Such league tables are implicated in reproducing global inequalities. While global higher education has become a key development priority and, in theory, should promote greater economic and social equality, it is being provided as a private good by way of international trade rather than as a public good (Robertson, 2009). Global league tables encourage competition in an international higher education market and favour the already wealthy nations. The belief that students receive a better quality education in the US or UK has resulted in benefitting developed economies rather than low-income countries: poorer countries pay richer countries for education, and league tables based on spurious notions of pedagogic quality provide a justification.

League table positions conform to public and media assumptions about the 'quality' of universities and countries, mirroring global as well as local hierarchies (Ashworth et al., 2004; Archer, 2007). Quality systems that are not designed to acknowledge or alleviate inequalities in economic and social capital are being replicated across the world (Avnet Morse, 2006; Cook et al., 2006; Harvey, 2006; Heusser, 2006). They bolster the common belief that the less prestigious a university or the poorer the country in which a university is located, the worse the quality of education provided. From the perspective presented here, orthodox judgements about university pedagogy cannot be justified without investigation: institutional prestige is no guarantor of actual pedagogic quality (Strathern, 2000; Morley, 2003; Crook et al., 2006). Our goal is to provide a basis for debate about how to evaluate pedagogic quality using alternative, fairer measures than those currently used.

▶ Conceptual framework: Basil Bernstein

The study reported here is based on in-depth interviews with eight sociology lecturers in six UK universities of different social status (identified by their position in league tables).[2] We have been drawn to testing Bernstein's theory, which proposes that knowledge is differentially distributed in formal education settings to reflect social and economic injustices in society. His oeuvre (1971, 1973, 1975, 1990, 2000) and the work of Bernsteinian scholars, mainly focusing on the school sector, demonstrate how education is central to the production and reproduction of distributive injustices (see e.g. Atkinson et al., 1995; Sadovnik, 1995; Muller et al., 2004; Moore et al., 2006 and the Special Issue of the *British Journal of Sociology of Education*, 2002). An earlier study comparing the documentation of two sociology degrees, one in an elite university and another in a university near the bottom of the league tables, convinced us of the power of Bernstein's theory for investigating pedagogy in universities of different social status (Abbas and McLean, 2007).

It is beyond the scope of this chapter to present the full range of Bernstein's theoretical work, which is coherent, complex and wide-ranging. Here we shall introduce a limited number of concepts and as the chapter unfolds show how they illuminated what the sociology lecturers talked to us about.

According to Bernstein (2000, p. 28), distributive rules 'regulate relationships between power, social groups, forms of consciousness and forms of practice.' He proposes that different forms of human consciousness are distributed through different forms of knowledge. Although he acknowledges it is a crude, simplified representation of what goes on, Bernstein distinguishes between two classes of knowledge present in all societies (even if the content changes historically and culturally) that are unequally distributed according to socio-economic hierarchies. They are 'profane' and 'sacred' knowledge and the table below lists the characteristics of each. Types of knowledge are distributed according to power relations, which differentiate between and stratify groups in society. Unthinkable or sacred knowledge, traditionally produced and reproduced in universities, empowers the groups that possess it because it bestows on them agential capabilities: namely, to reflect on society or a particular aspect of it, to fully participate in the democratic process, and to act to change society. The means by which the two classes of knowledge are differentially distributed in society is the 'pedagogic device' that explains the social bases for knowledge transmission, acquisition and evaluation (generally called 'assessment' in the UK system) in formal education.

Profane knowledge	Sacred knowledge
managed by secondary and primary school	major control and management in universities
thinkable	unthinkable
mundane	esoteric
knowledge of how it is	possibility of the impossible
knowledge of the other	otherness of knowledge
expressed through 'vertical' everyday discourse	expressed though specialized 'horizontal' discourse

We want to explore how far Bernstein's concepts assist an understanding of university-acquired knowledge for thinking about possibilities in an 'economised' (Jones, 2004) higher education system by which a (now very troubled) global capitalism drives forward a managerial and marketised quality agenda which, although associated with some positive changes, does not incorporate the redistributive principles necessary to address inequality (Morley, 2003).

To be simple, in Bernstein's framework the 're-centred' state – marked by new forms of central regulation – and its selected agents and ministries produce and control with 'official regulative discourse'. And here we use the expression 'profane' to denote discursive practices that flow, in contemporary times, not only from government agencies' requirements of universities, but also from higher education becoming international big business (for example, the World Trade Organization has included higher education in its General Agreements on Trade in Services (GATS)). According to Bernstein, lecturers and other pedagogic agents are the custodians of 'sacred' 'pedagogic discourses', which can be identified by different and usually oppositional language and practices. Bernstein's theory predicts a struggle between the two discourses.

A pedagogic identity is 'the result of embedding a career in a collective base' (Bernstein, 2000, p. 66), and educational reforms can be seen as attempts 'to produce and institutionalise particular identities' (ibid., p. 20). From a matrix of pedagogic identities that Bernstein identifies, we have employed 'retrospective' and 'de-centred market' identities. 'Retrospective' identities are shaped by grand narratives of the past and 'by hierarchically ordered, strongly bounded, explicitly stratified and sequenced discourses and practices' (ibid., p. 67) associated with academic disciplines. 'De-centred market' pedagogic identities are constructed, according to Bernstein, in institutions where pedagogic practice is contingent on the market. The de-centred market position is driven to become a 'reflection of external exigencies' (ibid., p. 70) and is a 'responsive identity rather than one driven by inner dedication' (ibid., p. 69).

These concepts suggest overarching research questions: What and how pedagogic identities are invoked in lecturers? What significance might this have for the distribution of good pedagogic quality in different universities for students from different socio-economic and cultural backgrounds?

▶ Methodology

A note about why we focus on sociology is worthwhile. First, university sociology is increasingly taught in courses in which the discipline is applied to fields of practice (which might render it more 'profane'); and, at the same time, it is a discipline that historically pursues social and moral ambitions (Halsey, 2004). Given that sociology is not a discipline more or less accessible to different socio-economic classes (Houston and Lebeau, 2006), this combination of characteristics helps an exploration of the usefulness of a degree to individuals from diverse backgrounds and to society beyond economic goals. Secondly, we teach and research sociology and sociology of education. There are important limitations to the generic features of pedagogic quality, so an understanding of the subjects under discussion enhances the research process. Finally, researching the quality of university teaching is extremely sensitive for colleagues, so prior professional relationships ease access to staff and students.

Our first principle for selecting the six sociology departments was that they should be in universities located quite differently in UK league tables.[3] Everley, Maplin and Pursgrove[4] are known as 'new universities' which means that their status changed from polytechnic to university after 1992: these universities are referred to as 'teaching-intensive' and there is a strong tendency for them to appear lower down league tables (and they do not appear in international rankings). Larcia, Nicocia and Movia are 'old universities', that is they have been universities since their establishment and two are members of the elite Russell Group 'an association of 20 research-intensive universities':[5] these universities tend to come higher in league tables (see e.g. THE-QS, 2009).

We invited sociology colleagues with whom we have some connection to take part. Whether or not they work in teaching- or research-intensive universities, all eight are research active, producing publications. An important methodological point is that the lecturers we interviewed are disciplinary colleagues who are familiar with our methods and so we see them as reflexive, with the self-knowledge and personal, professional experience to contribute to interpretation of data (Van Maanen et al., 1988; Bolak, 1997).

Each lecturer was interviewed for approximately one hour and tapes of the interviews were transcribed in full. The questions covered were: What do lecturers think are the purposes of the courses? What influences the curriculum and pedagogic design of courses? How do lecturers evaluate the outcomes of the courses? How do lecturers experience teaching? By way of an iterative, collaborative process we themed the transcripts exhaustively using Nvivo.[6] Themes were compared and contrasted across institutions to deepen our understanding of lecturers' interpretations of the quality of their degrees and to unpick possible relationships between the discursive practices of lecturers and the location of their institution in the hierarchy. Bernstein's concepts were used to assist the analytic process. We present here interpretations based on a selection of themes.

▶ Findings

Overall, although there are ambiguities, university lecturers use strong academic and sociological values both to resist and to accommodate profane market-driven, official pedagogic discourse. In the case of sociology lecturers in the lower status universities, the accommodation is partly motivated by seeing their students as socially disadvantaged. All the lecturers hold out against official regulatory constructions of the pedagogic social order and of pedagogic identities: in Bernstein's (2000) words, 'resources, positions and identities [are] in the struggle for dominance within the official arena of educational policy and reform' (2000, p. 72). As predicted by Bernstein, the struggle is generally harder in the new universities than in the old. There is, however, a complex interplay between how the sacred and profane knowledge is used which depends partially on the market position of universities, and, also on the position of lecturers within institutions (that is, how high in the internal hierarchy they are, or their role in relation to teaching).

For lecturers, academic and sociological values and principles constitute sacred knowledge. What university lecturers think of as 'quality' (though they might not use the word) is expressed in their goals for students. Regardless of the type of university, the university lecturers expressed markedly similar aspirations for students: broadly, they are interested in individual transformation through critical self-reflective thinking and in the transformation of society through students' understanding of societal injustices and the workings of power. The commonality of pedagogic goals is illustrated in quotations from both 'new and old universities':[7]

> Most people [...] who teach sociology have some kind of commitment to the discipline itself and to [...] the kind of analyses of both contemporary society and also social change. [...] it is about transformative education[...] you are giving them a new awareness and tools [and] knowledge about the society in which they're located. (Hannah, Everley, [N])

> There's [...] content, knowing what sociologists say about X and what X is [...]. Then there's all the transferable skills [...] critical analysis, writing, all the skills. [... We ask the students] what is it they wanted to get from their degree and what they got out of it. And they're always saying that they become more annoying to live with after three years of sociology [because of their] critical analysis. (Theresa, Movia, [O])

These quotations typify what the lecturers claim as pedagogic goals and, in part, reveal what Bernstein calls a 'retrospective pedagogic identity'. As active academic researchers of sociology these lecturers are producers of the discourse of sociology, and as such they belong to an established collective social base which, to quote Bernstein, is made up of: 'an amalgam of knowledge, sensitivities, manners [it] requires a very long and arduous apprenticeship into the aesthetic mode [...] it refuses to engage with the market' (Bernstein, 2000, pp. 75–76). In the case of sociology, there is a paradox. While a 'retrospective identity' is essentially elitist, sociology itself has a strong tradition as a subversive even disreputable 'critic of the established social order' (Halsey, 2004, p. 144) which also influences lecturers' evaluation of students' educational achievements. Furthermore, in the case of the new university lecturers, this tradition might influence their motivation to counter the social disadvantages of their students by helping them to acquire the resource of the sacred knowledge of sociology.[8]

As the quotations above illustrate, lecturers' goals for their students, whatever the type of university, can be expressed both in the official regulatory discourse of employability (for example, transferable skills) and in terms of a transformation by the sacred knowledge of sociology. (All have taken on the new language of teaching and learning to some extent.) While some lecturers acknowledge students' achievements, there is a general view that, within the terms of pedagogic disciplinary discourse, the students fail to reach goals. For example, Tristan from Pursgrove (N) draws an explicit distinction between achieving 'learning outcomes' and 'excelling' which students do not because of constraints imposed by features in the rest of their lives:

> Because of the way in which students have changed and the pressures upon them and the way in which their degree is just one part of their life and that they can't [...] devote their whole lives to. A lot of them are working almost full-time [...] They're still meeting the learning outcomes [which] are the sort of baseline [...], if they don't meet the learning outcomes they will fail. But they're not [...] excelling [...] One or two do, but not in the same numbers that they were five years ago.

Susannah from Maplin (N) points to a transformation in some 'extraordinarily good' students:

> I mean we get some extraordinarily good students and we see some incredible transformations. [...] They don't look flatly at themselves [...] they've challenged their commonsense understandings of the world, they read things differently.

Yet, later in the interview she indicates that she is dissatisfied with what the majority of students gain from their degree:

The whole education system now is geared up towards pass-
ing exams[...]. So there's not always a critical eye and not
always a critical edge. And we're living in a time of political ambivalence [...] and it's hard to kind of stir [students]
up and say [...] what we've got now needn't be like that,
you know, it was different twenty years ago and it will be
different twenty years from now.

The idea that sociology students are not as good as they used
to be is echoed in all interviews, but with different inflections in
new and old universities. In the new, the students' life difficulties
and their lack of experience with academic study is emphasized:

I've always taught at the same sort of institution and they
don't read as much now as they used to. [...] some of them
come with less skills, that's problematic 'cos it's sort of in
the '70s and '80s[they] used to have lots of Access courses
where people [...] got the skills and the motivation grew
during the Access programme. [...] Once they came in they
were often extremely good students and [...] a lot of our
sociology students now are really struggling just to manage
the whole [of] their lives. It doesn't mean that some of them
don't perform very well. (Hannah, Everley)

Michael from Larcia is the only lecturer from the old universities
who is unequivocally positive about his students, and we speculate that his view is influenced by doing little teaching and not
being responsible for a course:

In our discipline you'd expect them to be doing a lot of
reading and we do have very good students that are very
committed. [...] I can certainly say that this is different to
other universities I've worked in. There's lots and lots of evidence of really, really deep reading and thinking that our
students do.

Martha at Nicocia is more typical of the old university lecturers
by bemoaning the students' desire for structure and guidance
(this was mentioned by others too):

They arrive less used to it, they ask for lots of structure,
we resist up to a point. [...]. For example, [...] I produce

summaries of my lectures and [...] send them out electronically [...]. Other people are more generous than that. But [...] there is an area of struggle here.

The decline is not the students' fault: they have become instrumental because they must do paid work or because of their experience of schooling or because they are now tainted by the institutional context which constructs the student as consumer. The phenomena of what has been called the 'student deficit model' might be more usefully construed as a perception on the part of lecturers that the task of inducting students into sacred knowledge has become more difficult in times when commonsense official regulatory discourse permeates society and infiltrates the university. Yet there are conscious teaching efforts to engage students by connecting sociology to their own lives:

[In] one of the first year courses they always have to produce identity boxes and then there would be an exhibition of identity boxes.(Hannah, Everley, [N])

He created a narrative of somebody's life story that he presented to the group and then said 'Right okay this is an example of a narrative, now you need to go and find an older person of your own and create a narrative based on this and compare the two narratives. It's creating a more sophisticated way of them relating to [...] sociological issues of being an older person, through their own people they know themselves. (Michael, Larcia, [O])

This was somebody from Northern Ireland who looked at the life of [...] a member of their family whose life was very much affected by alcohol abuse.[...] And I think in terms of moving the students on in terms of their confidence in research and their confidence in presentation, but also an understanding of the kind of structure and action of the individual within the wider context. It did take students on a kind of leap.(Susannah, Maplins, [N])

The capacity of students to connect the insights of sociology to their own or others' everyday lives is highly valued by all the lecturers.

Official knowledge peddled by the re-centred state is distributed by way of particular management discourse and practices which arise from needing to market and control the quality of the educational 'goods'. Bernstein proposes that a 'de-centred market identity' is seen in educational institutions which have three characteristics (1) they are relatively autonomous (2) they respond to externally imposed criteria and (3) they are in competition with other similar institutions for students – precisely the institutions our eight lecturers work in. Bernstein, though, predicts that elite universities will be better able than non-elite universities to protect pedagogic retrospective identities because they can afford to buy in leading producers of knowledge (researchers). So we should see more de-centred market identities in the new universities. Yet, as we have seen, whatever the university, the lecturers display the same commitment and 'inner dedication' to their discipline. All universities respond to market contingencies in an effort to secure student numbers and also, at least to some extent, appropriate profane official regulatory discourse for the sake of inducting their students into sacred disciplinary ways of knowing and being.

The need to respond to the student market appears to have an impact on how sociology is classified in all six universities. In Bernstein's terms 'classification' refers to how boundaries are created and maintained between categories. The categories could be agencies, practices or discourses: in this case, it is the pedagogy and curriculum of university sociology. For Bernstein sociology is a 'singular': that is, a discourse that has appropriated a space and given itself a unique name, unlike, for example, physics, it is a weakly classified 'singular' with a horizontal knowledge structure, encompassing a wide range of theoretical stances and methodological approaches. 'Regions' are contrasted to singulars and ' ... are the interface between the field of production of knowledge and any field of practice' (2000, p. 9). As a result of the demands of the student market in almost all universities at the present time, we can see that pure sociology is giving way to a range of 'regions' – criminology; social policy; and courses of applied sociology. In the following quotations we can hear how sociology is shifting to become more applied to fields of practice. Wanda at Larcia and Hannah at Everley draw attention to how fewer students are registering for pure sociology in favour of degrees that hold out more promise of a job:

> The straight sociology degree is one which attracts quite a few people but not anything near as many as the criminology, a third of that number. [...] the younger students coming in [...] see criminology as a route into a sort of social policy sort of studies. (Wanda, Larcia, O)

> We noticed with recruitment the enormous amount of people who want to do social work obviously for vocational reasons [...] Some recruitment in sociology was falling because of people thinking it wouldn't get them jobs. [...] So it's got probably less social theory and more skills, policy, practice kind of modules within it. (Hannah, Everley, N)

Taking a different approach to marketing, Chris at Pursgrove (N) where there is a high proportion of working-class students, sees it as an opportunity to get students to make connections between sociology and their own lives:

> [...] because of my involvement with the marketing and promotion of sociology [...] I [see that] the discipline has drifted [...] in how it markets itself [...] It's about suggesting that [...] being disempowered happens to all sorts of individuals and you're not selling it in terms of traditional notions of class 'cos young people don't relate to class like they used to. So [...] you sell it in terms of [...] why've you done badly in your exams.

Bernstein sees dealings with both the market and regionalization as a movement towards 'profane' less high status knowledge, which undermines capacities for thinking about possibilities. Yet, Chris alludes to the idea that the growth of a more diverse student body offers the potential for relatively disadvantaged students to become empowered through learning the sacred knowledge of sociology; and, he expresses a belief that his students, unlike more advantaged students, have the chance to use this knowledge directly. All the lecturers from new universities see transformation brought about by academic engagement with sociology as particularly significant for less advantaged students. Tristan also from Pursgrove (N) demonstrates this when he compares students at his university with students from an old university where he taught before:

> What was different [in the old university] was that the students didn't lack anything in terms of basic study skills for higher education and could all write very well, they could all present an argument, they were all very coherent and articulate. But I found them quite closed in terms of their ability to take on new ideas or new perspectives and think differently. And that when you talk about sociology [...] it's something out there but not something directly connected with their concerns [for example] class inequalities or gender power relations or ethnic conflicts. The students [here in the new university] are very quick to see how they're directly sort of involved in these things.

This empowering-the-disempowered aspect of the sociological enterprise is usually seen as being achieved through research or by educating middle-class students to work empathetically with disenfranchised groups. Here, though, Chris and Tristan (in a highly market-driven institutional environment) reconfigure the sacred knowledge of sociology to sell the discipline to relatively disenfranchised students, who are presented not only as difficult to teach, but also as particularly worthwhile to teach because their success in learning sociology can result in empowerment.

Bernstein argues that in an institution where de centred market identities are being invoked, management operates to:

> facilitate the survival of the fittest as judged by market demands. The focus is on the short term rather than the long term, on the extrinsic rather than the intrinsic, upon the exploration of vocational applications rather than upon exploration of knowledge.[...] Personal commitment and particular dedication of staff and students are regarded as resistances. (2000, p. 69)

Some of this resistance and its costs can be heard in Susannah's description of her head of department's efforts to get something done about lack of resources and support:

> So our team leader [...] goes over there and blows a gasket on a regular basis [...]. And he does his damndest. [...] And actually we don't see our direct managers very often [...] I know they've got a lot to do, but what I tend to feel, as a foot soldier, is that there are some people in the team who have that connection with associate deans or deans or head of research or whatever and I don't have it, I'm just a prole [...] So [...] we do our best [...] to try and resist that, but it falls on the shoulders of our team leader [...] (Maplin, [N])

On the other hand, in a similar university, Tristan's experience of responding to management imperatives is benign:

> The last review and validation? [...] It was a fairly collective and democratic process across the whole sociology subject, even though the task of actually writing the documents tended to fall to two or three people. (Pursgrove [N])

The imposition of the quality regimes in universities fits with Bernstein's observation that 'contemporary educational reforms aim to achieve control [...] by tight and public evaluation' (2000, p. 69). In practice, there is ambivalence and an uneasy accommodation with the de-centred market colonizers. Here Susannah at Maplin (N) describes how she and her colleagues combine two sets of imperatives and make it fit with their own 'vision':

> We've got a profile handed from above here and we've also got to go on the national kind of benchmarks with which to relate our ideas [...]. And we've also got a vision of who we are and what we're doing here and what we're good at[...] the programme will provide, x, x, x, x, or whatever in terms of learning outcomes and we need to ensure that we're actually assessing that as it were. I think a lot of it's top down. We're being told by eminent sociologists [...] what a sociologist should look like and we've been told by this university

what a graduate should look like, but we do still have a good deal of discretion to try and make that our own.

Chris at Pursgrove (N) is well-schooled in official pedagogic discourse, using it skilfully to talk about student learning and progress:

> The aims and how they're linked into the learning out-
> comes at different levels of the degree I think are useful
> [...] because it's a condensed version of what you're hop-
> ing the students are working towards [...]. So what is a
> year-one student working towards in terms of analysis, eval-
> uation, and a range of other skills, reading skills. [...] 'Cos
> the notion of progression is something that you're trying to
> achieve.

In contrast, lecturers at the old universities appear to have less official and regulatory demands: it is easier to keep managerial and quality discursive practices at arm's length:

> I read the [student evaluation forms] and I certainly do con-
> sider what they say [...]. First of all you read them at one
> level thinking 'oh do they like my module, do they like
> me'. And then you think 'is there anything I can use to
> make this a better module'. It is useful but I don't think
> it's used as rigorously and proactively as possible. (Michael,
> Larcia, [O])

Old university lecturers have more administrative support for 'quality work' (Morley, 2003): it is administrators rather than lecturers who take on the burden. In the new universities, administrative staff advise and support academic staff who themselves undertake the 'quality work'. But, we must not overstate the distinction between the two categories of univer-sity here, for the burden varies according to role. Theresa and Michael work in the same old university, yet, while Michael has no responsibility for a course and makes little reference to official regulatory discourse, Theresa is a course leader for one of the sociology degrees and she is conversant with the language of quality, describing the mundane nature of the work:

> We have the Annual Management Review, every year. And as the director it's huge. [...] You get [a] set agenda, you need to cover various things. [...] I was just finalising stuff today and I realised that we haven't had semester two evaluation questionnaires back. I can't tick it off. (Theresa, Novia, [O])

So within one department there can be varying perspectives on quality procedures and different levels of familiarity with its discursive practices. At the same time both Hannah at Everley (N) and Martha at Nicosia (O) report that as soon as there is a relaxation there is a retreat:

> We wrote it all out a few years ago in a large handbook and it's still there, but no-one refers to it anymore. I don't think any of the new, younger staff even know it exists. In fact none of my colleagues could tell you about all the degree programmes [...] even if they were a convenor of one of our programmes. (Hannah, Everley, [N])

On the ground, it appears, all eight lecturers, to a lesser or greater extent take measures to protect sacred disciplinary and academic knowledge. Organizational variations can be discerned. As Bernstein puts it, 'the resources which construct DCM [de-centred market] identities [...] also create [...] stratification' (2000, p. 69) and the less prestigious, less resourced universities are more invaded from the outside by official regulatory knowledge, which impinges on pedagogic discourse. But, there is also variation *within* institutions of the extent to which individual sociology lecturers are 'invaded'. Nevertheless, the lower status new universities do appear to be rather more permeable: particularly insofar as lack of resources puts pressure on lecturers to use their time on administrative duties while they strive to preserve time for academic activity. But, importantly, at the same time, they manipulate quality discourses to subvert the official regulatory colonizations in order to protect core values, which they believe they perpetuate by teaching relatively disadvantaged students.

As we have seen, two pedagogic identities identified by Bernstein can, to a degree, describe the lecturers to whom we talked. On the one hand, Bernstein leads us to expect to see, 'the de-centred market position construct[ing] an outwardly responsive identity rather than one driven by inner dedication. Contract replaces covenant' (2000, p. 69); and this pedagogic identity tends towards a 'reflection of external exigencies' (ibid., p. 70); on the other hand, there is the 'retrospective pedagogic identity' which is orientated towards deeply held academic and sociological values. A tension between these two identities or between external and internal imperatives led Bernstein to assert: 'We have a new pathological position at work in education: the pedagogic schizoid position' (ibid., p. 71). He appears to be using 'schizoid' in the vernacular rather than specialized sense to convey a 'split personality' rather than a cluster of psychological symptoms. We prefer the metaphor 'cognitive dissonance',[9] a psychological term that refers to the tension felt when thoughts, values or emotions are in potential conflict.

Cognitive dissonance is a useful metaphor when we consider the struggle that we witness of the two social orders (official regulative and pedagogic). At one and the same time, the lecturers long for and make provision for students to take on the moral dispositions, motivations and aspirations of their discipline; and, they accommodate new quality discourses as a form of defensive action, particularly in the new universities where the directives of the re-centred state and the exigencies of the market impinge more. A feature of cognitive dissonance is that it drives people to be inventive in order to reduce the discomfort it provokes. The lecturers in the new universities tend to frame the curriculum (as we have interpreted it) 'to do the best we can for our working-class students': the curriculum in these institutions incorporates innovation, variety and methods which engage students personally. Pedagogic ideas are drawn from a specific part of the new quality discourses called the 'professionalisation of teaching':

> Our students do come from diverse backgrounds and particularly from backgrounds where there isn't a tradition of higher education [...]. And the traditional formal lecture/ seminar format [...], I think there's a danger that they might find that quite alienating, they may not be able to engage

with it in the way that they would with some of the more participative forms of delivery. But I think, in general, variety is good anyway in that it enables students to engage and see things in a different perspective.' (Tristan, Pursgrove [N])

Staff are conscious of a more diverse range of students [and of the] need to think more about their classroom delivery than they would have done ten years ago. (Chris, Pursgrove [N])

So there is quite a lot of emphasis on presentations, we do quite a lot of fieldtrips. In the first year the students have to go off to the Tate Modern and they have to do a whole lot of exercises. And I used to take them to the Imperial War Museum, again some of them they had to do quite a lot of exercises through the day. And they also go to the shopping centre and there's various things. (Hannah, Everley, [N])

'Doing the best for working-class students' can be seen as a part of the broader project for sociology of empowering the disenfranchised. This is significant in terms of thinking about lecturers' relationship to sacred knowledge. Arguably the pressure to do justice to such students leads to even greater dissonance for these lecturers who are trying hard to do so in difficult circumstances and in the face of increasing and conflicting demands. Quality concerns in the old universities tend to focus the lecturers away from teaching and towards research in the form of the Research Evaluation Framework (REF). The quality focus on teaching mentioned by all the lecturers in the old universities is towards increasing the number of 1st class degrees awarded, which they interpreted as pressure to award higher marks than students deserve. Nevertheless, such foci appear to create less dissonance than for the new university.

▶ Concluding discussion

We set ourselves the task of exploring the significance of the pedagogic identities of sociology lecturers for the pedagogic quality of sociology in universities of different social status for students from different socio-economic and cultural backgrounds. We have found no evidence of a poorer quality education (that is, of an unequal distribution of sacred knowledge) in resource-poorer universities, which tend to provide education for students from lower socio-economic groups. For now, it can be said that for *all* the lecturers we spoke to good pedagogic quality is the space and capacity to make adjustments to preserve and to communicate to students core academic and disciplinary values. And it is the unequal distribution of resources of time and peace to contemplate the 'sacred' that reflects the hierarchy of institutions.

Going further, we want to speculate that, wherever they work, most sociology university lecturers want their students to gain the power that emanates from esoteric, sacred, disciplinary knowledge. A small piece of evidence is the organization 'Sociologists Without Borders' which advocates that the modern world needs sociologists who are 'engaged and committed, and also reflective and critical' (Sociologists Without Borders, 2009). It is not unlikely that in low-income countries where higher education is 'fragile' and underfunded (ibid.) we can further speculate that lecturers connect such knowledge to possibilities for human development in their countries. Robertson makes the point that:

> A new model of higher education for developing countries that rethinks, defines and reclaims knowledge, is necessary to promote higher education not as a commodity but as a resource for building the kind of capacity that is able to respond to an array of local economic, social and political projects in ways that are emancipatory rather than those that feed into global markets. (2009, p. 16)

This view connects to our investigation which shows that pedagogic quality emerges from a set of complex relationships between staff, students, the discipline and the institutional, national and international contexts. It connects, too, to the OECD's proposal that quality systems should be sensitive to specific national policy contexts (OECD, 2008). Bernstein's concepts offer a way of making judgements about pedagogic quality which can incorporate both such complexity and notions of social justice. The gap between the material/mundane world (the world of markets and quality regimes) and the immaterial/transcendental (the academic discipline) world has the potential for 'an alternative order, an alternative society, and an alternative power relation' for the pedagogic device can never be wholly effective or deterministic. It should be possible to explore the extent to which in different settings higher education is contributing to transformation in society, rather than to benefitting the already rich and comfortable.

▶ Notes

1. In this chapter, we mainly use the term 'pedagogy' to denote the teaching/learning relationship and Bernstein's trio of transmission, acquisition and evaluation in education.
2. It is the result of a pilot study for the 3-year Economic and Social Science Research Council (ESRC)-funded project 'Quality and inequality in university first degrees' which started in November 2008 and runs until November 2011. Its aim is to articulate a definition of the quality of university pedagogy and curriculum for first degree courses that encompasses a full range of educational goals and incorporates a concern for social inclusion.
3. For example, in the Times Good University Guide' of 113 universities Nicocia and Movia are in the top 20, Larcia in the top 40, Maplin in the top 80 and Pursgrove and Everley in the top 100 (http://extras.timesonline.co.uk/gug/gooduniversity guide.php, accessed 14 November 2007).
4. Pseudonyms are used both for the universities and for the lecturers.
5. http://www.russellgroup.ac.uk.
6. We arrived at the following: biographical details; goals of teaching; framing the curriculum; assessment; disciplinary and pedagogic identities; decision-making/governance/management; 'evaluation of what is acquired' (Bernstein's phrase) including gauging standards; experience of teaching; comparisons with other institutions; and, constructing students.
7. From now 'N' denotes new university, while 'O' denotes old.
8. We are not in a position to say whether or not lecturers in other disciplines would be similarly motivated, we can only speculate.
9. The seminal research was by Leon Festinger. Festinger, L. (1957) *A Theory of Cognitive Dissonance* (Stanford: Stanford University Press).

► References

Abbas, A. and McLean, M. (2007) 'Qualitative Research as a Method for Making Just Comparisons of Pedagogic Quality in Higher Education: A Pilot Study', *British Journal of Sociology of Education*, 28(6), 723–737.

Aelterman, G. (2006) 'Sets of Standards for External Quality Assurance Agencies: A Comparison', *Quality in Higher Education*, 12(3), 227–233.

Ainley, P. (2004) 'The New Market State and Education', *Journal of Education Policy*, 19(4), 497–514.

Archer, L. (2007) 'Diversity, Equality and Higher Education: A Critical Reflection on the Ab/Uses of Equity Discourse within Widening Participation', *Teaching in Higher Education*, 12(5–6), 635–653.

Archer, L. and Leathwood, C. (2003) 'Identities, Inequality and Higher Education', in Archer, L., Ross, A. and Hutchings, M. (eds) *Higher Education and Social Class: Issues of Inclusion and Exclusion* (London: RoutledgeFalmer).

Archer, L., Hutchings, M. and Ross, A. (2003) *Higher Education and Social Class: Issues of Exclusion and Inclusion* (London: RoutledgeFalmer).

Ashworth, P., Clegg, S. and Nixon, J. (2004) 'The Redistribution of Excellence: Reclaiming Widening Participation for a Just Society', paper presented at the 12th *Improving Student Learning Symposium, Inclusivity and Difference*, Birmingham, 6–8 September 2004.

Atkinson, P., Davies, P. and Delamont, S. (eds) (1995) *Discourse and Reproduction: A Festchrift for Basil Bernstein* (Broadway: Hampton Press).

Avnet Morse, J. (2006) 'The INQAAHE Guidelines for Good Practice for External Quality Assurance Agencies: Assessment and Next Steps', *Quality in Higher Education*, 12(3), 243–252.

Beck, U. (1992) *Risk Society: Towards a New Modernity* (London: Sage).

Bekhradnia, B., Whitnall, C. and Sastry, T. (2006) *The Academic Experience of Students in English Universities* (Leeds: Higher Education Policy Unit, University of Leeds).

Bernstein, B. (1971) *Class, Codes and Control* (London: Routledge and Kegan Paul).

Bernstein, B. (1973) 'On the Classification and Framing of Educational Knowledge', in Brown, R. (ed.) *Knowledge, Education and Cultural Change* (London: Tavistock).

Bernstein, B. (1975) *Towards a Theory of Educational Transmissions* (London: Routledge and Kegan Paul).

Bernstein, B. (1990) *The Structuring of Pedagogic Discourse* (London: Routledge).

Bernstein, B. (2000) *Pedagogy, Symbolic Control and Identity*, 2nd Revised Edition (London: Rowman and Littlefield Publishers).

Billing, D. (2004) 'International Comparisons and Trends in External Quality Assurance of Higher Education: Commonality or Diversity?', *Higher Education*, 47, 113–137.

Bolak, H. C. (1997) 'When Wives are Major Providers: Culture, Gender and Family Work', *Gender and Society*, 11(4), 409–433.

Bottery, M. (2000) *Education, Policy and Ethics* (London: Continuum).

Bowl, M. (2003) *Non-traditional Entrants to Higher Education: 'They Talk about People Like Me'* (Stoke on Trent: Trentham).

Brennan, J. and Shah, T. (2000a) 'Quality Assessment and Institutional Change: Experiences from 14 Countries', *Higher Education*, 40, 331–349.

Brennan, J. and Shah, T. (2000b) *Managing Quality in Higher Education: An International Perspective on Institutional Assessment and Change* (Buckingham: Society for Research into Higher Education and Open University Press).

British Journal of Sociology of Education (2002) *Special Issue: Basil Bernstein's Theory of Social Class, Educational Codes and Social Control.*

Brookes, R. (2006) 'Young Graduates and Lifelong Learning: The Impact of Institutional Stratification', *Sociology*, 40(6), 1019–1037.

Cook, R., Butcher, I. and Raeside, R. (2006) 'Recounting the Scores: An Analysis of the QAA Subject Review Grades 1995–2001', *Quality in Higher Education*, 12(2), 135–144.

Crook, C., Gross, H. and Dymott, R. (2006) 'Assessment Relationships in Higher Education: The Tension of Process and Practice', *British Educational Research Journal*, 32 (1), 95–114.

Forsyth, A. and Furlong, F. (2000) *Socioeconomic Disadvantage and Access to Higher Education* (Bristol: The Policy Press).

Forsyth, A. and Furlong, F. (2003) *Losing Out? Socioeconomic Disadvantage and Experience in Further and Higher Education* (Bristol: The Policy Press).

Furlong, A. and Cartmel, F. (2005) *Graduates from Disadvantaged Families: Early Labour Market Experiences* (Bristol: The Policy Press for the Joseph Rowntree Foundation).

Halsey, A. H. (2004) *A History of Sociology in Britain* (Oxford: Oxford University Press).

Harvey, L. (2006) 'The End of Quality?', *Quality in Higher Education*, 8(1), 5–22.

Heusser, R. (2006) 'Mutual Recognition of Accreditation Decisions in Europe', *Quality in Higher Education*, 12(3), 253–256.

Higher Education Statistic Agency (HESA) (2005) www.hesa.co.uk/holisdocs/homehtm (accessed 18 February 2006).

Houston, M., and Lebeau, Y. (2006) *The Social Mediation of University Learning* (York: Teaching and Learning Research Programme Occasional Publication) available at http://www.tlrp.org/dspace/handle/123456789/616   (accessed May 2009).

Hutchings, M. (2003) 'Information and Advice and Cultural Discourses of Higher Education', in Archer, L., Ross, A. and Hutchings, M. (eds) *Higher Education and Social Class: Issues of Inclusion and Exclusion* (London: RoutledgeFalmer).

Jones, K. (2004) 'Higher Education in Crisis: The English Experience', Contribution to *SIPTU Seminar, Irish Universities and the Threat of Privatisation*, Liberty Hall, Dublin 22 May.

Lemaitre, M. J. (2002) 'Quality as Politics', *Quality in Higher Education*, 8(1), 29–37.

McCarthy, C. and Dimitriadis, G. (2000) 'Governmentality and the Sociology of Education: Media, Educational Policy and the Politics of Resentment', *British Journal of Sociology of Education*, 21(2), 169–184.

Moore, R., Arnot, M., Beck, J. and Daniels, H. (2006) *Knowledge, Power and Educational Reform: Applying the Sociology of Basil Bernstein* (London: Routledge).

Moreau, M-P. and Leathwood, C. (2006) 'Balancing Paid Work and Studies: Working (-Class) Students in Higher Education', *Studies in Higher Education*, 31(1), 23–42.

Morley, L. (2003) *Quality and Power in Higher Education* (Buckingham: Society for Research into Higher Education and Open University Press).

Muller, J., Davies, B. and Morais, A. (2004) *Reading Bernstein, Research Bernstein* (London: RoutledgeFalmer).

Organisation for Economic Co-Operation and Development (OECD) (2008) Tertiary *Education for the Knowledge Society:*

Volume 1 (Paris: Organisation for Economic Co-Operation and Development).

Reay, D., David, M. and Ball, S. (2005) *Degrees of Choice: Social Class, Race and Gender in Higher Education* (Stoke on Trent: Trentham Books).

Rhoades, G. and Sporn, B. (2002) 'Quality Assurance in Europe and the U.S.: Professional and Political Economic Framing of Higher Education Policy', *Higher Education*, 43, 355–390.

Robertson, S. (2009) 'Market Multilateralism, the World Bank Group and the Aysymmetries of Globalising Higher Education: Towards a Critical Political Economy Analysis', in Bassett, R. and Maldonado, A. (eds) *Thinking Globally, Acting Locally* (London and New York: Routledge).

Saarinen, T. (2005) 'From Sickness to Cure and Further. Construction of "Quality" in Finnish Higher Education Policy from the 1960's to the Era of the Bologna Process', *Quality in Higher Education*, 11(1), 3–15.

Sadovnik, A. R. (ed.) (1995) *Knowledge and Pedagogy: The Sociology of Basil Bernstein* (Westport, Connecticut: Ablex Publishing).

Sociologists Without Borders (2009) *Homepage* http://www.sociologistswithoutborders.org/ (accessed November 2009).

Strathern, M. (2000) *Audit Cultures: Anthropological Studies in Accountability, Ethics and the Academy* (London: Routledge).

Times Higher Education-QS (THE-QS) (2009) 'World University Rankings'. www.topuniversities.com/worlduniversityrankings/ (accessed 25 February 2009).

van Damme, D. (2001) 'Quality Issues in the Internationalisation of Higher Education', *Higher Education*, 41, 415–441.

Van Maanen, J. (1988) *Tales of the Field: On Writing Ethnography* (Chicago: University of Chicago Press).

Vidovich, L. (2004) 'Global-National-Local Dynamics in Policy Processes: A Case of "Quality" Policy in Higher Education', *British Journal of Sociology of Education*, 25(3), 341–354.

Vidovich, L. and Slee, R. (2001) 'Bringing Universities to Account? Exploring Some Global and Local Policy Tensions', *Journal of Education Policy*, 16(5), 431–453.

Vignoles, A. and Feinstein, L. (2009) 'Unexpected individual differences in the pathways into Higher Education in the

UK: a lifecourse approach, *Journal of Social Issues,* 64(1), pp. 115–132

Voight, K. (2007) 'Individual Choice and Unequal Participation in Higher Education', *Theory and Research in Education*, 5(1), 87–112.

10 Development Education, Sustainable Development, Global Citizenship and Higher Education: Towards a Transformatory Approach to Learning

Douglas Bourn and Alun Morgan

▶ Introduction

Over the past decade universities have begun to address their role and relationship to a wider world. Many conceive this now goes beyond the recruitment of students and sharing academic debates. Globalization, new technology and increased economic mobility all impinge on university policy. In addition, the need to address sustainable development has increasingly come to the fore.

In the UK, universities as diverse as Bournemouth, University College London (UCL), Leeds Metropolitan, Gloucester and Plymouth have undertaken policy and curriculum reviews to address sustainability concerns (Bourn et al., 2006; Dyer et al., 2006; Caruana and Spurling, 2007; Jones and Brown, 2007; Roberts and Roberts, 2007; UCL, 2007). Elsewhere in the world it is evident many universities are re-thinking their role in relation to the impact of globalization, global citizenship and the environmental challenges of the twenty-first century (Corcoran and Wals, 2004; Gough and Scott, 2007; Schattle, 2008; Stearns, 2009).

These initiatives are partly a response to government, students and employers who, for differing reasons, are calling on universities to recognize their role within a rapidly changing global society and economy. For a variety of reasons, universities promote terms like 'preparing students to be global citizens' (Shiel, 2006; Abdi and Shultz, 2008; Bourn, 2009; Stearns, 2009). This chapter will explore how and in what ways ideas about sustainable development have begun to influence higher education, and how being a 'global university' may relate to wider debates and questions regarding the transformatory roles universities can play.

▶ Some antecedents: Development education

The term 'development education' emerged in the UK during the 1970s. Partly it was a response to decolonization and the emergence of aid as an area of public debate. However, as Harrison (2005) has commented, the influence of UNESCO and the United Nations gave a particular emphasis and in 1975 defined 'development education' as '... concerned with issues of human rights, dignity, self-reliance, and social justice in both developed and developing countries' (United Nations 1975, quoted in Osler, 1994).

In the 1980s, development education came to be influenced by the thinking of Paulo Freire, with his emphasis on participatory learning and the relationship between education and social change. Critical pedagogy was used as many themes and topics, such as fair trade and climate change, engendered personal and social action. But in the 1980s the growing influence of neoliberal theories led to criticisms that development and global education were (too) political. Work in this field thus was not undertaken by state-funded institutions, but by NGOs (Arnold, 1987; McCollum, 1996; Marshall, 2005).

However, in 1997, the newly elected Labour government published 'Building Support for Development' (DFID, 1998). It advocated learning inside and outside schools about trade, debt, climate change and global poverty. The newly formed Department for International Development (DFID) stressed that development entailed recognizing we live in an 'interdependent world'. This entailed a need to promote social justice, rather than charity to help the poor. Explaining these changed emphases gave development education a new rationale.

However, for decades development education in the UK had generally been the preserve of NGOs. Individual academics were supportive, but there were few initiatives that attempted to make connections between learning, teaching and research on international development. Similar observations could be made about other countries in Europe, North America or the Pacific region (Cronkhite, 2000; Hartmeyer, 2008). As a discipline development studies in the UK and other industrialized countries has tended to focus on research on developing countries rather than the question of learning. Where there was dialogue between development studies and development education, it tended to be in areas related to the role of the media, images and public perceptions of development (Smith and Yanacopulos, 2004). However, the University of Ulster through its International Development Centre and an undergraduate minor course on international development, attempted to make closer teaching and learning connections between development education and development studies. This course can be taken alongside other courses as a contribution towards a BA degree. The creation of the Development Education Research Centre at the Institute of Education in 2008 was the first research centre dedicated to this field in higher education in the UK (Bourn, 2008).

Development education has had some impact on professional training. In teacher education a variety of initiatives and courses have encouraged understanding of a global dimension as an element in qualification to be an effective teacher (Hicks and Holden, 2007; Wade and Parker, 2008). Medicine and engineering have been other areas where there has been an expansion of interest in global issues. External bodies such as Skillshare International in global health and Engineers Against Poverty and the Global Engineer have helped nurture this new emphasis (Bourn and Neal, 2008).

Development education has also had some influence on university responses to the challenges of globalization. The Development Education Association (DEA) has influenced a number of universities to look at international development and globalization not as areas of study but as drivers for re-thinking how an institution relates to global forces and influences. Through a range of publications and events between

1997 and 2006, the DEA evolved a development education approach towards higher education that came under the heading 'global perspectives'. The approach entails '...promoting ways of understanding society by making connections between local and wider world issues. It means looking at an issue or area of learning through the impact of globalisation and international development' (McKenzie et al., 2003, p. 7). The DEA gave its rationale for promoting global perspectives that it enabled the learner to 'understand their own situation in a wider context', to 'develop skills and knowledge to interpret events affecting (their) lives' and to 'learn from experiences elsewhere in the world' (Bourn et al., 2006, p. 7). The DEA framework emphasized the interrelationship of knowledge and learning, cognitive, social and practical skills and values and attitudes. It stressed one cannot learn about the cause of poverty and inequality without the development of critical and analytical thinking, respecting views and having a commitment to social justice (McKenzie et al., 2003).

Government funding and support from DFID in the UK thus played an important role in promoting a range of projects that moved beyond merely accommodating learning about development within the existing curriculum. Some critical perspectives that had been nurtured within the development education projects of NGOs thus came to be introduced to schools and higher education.

▶ Education for sustainable development

Education for Sustainable Development (ESD) emerged in the 1990s through the combination of environmental education with development education. NGOs and later national and international initiatives on the environment were key influences promoting the term 'sustainable development'. The UN Summit on environment and development in 1992 (the Rio Summit) called upon governments and civil society bodies around the world to give a new focus to protecting the planet. This built on the work of the Brundtland Commission in the previous decade (WCED, 1987). A key element of the Rio meeting and its core document Agenda 21 (UNCED, 1992) was a focus on education. A whole chapter (chapter 36) of Agenda 21 dealt with this area.

In the early 1990s, ESD gained a foothold within higher education. The Talloires Declaration in 1990 and declarations at Thessaloniki in 1997 and Luneburg in 2000 (Wright, 2004) had catalysed a strong international academic movement in support of environmental education, which later became subsumed into ESD. Within the UK, a number of research centres with a focus on sustainable development were established, most notably at Bath (Centre for Research in Environmental Education), Plymouth (Centre for Sustainable Futures) and Gloucestershire (International Research Institute in Sustainability). The Environmental Association of Universities and Colleges (EAUC) supported these Centres and other initiatives. The Higher Education Funding Council for England, the Higher Education Academy and the UK government's Sustainable Development Commission all supported further work in higher education on ESD.

The UK government's Sustainable Development Education Panel (1997–2002) defined ESD as 'about developing the knowledge, skills, understanding and values to participate in decisions about the way we do things individually and collectively, both locally and globally, that will improve the quality of life now without damaging the planet for the future' (DETR, 1998). ESD is thus about working towards a more environmentally friendly, equitable and sustainable world.

But ESD is also a construction as Rost has stated that stems

> ... from an expression of (international) political will. It could be understood as a kind of mission from the political arena, given to education professionals and academics, to design an educational concept that correctly deals with the necessary requirements for sustainable development in our world. (Rost, 2004)

Thus there has been political pressure for education institutions to include sustainability within the curriculum, but there is also an assumption that this will lead to changes in individual behaviour and society.

The creation of the Decade on Education for Sustainable Development (DESD) from 2005 to 2014, led by UNESCO, aims to promote education as a basis for a more sustainable human society and to integrate sustainable development into education systems at all levels. The plan for the decade sees:

Education for sustainable development as a dynamic concept that utilises all aspects of public awareness, education and training to create or enhance an understanding of the linkages among the issues of sustainable development and to develop the knowledge, skills, perspectives and values which will empower people of all ages to assume responsibility for creating and enjoying a sustainable future. It is about the way we live our lives, the way we respect the lives of others – far and near, present and future – and our attitudes to the world around us. (UNESCO, 2005)

ESD has been interpreted in a number of different ways in higher education. It has prompted inclusion of courses or activities that address specific issues such as climate change. In some cases, as Sterling (2001) has suggested, it has generated a new way of thinking about learning and engaging in society. It has also been seen as a mechanism for promoting a more sustainable way of working. Across the UK, examples can be found within universities that make reference to ESD including Gloucestershire (Roberts and Roberts, 2007, 2008), Bradford (Hopkinson et al., 2008) and London South Bank (Wade and Parker, 2008). Examples can also be found in Sweden, Denmark, Australia, Germany and the United States (Corcoran and Wals, 2004; Gough and Scott, 2007).

But most of these ESD initiatives are not set within wider questions about approaches towards learning. Sterling (2001) suggests that ESD or what he calls 'sustainable education' needs to be much more radical than just tinkering with the specifics of a course. According to him, we need to think 'out of the box' to shift our focus and attention 'from things to processes, from static states to dynamics, and from parts to wholes' (Sterling, 2004a). Sustainability has to be seen as the 'ability of a system to sustain itself in relation to its environment' (Sterling, 2004b). He goes on to suggest that sustainable development, if it has to have any impact within society beyond 'cosmetic reform', or even 'serious greening', has to be seen as learning as change. This engages both the individual and the whole institution.

Gough and Scott (2007), whilst perhaps not going as far as Sterling, suggest that sustainable development is significant not as a specialism within departments but as a 'fresh and necessary challenge to the way that ideas are classified into economics, environmental science, sociology, politics and so on' (ibid., p. 167). They also question aspects of current ESD practice in higher education in the UK, most notably aspects of the work of Forum for the Future, which, as an NGO working with universities, developed a prescriptive model closely linked to environmental management indicators (Scott and Gough, 2004).

Aspects of these debates can be seen in the ways in which two national bodies in the UK have addressed the challenges of ESD. The Higher Education Funding Council in England (HEFCE) has developed a series of strategies and action plans in this area (HEFCE, 2005, 2008, 2009) with a recognition of the need to address learning and curriculum, policy and management. However, whilst the Council has recognized the important role higher education institutions can play in 'improving the environment, preserving natural resources and making an economic and social impact' (HEFCE, 2009), the emphasis on capacity building in terms of resource allocation is on capacity building in terms of management of institutions, changes in student behaviour and encouraging greater employment engagement.

In contrast, the Higher Education Academy, which provides curriculum support and advice to academics in the UK, has supported a range of projects on sustainable development related to academic disciplines. This has resulted in curriculum development projects that have links to specific subjects, for example English at Bath Spa, bioscience at Leeds, geography and earth science at Brighton and art and design at University College, Falmouth (Sterling and Witham, 2008).

Thus, there is evidence of considerable activity on ESD in higher education in the UK. But the extent to which this has led to any radical re-thinking of where and how sustainable development contributes to addressing questions of global inequality and higher education is less frequently discussed.

▶ Global citizenship

Global citizenship as an area of focus in higher education has links with ideas associated with development education and education for sustainable development (Sterling, 2004a, 2004b; Bourn et al., 2006; Gough and Scott, 2007; Bourn, 2008) but its origins and discourses in Europe and North America have followed a somewhat different stream.

In North America, global citizenship emerged in a number of universities in the 1990s in response to globalization and the need for graduates to be more globally aware, to travel and have the skills to work anywhere around the world. The events of 9/11 reinforced this notion, although giving it a particular slant in some institutions. Thus, in some institutions such as George Mason University (Stearns, 2009) and Chapman and Tufts universities (Schattle, 2008) there is a desire to equip students to have greater knowledge, experience and positive outlook on wider world affairs.

A variety of sources have supported these initiatives. At Soka University of America (Schattle, 2008), Buddhism was a key influence. In others, economic forces prompted an institution to be more globally competitive. Sometimes the changing nature of the international student body and the promotion of international volunteering prompted change (Stearns, 2009). One initiative to promote the concept of global citizenship has been sponsored by the American Association of Colleges and Universities (AAC&U). 'Shared Futures: Liberal Education and Global Citizenship' has supported initiatives at 11 universities to give the specific idea of global citizenship a higher profile in university education. This initiative drew on a desire to move beyond international exchanges and language learning to that of interdependence and viewing the planet as a single unit (Schattle, 2008).

In the UK, UCL, one of the leading proponents of the term 'global citizenship', clearly sees a connection between the usage of the term and its mission to be one of the leading universities in the world. For many other universities use of the term was prompted by larger numbers of international students and an emphasis on concerns with global inequality.

Studies at UCL and other higher education institutions (Bourn, 2009) suggest that students' interest in global issues has often to be developed outside of formal teaching and learning environments with the support of student networks. This sense of frustration can be summarized by the following extract from a text produced by a coalition of UK-based student groups:

> How are today's students going to understand and to respond to the freedoms, problems and the responsibilities they are inheriting? How are today's students going to find their individual roles in a global society? And where do

they start? ...Awareness of the world has heightened the curiosity of students about their role in a global society. They travel across the world, absorb news from across the world and communicate with people from across the world. Unless students find themselves roles to play, there is a risk of disenfranchisement or of disillusionment: that they are aware of global issues but do nothing about them. (Lamb et al., 2007, p. 17)

The idea of global citizenship has been elaborated in Nigel Dower's (2003) work on the ethical and moral support for global citizenship. In addition, campaigns by the NGO, Oxfam, have helped to popularize the idea. Oxfam sees the Global Citizen as someone who respects and values diversity, is outraged by social injustice and takes responsibility for their actions (Oxfam, 2006).The term has been linked to a set of pedagogical principles which aim to empower students to develop as critical beings, to show relevance of global issues to their own lives and to demonstrate the relationship between local actions and global consequences (Killick, 2006; Lunn, 2006; Shiel, 2006; Caruana and Spurling, 2007).

But critics of the term 'global citizenship' suggest that it is elitist, not grounded in realities of political systems and makes assumptions, usually by people in the North on behalf of the rest of the world, about best forms of global social change (Dobson and Valencia, 2005). Carter (2001) suggests that if the term is seen to open up dialogue and debate across a spectrum of theories and interpretations, it can become the basis for a constructive discourse. Andreotti and de Souza (2008) make a distinction between a 'soft' or passive form of global citizenship versus a 'hard' or more active form linked to notions of social justice and critical thinking.

▶ **The global university**

Development education, sustainable development and global citizenship have been put into practice in a number of universities. Some salient questions for policy emerge.

Bournemouth University has taken forward all three agendas. Initially influenced by a project with a local Development

Education Centre, DEED, the university developed a Global Vision strategy (Bournemouth University, 1999). The strategy connects concerns about wider world agendas with critical thinking and valuing different methodologies and approaches. The approach questions the dominance of Eurocentric and rich world viewpoints and prompts 'challenging and discarding prejudice' while acknowledging the 'global forces that affects us all and promotes justice and equality' (Shiel, 2007).

Developing a global perspective is therefore seen as about broadening curricula and incorporating pedagogic approaches that empower students to develop as critical beings who are able to challenge orthodoxy and bring about change. This involves a 'shift in approach, rather than a radical change of content' (Shiel and Jones, 2004).

At Leeds Metropolitan University, students are enabled to 'develop both an awareness of the global context of their subjects and themselves as global citizens' (Killick, 2006, p. 12). Their internationalization strategy which includes linkages to sustainable development (Jones and Brown, 2007) reflects a strong values-based approach, with the aim of ensuring an international, multi-cultural ethos and the development of graduates with 'world-wide horizons' (Leeds Metropolitan University, 2008).

UCL is a very different type of institution to Bournemouth and Leeds Metropolitan. The latter two are post-1992 universities, that is institutions that were formerly polytechnics, where interdisciplinary courses and initiatives were encouraged. UCL, by contrast, is an old university, part of an elite group of British universities with a strong emphasis on disciplinary engagement. Nonetheless, since 2005, UCL has begun a programme of promoting itself as a global university and the university for global citizenship. It states that as an institution with a strong liberal tradition, going global should mean 'actively promoting a sense of global citizenship, social justice and environmental responsibility' (UCL, 2007). The goal of UCL's strategy is to develop graduates who are:

- critical and creative thinkers;
- ambitious – but also idealistic and committed to ethical behaviour;
- aware of the intellectual and social value of culture difference;

- entrepreneurs with the ability to innovate;
- willing to assume leadership roles: in the family, the community and the workplace;
- highly employable and ready to embrace professional mobility. (UCL, 2007)

Behind these different approaches in the universities described, there is a recognition that promoting global perspectives and global citizenship potentially opens space for a more transformatory perspective in higher education. The authors of this chapter are not suggesting this is happening. We are not in a position to make such judgements and nor has there been any substantial research, as yet, that has looked at the impact of these initiatives. Nonetheless, we suggest these initiatives create a potential space for engagement in debates regarding a transformatory university.

▶ **Shifting learning**

At a general level, all forms of education may be seen as transformative if they involve 'a shift of consciousness that dramatically and permanently alters our way of being in the world' (Morrell and O'Connor, 2002). Learning may now be understood as a socially facilitated process by which an epistemological frame is either constructed and consolidated or, more importantly, is transcended leading to a new, more adequate, frame. However, according to transformative learning theory, there are a number of different, ever more adequate 'orders' of consciousness or epistemological 'frames' through which we relate to reality. Sterling discusses three orders of learning:

> First order change and learning takes place within accepted boundaries; it is adaptive learning that leaves basic values unexamined and unchanged...By contrast, second order change and learning involves critically reflective learning, when we examine the assumptions that influence first order learning...At a deeper level still, when third order learning happens we are able to see things differently. It is creative, and involves a deep awareness of alternative world-views and ways of doing things. (Sterling, 2001, p. 15)

This notion also relates to 'multiple loop' learning:

> ... [s]ingle-loop learning refers to learning concerned with changing skills, practices and actions. Double-loop learning facilitates the examination of underlying assumptions and models driving our actions and behaviour patters. Triple-loop learning allows us to question and change values and norms that are the foundation of our operating assumptions and actions. (Keen et al., 2005, p. 16)

Transformative formulations of Development Education, Education for Sustainable Development and Global Citizenship require all three orders, or loops, of learning. Thus, learners will need to engage in first order/loop learning with the support of 'first order/loop' teaching/teachers in order to be apprenticed to the skills and practices prevalent in society generally or within specific professions or academic disciplines specifically. Traditional (western) pedagogy across all educational phases and sectors has functioned reasonably well at achieving this level of transmission learning. However, if learning were to end here, it would merely result in a continuation of the same values, attitudes and practices which have led to the prevailing conditions of social and ecological unsustainability. Consequently, second order/loop learning is necessary to critique the prevailing situation. The practice of 'deconstruction' associated with postmodern discourse and applied in educational situations by radical/critical educators who have achieved 'second order' learning themselves represents key pedagogical attempts to conscientize learners, that is bring to consciousness hidden assumptions informing the prevailing situation/worldview.

However, critique is not enough and the opportunity must be taken to transform those attitudes and values which are found wanting. This process – third order learning (understood here in terms of postmodern reconstruction) – will entail the development of a whole new worldview which is more adequate in terms of the achievement of ecocultural sustainability. Such is the understanding of transformative development education learning advocated in this chapter. It represents an initiation into authentic, mature and fully human existence – wisdom – which represents a necessary motivation towards the achievement of the 'Good Life' both individually and collectively, and represents a move away from merely self-serving behaviour towards the performance of service in support of the 'Greater Good'.

A particular challenge for the higher education sector is, however, that such learning will require 'third order' teaching and teachers or what has been referred to as 'transformative education' and 'transformative' or 'vanguard' educators (Lister, 1987). Whilst the term 'vanguard' could be seen as elitist, it does convey the fact that such educators represent the 'leading edge' of societal transformation needed in the twenty-first century. Unfortunately, they are relatively few in number and what is required is for 'sufficient members of society to have experienced some form of transformative, epistemic [third order] change in order to facilitate and stimulate second order learning amongst a greater numbers' (Sterling, 2007).

What is evident from developments at Bournemouth University and to a lesser extent at UCL and Leeds Metropolitan in the UK and from recent research in Ireland (Khoo, 2006; Tormey and Kiely, 2006) is that potential spaces and openings concerning transformative learning for both students *and* teachers/lecturers are emerging. Sterling notes that whilst there is evidence of examples of changes within faculties and courses, there is much less in terms of institutional change. He gives an example of Hawkesbury College in Australia, an agricultural college, where the mission became one of learning to think not only critically but also in a way that necessitated a change in perception about engagement in the world (Sterling, 2004b). Similarly, Engineers Against Poverty in the UK as a partnership with a range of academics has evolved the concept of the 'global engineer' (Bourn and Neal, 2008). This suggests there is a need to look at engineering in a fundamentally different way based on moving from:

- fixed content and skills to conform to a pre-determined idea of society and the future towards concepts and strategies to address complexity, difference and uncertainty;
- the mere absorption of information, reproduction of received knowledge and acceptance and adaptation to existing structures and models of thinking, knowing and being to assessing, interrogating and connecting information, generating knowledge, living with difference and conflict and shifting positions and perspectives according to contexts;

- structured, ordered and stable, predictable, comprehensible and universal meanings and interpretations to complex and changing, uncertain, multifaceted and interconnected, different meanings and interpretations. (Bourn and Neal, 2008, p. 12)

Behind this approach is a challenge to engineers to move beyond seeing their work just in terms of solving problems. Instead they need to critically understand what the problems are – and to recognize different interpretations of issues and challenges.

▶ Conclusion

This chapter has outlined the ways in which development education, sustainable development and global citizenship are having an impact within higher education. This takes a number of forms ranging from reformist and adaptive to transformative. What is perhaps surprizing is that the role of government, in encouraging initiatives in these areas, has not necessarily restricted the debates and interpretations of these terms. Thus, a number of universities have used government funding to engage with these terms and to create for more transformative approaches to learning. It is too early, however, to assess whether this government support has limits and drawbacks. At present, promising initiatives are evident of a transformative experience in some higher education that moves beyond learning about global inequalities to critical pedagogy and appreciating multiple perspectives.

▶ References

Abdi, A. and Shultz, L. (2008) *Education for Human Rights and Global Citizenship* (Albany: State University of New York Press).

Andreotti, V. and De Souza, L. M. (2008) 'Translating Theory into Practice and Walking Minefields', *International Journal of Development Education and Global Learning*, 1(1), 23–36.

Arnold, S. (1987) 'Constrained Crusaders- NGOs and Development Education in the UK', *Occasional Paper, Institute of Education, University of London* (London: Institute of Education).

Bourn, D. (2008) *Development Education: Debates and Dialogue* (London: Bedford Way Papers-Institute of Education).

Bourn, D. (2009) 'Students as Global Citizens', in Jones, E. (ed.) *Internationalisation: The Student Voice* (London: Routledge).

Bourn, D., McKenzie, A. and Shiel, C. (2006) *The Global University: The Role of the Curriculum* (London: Development Education Association).

Bourn, D. and Neal, I. (2008) *The Global Engineer* (London: Engineers Against Poverty).

Bournemouth University (1999) *A Global Vision for Bournemouth University* (Bournemouth: Development Education in Dorset).

Carter, A. (2001) *Political Theory of Global Citizenship* (London: Routledge).

Caruana, V. and Spurling, N. (2007) *The Internationalisation of UK Higher Education: A Review of Selected Material* (York: Higher Education Academy), http://www.heacademy.ac.uk/assets/York/documents/ourwork/tla/lit_review_internationalisation_of_uk_he.pdf (accessed 6/4/09).

Corcoran, P. B. and Wals, A. E. J. (eds) (2004) *Higher Education and the Challenge of Sustainability* (Dordrecht: Kluwer).

Cronkhite, L. (2000) 'Development Education: Making Connections North and South', in Selby, D. and Goldstein, T. (eds) *Weaving Connections* (Toronto: Sumach Press).

DETR (1998) *Sustainable Development Education Panel – First Annual Report* (London: DETR).

Department for International Development (UK) (DFID) (1998) *Building Support for Development* (London, UK Department for International Development).

Dobson, A. and Valencia, A. (Eds.) (2005) *Citizenship, Environment and Economy* (London: Routledge).

Dower, N. (2003) *An Introduction to Global Citizenship* (Edinburgh: Edinburgh University Press).

Dyer, A., Selby, D. and Chalkley, B. (2006) 'A Centre for Excellence in Education for Sustainable Development', *Journal of Geography in Higher Education*, 30(2), 307–312.

Gough, S. and Scott, W. A. H. (2007) *Higher Education and Sustainable Development* (London: Routledge).

Harrison, D. (2005) 'Post-its on History of Development Education', *Development Education Journal*, 13(1), 6–8.

Hartmeyer, H. (2008) *Experiencing the World. Global Learning in Austria: Developing, Reaching Out, Crossing Borders* (Munster/ New York, Waxman Verlag).

Hicks, D. and Holden, C. (2007) *Teaching the Global Dimension* (London: Routledge).

Higher Education Funding Council for England (HEFCE) (2005) *Sustainable Development in Higher Education: Consultation on a Support Strategy and Action Plan* (Bristol: Higher Education Funding Council for England).

Higher Education Funding Council for England (HEFCE) (2008) *Sustainable Development in Higher Education: Consultation on 2008 Update to Strategic Statement and Action Plan* (Bristol: Higher Education Funding Council for England).

Higher Education Funding Council for England (HEFCE) (2009) *Sustainable Development in Higher Education: 2008 Update to Strategic Statement and Action Plan* (Bristol: Higher Education Funding Council for England).

Hopkinson, P., Hughes, P. and Layer, G. (2008) 'Sustainable Graduates: Linking Formal, Informal and Campus Curricula to Embed Education for Sustainable Development in the Student Learner Experience', *Environmental Education Research*, 14(4), 435–454.

Jones, E. and Brown, S. (eds) (2007) *Internationalising Higher Education* (London: Routledge).

Keen, M., Brown, V. A. and Dyball, R. (2005) 'Social Learning: A New Approach to Environmental Management', in Keen, M., Brown, V. A. and Dybal, R. (eds) *Social Learning in Environmental Management: Towards a Sustainable Future* (London: Earthscan).

Khoo, S. (2006) 'Development Education, Citizenship and Civic Engagement at Third Level and Beyond in the Irish Republic', *Policy and Practice* (*Centre for Global Education, Belfast*), 3, 26–39.

Killick, D. (2006) 'The Internationalized Curriculum: Making UK HE Fit for Purpose', *Academy Exchange: Supporting the Student Learning Experience*, 5, Winter, 13–15.

Lamb, A., Roberts, E., Kentish, J. and Bennett, C. (2007) 'Students as Active Global Citizens', *Zeitschrift fur Internationale Bildungsforschung und Entwicklungspadagogik*, 30(1), 17–19.

Leeds Metropolitan University (2008) Internationalisation Strategy 2008–2012: World Wide Horizons at Leeds Met, http://www.leedsmet.ac.uk/Revised_Internationalisation_Strategy_2008_-_2012.pdf (accessed 10/3/10).

Lister, I. (1987) 'Global and International Approaches in Political Education', in Harber, C. (ed.) *Political Education in Britain* (London: The Falmer Press).

Lunn, J. (2006) *Global Perspectives in Higher Education* (The Royal Geographical Society with Institute of British Geographers Project Report) (London: Royal Geographical Society-Institute of British Geographers).

Marshall, H. (2005) 'Developing the Global Gaze in Citizenship Education: Exploring the Perspectives of Global Education NGO Workers in England', *The International Journal of Citizenship and Teacher Education*, 1(2), 76–92.

McCollum, A. (1996) *On the Margins? An Analysis of Theory and Practice in Development Education in the 1990s*, unpublished PhD thesis (London: Open University).

McKenzie, A., Bourn, D., Evans, S., Brown, M., Shiel, C., Bunney, A., Collins, G., Wade, R., Parker, J. and Annette, J. (2003) *The Improving Practice Series: Global Perspectives in Higher Education* (London: Development Education Association).

Morrell, A. and O'Connor, M. A. (2002) 'Introduction', in O'Sullivan, E., Morrell, A. and O'Connor, M. A. (eds) *Expanding the Boundaries of Transformative Learning: Essays on Theory and Praxis* (New York: Palgrave).

Osler, A. (1994) *Development Education* (London: Cassells).

Oxfam (2006) *Education for Global Citizenship* (Oxford: Oxfam).

Roberts, C. and Roberts, J. (2007) *Greener by Degrees: Exploring Sustainability through Higher Education Curricula* (Cheltenham: Geography Discipline Network, University of Gloucestershire).

Roberts, C. and Roberts, J. (2008) 'Starting with the Staff: How Swapshots Can Develop Esd and Empower Practitioners', *Environmental Education Research*, 14(4), 423–434.

Rost, J. (2004) 'Competencies for Global Learning', *The Development Education Journal*, 11(1), 6–8.

Schattle, H. (2008) *The Practices of Global Citizenship* (Lanham, Maryland: Rowman and Littlefield).

Scott, W. A. H. and Gough, S. R. (2004) 'Education and Sustainable Development in UK Universities: A Critical Exploration Post-Rio', in Corcoran, P. B. and Wals, A. E. J. (eds) *Higher*

Education and the Challenge of Sustainability (Dordrecht: Kluwer).

Shiel, C. (2006) 'Developing the Global Citizen', *The Higher Education Academy: Academy Exchange*, 5, 18–20.

Shiel, C. (2007) 'Developing and Embedding Global Perspectives Across the University', in Marshal, S. (ed.) *Strategic Leadership of Change in Higher Education* (London and New York: Routledge).

Shiel, C. and Jones, D. (2004) 'Global Perspectives and Higher Education: Taking the Agenda Forward in a Business School', *The Development Education Journal*, 10(3), 10–12.

Smith, M. and Yanacopulos, H. (2004) 'The Public Face of Development: An Introduction', *Journal of International Development*, 16(5), 657–664.

Stearns, P. (2009) *Educating Global Citizens in Colleges and Universities* (New York: Routledge).

Sterling, S. (2001) *Sustainable Education: Re-visioning Learning and Change* (Dartington: Green Books and the Schumacher Society).

Sterling, S. (2004a) 'Thinking Systematically', in Tilbury, D. and Wortman, D. (eds) *Engaging People in Sustainability* (Gland, Switzerland and Cambridge: IUCN).

Sterling, S. (2004b) 'Higher Education, Sustainability and the Role of Systematic Learning', in Corcoran, P. B. and Wals, A. E. J. (eds) *Higher Education and the Challenge of Sustainability* (Dordrecht: Kluwer).

Sterling, S. (2007) 'Riding the Storm: Towards a Connective Cultural Consciousness', in Wals, A. E. J. (ed.) *Social Learning Towards a Sustainable World: Principles, Perspectives, and Praxis* (Wageningen: Wageningen Academic Publishers).

Sterling, S. and Witham, H. (2008) 'Pushing the Boundaries: The Work of the Higher Education Academy's ESD Project', *Environmental Education Research*, 14(4), 399–412.

Tormey, R. and Kiely, M. (2006) 'Development Education in Higher Education: Ethnographic Research as a Development Education Methodology', *Policy and Practice*, 2, 15–23.

United Nations Conference on Environment and Development (UNCED) (1992) *Agenda 21: Programme of Action for Sustainable Development: Rio Declaration on Environment and Development* (Rio De Janeiro, Brazil: United Nations Conference on Environment and Development).

UNESCO (2005) *Implementation Plan for the Decade on Education for Sustainable Development* (Paris: UNESCO), http://www.desd.org/index.htm (accessed 30/4/2009).

University College London (UCL) (2007) *Global Citizenship* (London: University College London), http://www.ucl.ac.uk/global_citizenship (accessed 22/4/09).

Wade, R. and Parker, J. (2008) *Learning Journeys Towards Sustainability* (London: London South Bank University, World Wildlife Fund and Oxfam).

World Commission of Environment and Development (WCED) (1987) *Our Common Future, Report of the World Commission on Environment and Development* (Oxford: Oxford University Press).

Wright, T. (2004) 'The Evolution of Sustainability Declarations in Higher Education', in Corcoran, P. B. and Wals, A. E. J. (eds) *Higher Education and the Challenge of Sustainability* (Dordrecht: Kluwer).

11 Globalization and the Professional Ethic of the Professoriat

Harry Brighouse

All rich countries subsidize undergraduate participation in higher education, through direct subsidies to tuition, tax breaks for tuition expenditures, government guarantees for loans, and grants of various kinds.[1] But undergraduates come mainly from households in the upper quarter of the income distribution. And college degrees are required for most well-paid and high-status jobs, and the security, control over one's own life, freedom from stress, and health advantages that accompany such jobs. Access to the public subsidies available for this process is conditional on having already met certain academic requirements, which depends on having attended good enough schools and on having had the traits that education rewards. No comparable public subsidies are available for young people who seek to enter the more advantaged positions by some other method. For example, whereas the State of Wisconsin subsidizes undergraduate tuition for resident students at its flagship state university at a rate of about $58,000 over 4 years,[2] there is no program for 18-year-olds who either had poor quality k-12 education or did not take good advantage of it to access a grant *or even a loan* of $58,000 to start a small business.

Academics, then, are complicit in a complex practice that involves using public resources to facilitate the entry of children from the more advantaged backgrounds in society into the more advantaged positions that society makes available. They are complicit in the practice of social closure – of making opportunity unequal in a way that is, *prima facie*, unfair to those whose opportunities are less.

The globalization of higher education, and especially of the undergraduate market, adds a further wrinkle to this story. Universities in rich countries compete for undergraduate students from developing countries. This yields revenue because, unlike domestic students, such students can be charged at a market rate. But whereas domestic students tend to be merely from the upper levels of their society, overseas students tend to be from the elites of their own societies. Some return to elite positions, others remain in the elites of the societies they move to. As the elite labour market has become increasingly internationalized, universities, and especially elite universities, play an increasing role in facilitating entry into that globalized elite labour market. Few enter that elite from the bottom half of whatever society they come from, and few from the bottom half of any society attend universities.

I have two aims here. First an exploration of the moral character of the function of globalized higher education. Then to propose that academics, especially those in elite universities (those that teach the 20 per cent or so of students who are most likely to fill elite positions), should adopt an ethical stance towards their work as teachers that involves them in shaping the values and future direction of their students. Academics are complicit in a practice that, while unfair, could be justified all-things-considered, but only if it produces members of elites who embrace an obligation to serve society's interests, rather than their own. This is what obliges them to adopt such an ethic.

▶ Two conceptions of the purposes of higher education

Contrast two conceptions of higher education's purposes. On the first higher education is instrumental for the political and economic purposes of society; the point of it is to provide a way of producing a governing and technocratic elite. Students themselves go to university not so much to learn, as to get the credential and enter the social networks which provide them with access to membership of that elite. Universities admit students who have done well in compulsory education; that is, who have had the kind of home background that fits them well into compulsory education and students who have had good experiences within it.

I think of this as the Marxist view; it is Marxist in the sense that it sees higher education as playing a functional role in the maintenance of capitalist societies. But in fact most people who hold this view would be surprized to be thought Marxists. An informal survey of undergraduate students at my own university suggests to me, though, that most see the point of college broadly in terms of access to better jobs, higher incomes, and, for some, political power.

The rival approach to higher education is what I shall call the liberal conception. One nice account is provided by Derek Bok, a former President of Harvard University. Bok elaborates, but doesn't really defend, his conception of liberal education in his book *Our Underachieving Colleges* (Bok, 2006). The chapter titles, which I have amended very slightly, make the conception plain:

Learning to Communicate
Learning to Think
Building Character
Living with Diversity
Preparing for a Global Society
Acquiring Broader Interests
Preparing for a Career

Higher education, for Bok, is about enriching the intellectual lives of students and simultaneously inculcating a sense of responsibility to the society, which has provided them with this privilege. Colleges underachieve, in his view, because they do not call upon students to develop their capacities for higher level cognition, their inclination to participate in public life, their sense of responsibility to others, or even give them the means to think about their future lives in the whole. Preparing students for a career is, indeed, an appropriate part of the role of college, because a career plays a certain kind of role in a life, but that preparation should be subordinate to considerations of the career's contribution to the well-being of the student and making a contribution to the broader society (whether through the execution of the responsibilities involved in the career or through activities in their non-professional life).

In fact, I shall argue later that the two conceptions are not completely contradictory. It could well be that from the perspective of the student the point of higher education is to make them part of an elite; but from the point of view of professional academics, its point is somewhat different.

▶ The premium to higher education

The Marxist conception gains some credence not only from the fact that access to higher education is largely restricted to more advantaged students, but also from the fact that higher education makes an important contribution to success, as measured in terms of lifetime expected income, and access to interesting jobs. The precise amount of the wage premium attached to a degree is unclear: what is clear is that it is substantial. A recent OECD report claims a premium in the UK of 17 per cent (exceptionally high for OECD countries) (OECD, 2002), taking into account foregone earnings, costs of tuition, and tax rates. A Labour Force Survey study shows graduates aged between 20 and 24 earning (gross) 25 per cent more than those with A-level (and equivalent) qualifications (CSU, 2001). Even if we assumed as low as a 10 per cent all-things-considered premium, it is a substantial benefit, especially when combined with the relatively more interesting and autonomous jobs that are available to the higher education graduate. The premium attached to attending elite, as opposed to non-elite, institutions is almost certainly higher. In the US, the premium attached to completing higher education is even greater. Graduates with Bachelors degrees can expect lifetime earnings 70 per cent higher than high school graduates, and 100 per cent higher than high school dropouts. Professional (further) degrees (like MBAs, LLBs, and MDs) yield lifetime earnings three times that of a high school graduate (Cheeseman Day and Newburger, 2002). These gross figures obscure considerable differences among kinds of degree, and also among institutions. The premium is higher for science than for arts graduates, and may be higher for graduates of elite than for graduates of low-prestige institutions. And variation itself, of course, varies over time and across countries.

Is this premium caused by an increased supply of human capital? We don't know for sure, and certainly some of it must be. But a lot of it is driven by credentialism; universities play the role that employers used to play in preparing students for work, and playing another role, of assuring social closure. Rapid increases in higher education participation in wealthy democracies have usually been driven by government action, because governments are under pressure from non-college educated voters who see higher education as a route to social mobility for their children, and from college-educated voters who see it as a means of social closure. For example, the expansion in the US post World War II was driven by the GI bill; the two large expansions in the 1960s and the 1990s in the UK were both driven by government subsidy and government action (Wolf, 2002; Zemsky et al., 2004).

It is worth noting, further, that the premium is an artifice of the design of tax-transfer policy. As one would expect, the OECD estimates that higher education has a much lower monetary benefit in those countries with more progressive tax-transfer policies. It is also an artifice of the private costs of higher education; students having to pay the full cost of their tuition would make some inroads into the net monetary benefit. In principle it should be possible to design a tax-transfer regime in which the income-maximizer was indifferent to, or even averse to, higher education. All this gives us a reason to be rather cautious in assuming that much of the premium is about increased human capital (though this is not to deny that human capital might be being increased while students are in college).

For most of the past 150 years in the English-speaking world higher education was entirely an elite matter; now, in the US some 40 per cent of each cohort, and in the UK more than 40 per cent of each cohort, have some experience of higher education. So you might think that in an era of mass higher education it no longer plays the role which the Marxist assigns to it.[3] But the Marxist conception stands up well in an era of mass higher education. Although each particular boundary is porous and somewhat vague, higher education is highly segmented, and students, teachers, and employers are well aware of the purposes of the different segments. It is probably just as good if not better to go to the University of Wisconsin-Madison at a low price as to go to Harvard at a high price, partly because University of Wisconsin-Madison at a low price enables you, if successful, to enter a graduate program at Harvard or somewhere similar (Krueger and Dale, 2002). But attending the University of Wisconsin-Parkside is worse than Harvard at a high price, and everyone understands this. Similar segmentation occurs within the UK and other mass higher education markets, and is well-enough understood in the culture that it is able to play the sorting and social closure role that the Marxist conception assumes.

There is, however, another dimension to the expansion of higher education. It is no longer the case that higher education is required only to enter or stay in the elite; even securing a good sub-elite position requires higher education. Once it has become standard for large numbers of people to use higher education, employers can use college completion to screen potential employees. In terms of the skills, traits, and dispositions required, few jobs *intrinsically* require higher education. But if higher education is a general expectation, it makes sense for potential employers to allow governments and parents to bear the direct costs, and potential employees the opportunity costs, of education, and to disregard anyone who has not borne those costs: not only for lawyers, accountants, journalists, chemists, and engineers, but for managers, technicians, nurses and police officers. But once employers use college completion as a gatekeeping mechanism this creates insuperable barriers for those who do not take it up. To overstate the case, but not by much, there is a brief opportunity in one's late teens or early twenties missing which makes it near impossible to advance beyond a certain level within the occupational structure; mass higher education confirms this rigidly, which is especially serious for those children whom school does not suit.

▶ The international undergraduate market

Most elite universities in the rich world endeavour to welcome students from other countries, whether from other rich countries, or from the developing world. The motives are complex. International students add to the diversity of a campus, and can enrich the experience of domestic students; they are a source of income for most universities; and they enable universities to extend their influence into other countries. The economic globalization of the period 1990–2008, which may, or may not, have halted with the economic crisis which has engulfed the world as I write created a very substantial international market within which not only elite, but also sub-elite, universities started to compete heavily. Of course, the future may not resemble the past, but absent a massive and lasting economic collapse or very stringent protectionism (which would probably trigger the former) I expect this trend to resume in the near future. Universities, and countries, vary in where they draw international students from, but all rich countries are engaged in this competition.

To give a sense of how significant the numbers are, consider the US. The Institute of International Education (2004) reported that there were a total of 586,323 international students studying in the US during the 2002–2003 academic year. About half of these were undergraduates. This is, in the US at least, big business:

> International students and their dependents contribute nearly $13 billion to the U.S. economy each academic year. Not only do international students bring unique social, cultural, and academic perspectives and valuable insights to U.S. campuses; they also share their experiences about the institution they attend with colleagues back home and can serve as valuable friends and allies in the future. Most university administrators and American students would agree that international students provide educational benefits to American students and institutions that are priceless. (Institute of International Education, 2004)

The internationalization of the undergraduate student market is a natural, but delayed, corollary of the internationalization of the labour market, and in particular of the market for certain highly valued skills and traits. This means that in elite higher education, in particular, institutions are doing two things that for most of them are relatively new. They are educating people from far away, who have weak ties to both the place they are in and the place from which they came. And they are educating locals who also have the loosest ties, with the expectation that they will enter a labour market which will take them far from home.

Most of these institutions are subsidized by local taxpayers, even if the specific international students are not subsidized.

Who are the international students? It has been difficult for me to gather good data on the social origins and social destinations of international students, and it is not clear to me that anyone collects the kind of information that I want. Anecdotes, and everything we know about who takes up elite higher education within rich countries, suggest strongly that for the most part international students are the most advantaged in their countries of origin, and have the additional advantage of being enterprising and less embedded in their own countries of origin. American public universities and British universities both see international (in the UK, non-EU) students as income sources, because their ability to charge local students is limited by law; whereas they can charge international students at a market rate.

According to the Institute of International Exchange, 2/3rds of the international students in the US report no need for financial aid, whereas most domestic students do declare a need for financial aid (Taylor, 2005). If so, they come from the more advantaged sectors of their own societies. This should not be surprizing. Think about the situation in the UK, which is not especially distinctive. Higher education has expanded massively over the past decades, but the proportions of participants from different social class backgrounds have remained more or less constant, and participation is dramatically greater among children from high social class origins. According to the 1997 Report of the National Committee of Inquiry into higher education (NCI Higher Education, 1997) whereas in 1940, 8.4 per cent of the 18+ cohort from social classes I, II, and IIIA participated, only 1.5 per cent from social classes IIIB IV, and V participated. In 1950 the percentages are 18.5 and 2.7; in 1960, 26.7 and 3.6, and so on till 1995 when the figures are 45 per cent and 15.1 per cent. For 2001–2, the figures are 50 per cent and 19 per cent (National Statistics, 2004), while HESA figures for 2006/7 show that 29.8 per cent of young entrants to higher education come from the National Statistics 'Low Socio-Economic Classification' group (HESA, 2008). The NCI report explains:

> As Halsey (1980, 1993) points out, whenever the [Higher Education] sector expands – from 1963 or from 1987 – the fastest rates of growth go to the lower socio-economic

groups, but the absolute incremental growth goes to the higher socio-economic groups. The effect is to maintain nearly constant ratios of participation between higher and lower socio-economic groups, by volume, at approximately 75:25 for the pre-1992 universities and 68:32 for the 1992 universities. These ratios have remained broadly unchanged over a long period. (NCI Higher Education, 1997, p. 2)

International graduate and professional students in rich countries already have degrees from their home countries, so on the whole they are already privileged in their country of origin. If they come from developing countries, they are, very likely, quite privileged; and the longer they stay away, the more their relatively disadvantaged country is deprived of their skills. According to a World Bank study, fully one-fifth of scientists and engineers educated in developing countries live and work in rich countries; and about 3 million university graduates educated in developing countries live outside the developing world, a good number of them having taken further degrees at higher education institutions in the rich world (Bhargava, 2006, p. 114).

It is just not the case that students from disadvantaged social backgrounds in their country of origin are going abroad for university experience and spending between $20,000 and 40,000 a year for the privilege. The few that do, do so on scholarships, usually a sign that they have the talent to be highly advantaged in the international labour market. International students tend to be those best positioned to benefit from an increasingly fluid global skills market, because they are those for whom the costs of migration are least.

▶ Justifying an institution that gives more to those who already have

So higher education confers advantages in the competition for unequally distributed and highly desired social goods; specifically the elite positions in the society to which are attached high status, high salaries, high levels of control in one's work life and one's personal life, high degrees of interest and self-fulfilment through work, opportunities to contribute in a meaningful and publicly recognized way to society, and the better health and longevity that accompanies all those goods. It confers those advantages on young adults who were born into the more advantaged sectors of the societies they inhabit. What could possibly justify public involvement in such an institution?

One might think that this is an unanswerable question. But in fact such an institution could be justified, but only by its tendency to produce social goods that advantage those who do not make direct use of it. In other words, in order for public involvement in higher education to be justified, it must produce skills and knowledge that will, in fact, be turned to the benefit of the less advantaged members of society who do not directly participate. Those benefits, furthermore, must be so great that they outweigh the costs to those who do not participate of the competitive disadvantage that the institution puts them at.

This is not the place to make the case that higher education fails to do this; but I think that the consensus among economists of higher education that most of the financial return to higher education goes to participants suggests that we should be somewhat sceptical. Whether or not it succeeds depends on the structure of the society in question. In the case of overseas students, there are reasons to be sceptical that students who stay in the country where they study thereby, generally, benefit the less advantaged either in that society or in their society of origin; in the case of those who return, it is a complex question, and the truth depends on the economic and social structure of that country, the skills that the student has gained and the use to which they are put.

Conjectures about the likely contribution of an institution's students to the well-being of the least advantaged are complicated by the internationalization of the elite labour market. Whereas in the long period of 1918–1990 there was a relatively stable sense that the most likely outcome for students of even elite institutions was that they would find employment within the country they were raised in, the period 1990–2008 saw a rapid internationalization of the elite labour market, with the result that public authorities involved in supporting elite higher education were decreasingly able to rely on the assumption that whatever advantages their students gained would benefit the society in question. From a more cosmopolitan perspective this isn't a problem: cosmopolitans regard the global economy as a single entity, and the least advantaged in the world as the group in terms of whose benefit elite advantages need to be justified. But the internationalization of the elite labour market does not seem itself to have benefited the world's poor, and there is no reason to suppose that, in itself, it will do so in the future. In fact, it is not unreasonable to conjecture that the loosening of barriers between economies at the elite level has made it easier for elites to capture the return to their skills.

▶ Bringing the liberal conception back in

My conjecture is that there are few curbs on the ability of members of the elite to gain advantage for themselves, and fewer than there were prior to recent economic globalization. Someone might object that this is all to the good, because it increases efficiency of the global economy and ultimately economic growth, bringing those benefits to people from poorer countries. At the time of writing, this conjecture seems less plausible than it might once have done, but there is no need to reject it because I am not, here, proposing any large-scale reform of higher education or public involvement therein. What I am interested in is just what academics who participate in an institution that, I conjecture, does the wrong of creating social closure without producing countervailing benefits to the least advantaged should do; how they should see their own jobs, and their own relationships to their students. Whose interests should they serve?

In the previous section, I asked what could possibly justify public involvement in an institution that confers those advantages on young adults who were born into the more advantaged sectors of the societies they inhabited. The answer I gave was that it could only be justified if the institution, or public involvement in it, produced net benefits for the less advantaged, those who do not directly use it. But I also expressed scepticism that that is the case. So now I want to ask a different question: What could possibly justify *individual* involvement in an institution of this kind?

The problem is this. Academics in elite institutions, like it or not, are complicit in conferring unfair advantages to those who are already unfairly advantaged in the competition for unfairly unequally distributed goods and positions. Those in elite institutions enjoy the privilege of relatively high status, and of having jobs which give them a great deal of control over their working lives, and a fair amount of freedom in how and what to research and how and what to teach. They contribute, in other words, to injustice.

What should they do? One option, of course, is to abandon the profession. I'm not going to explore that option. Instead I want to explore what academics should do, given the structure of the institution in which they are embedded and its function in the world. Up to this point I have sounded very much as though I am wedded to the Marxist conception of higher education. But, in fact, I am committed to the liberal conception, and I want to deploy the liberal conception to construct what I think of as an ethics for the professoriate.

In order for our global society to become more just, there need to be more breaks on economically self-interested maximizing behaviour among the most advantaged. More of the productive efforts of the advantaged should be turned to the benefit of the disadvantaged. In the past century, egalitarians have relied on tax-transfer systems, and regulation of the economy, to guarantee that the productive efforts of the most advantaged redound somewhat to the benefit of the disadvantaged (Lowe, 2004). But academics in universities have no power to impose structural reforms, and exist in an environment in which equalizing structures have been, or are being, torn down. However, academics, and even more so the institutions they inhabit, *are* in a position to influence students' attitudes to preparation for their careers, and their stance towards the career they adopt. Academics are not only *in a position to influence* their self-understanding, but the institutions they inhabit *do influence* it by default.

The public ethos of the past couple of decades has permitted attitudes towards self-interest that work very much to further the disadvantage of the disadvantaged. Consider these two quotes, from a New York Times story about the very rich, written in 2007 at the height of the recent bubble:

> I think there are people, including myself at certain times in my career, who because of their uniqueness warrant whatever the market will bear.

In the current world there will be people who will move from one tax area to another. I am proud to be an American. But if tax became too high, as a matter of principle I would not be working this hard. (Uchitelle, 2007)

The first quote is from Leo Hindery Jr., managing partner of Intermedia Partners, a New York-based media industry private equity fund. The second is from Kenneth Griffin, founder and chairman of Citadel Investment Group, another private equity fund. I have been unable to find details of Hindery's income, but, according to Wikipedia, Griffin's '2004 compensation was reportedly $240 million, slightly higher than his 2003 compensation ($230 million). His 2005 compensation was ranked 13th at $210 million among the top 25 highest paid hedge fund managers. Reflecting the strong investment performance of his funds, Griffin's is reported to have taken home $1.7bn in 2006 and $2.8bn in 2007, of which salary was estimated to reach $1.5 billion in 2007' (Wikipedia, 2005). With the post-bubble perspective, of course, it is hard to be confident that the activities Hindery and Griffin have engaged in have produced any social benefit at all, and it is easy to suspect that they have caused social harm. But it is the remarkably unhumble public attitude to themselves that I want to highlight. Griffin actually threatens that he would move to a lower tax area, despite his patriotism, or simply be less productive, if he were disallowed from keeping a tiny increment more of the income his efforts yield for him. The reason to quote them is not that all or most students actively think of themselves in this way, but to highlight an aspect of the public ethos which has some influence on attitudes, and which an ethic of the professoriate should set itself against.

How does the liberal conception of higher education provide resources to combat such attitudes? According to the liberal conception, higher educational institutions are expected to foster critical thinking, higher cognition, and an ethic of service in return for the privilege that the student has been accorded. This purpose has, so far, played very little role in most of my story, just as it plays only a very limited role in the delivery and provision of higher education, even in the US, where it is the dominant self-understanding in universities. Even prior to the rapid internationalization of the undergraduate market, most colleges and universities were already engaged in intense competition for national-level undergraduates. In the US, a handful of private universities have the kind of endowment that allows them to be basically self-governing; Harvard, for example, could fund its entire operating expenses through the yield on its endowment. But the vast majority of institutions, public or private, which the vast majority of students attend, are highly dependent on market forces, and in order to stay in business they have to focus on competition for students. They also operate within a competitive market for professors; one which is pretty close to being unregulated in the US, and is increasingly, and of necessity, being de-regulated in other English-speaking countries (I say 'of necessity' for two reasons: in a more mobile world other English-speaking countries have to compete with the US, and with the return to talent outside of academia increasing dramatically, universities, like schools, have to compete with that external market for talent).

But the liberal conception, if upheld and taken seriously, could provide one small curb on the tendency of this new elite to enrich and empower itself. In one way my message here may seem to be quietistic. I am not advocating, here, that we radically restructure higher education, or restructure access to it. This is because I do not think that is possible, absent radical restructuring of domestic, and probably the world, order. I'd like to see both, because I believe that even wealthy liberal democracies are marred by serious injustices, and also that the distribution of power and resources between rich and poor countries is radically unjust (and that the rich use the excessive power they enjoy in ways that contribute to maintaining the more radical domestic injustices that many poorer countries endure). But academics work in a world in which neither kind of restructuring is on the policy horizon, and have to do what they can in the existing, highly imperfect, environment.

▶ **Towards a professional ethic for the professoriate**

What is a professional ethic for the professoriate? University teachers, certainly in elite institutions, although they participate in a wide range of established practices, lack a self-conscious ethic with regard to their role with students. If they have such an ethic, furthermore, they have it individually; there is not a collective common understanding, or even much of a discussion, of what it consists in and what it demands of them. There *is* a shared set of priorities: they typically think of research as coming first, graduate teaching, which is aimed at capturing people for the discipline, comes second, teaching undergraduates who are bound for graduate school, third, and teaching the rest comes last; elite academics are enculturated into this set of values. They do not typically see themselves as having a pastoral role, because students are adults, except in the very minimal sense that professors should introduce them to and get them excited about their subjects.

But the argument I have made is that universities play an enormous role in shaping the values and life-paths of those who attend them. They play the Marxist role of securing entry to an elite by default, and they have a hidden curriculum which is constituted by the way that they either approve of and support, or counteract, the influences and incentives the outside world exerts on the students. They still provide access to an approved pool of potential life (or perhaps these days just half-life) partners, and integration into a network that is extremely valuable for early career development. They provide these benefits for some, and exclude others from them; others who are usually less advantaged by their home background and will, usually, have less access over the course of their lives to the socially produced benefits our society distributes so unequally. We, as participants in the life of the institution, contribute to that role, or, if we dissent strongly, we might counteract it.

Most students enter the university influenced to a considerable extent by a social environment that validates competitive, professional, and financial success above service to others and, in particular, service to the less advantaged. Of course, this is not the only influence on them. Some are influenced by political or religious ideas that emphasize service over self-interest, but almost all are influenced by the self-interest validating messages that prevail in the public culture. In particular, the public service ethic which informed the formation of professional elites in my parents' generation (born 1940, 1943) was already weak in my own generation (born 1963), and is weaker still today; in my adopted country it was never as strong as in post-war Britain, and the weakening occurred earlier.

But universities and those of us who teach within them can and should play a modest countercultural role. Here are three features of the ethic I would propose:

1. We should take responsibility, individually and collectively, for the impact of our institution on the career aspirations of our students.
2. We should take responsibility, individually and collectively, for the impact of our institutions on the personal lives of our students.
3. We should take responsibility, individually and collectively, for the fact that our institutions confer unearned privileges on our students, and make sure that those students can be made aware of that privilege.

Adopting an ethic with these features has implications for the individual professor, the department in which she works, and the University itself. I'll make some brief comments about how I understand its implications at the individual and University level. They are, I should emphasize, very preliminary; I hope that readers will take a critical stance towards what I have to say, and will use it as a resource to think about, in developing other ideas.

What does the ethic mean for an individual professor? Here's a small anecdote I was told by an economist who has, himself, been president of a college:

> When I taught at X College [a very elite private university on the east coast] I once annoyed the President at a parents' day. We were making presentations about the purpose of college, and I told them that my main aim was to ruin Thanksgiving for them, by getting their sons and daughters to question absolutely everything they believed. He never really forgave me.

In fact, the ethic does not require that professors induce students to question *absolutely everything*. But getting them to take seriously their privilege and to think hard about whether their own aspirations really reflect their values, or good values, is entirely legitimate. In *Our Underachieving Colleges* Derek Bok describes the inadequacy of career guidance at our colleges; the professoriate does not take responsibility for helping students what to do with their working lives, with the result that students who do not know what career to adopt frequently end up applying to Law School by default (Bok, 2006, pp. 289–290). But Law School traps many students in a cycle of debt and relatively high-paying but relatively unrewarding and socially suboptimal work. One of the things that professors do is to facilitate this cycle by writing letters of recommendation. Impressed by Bok's analysis I began to ask every student who approached me for a letter why they wanted to go to Law School. The starkest, but most honest, version of the most common answer came from a student who had been raised in an evangelical Christian family in suburban Milwaukee: 'I don't have a good answer'. Asking someone raised with (and still committed to) Christian values why they want to be a lawyer is far more important role than trying to induce them to question their faith. If they attend an elite university, they have already made the commitment to be in an environment in which they will have no choice but to question their faith, and prompting them to do so more is not especially important. Prompting them, and atheist students, to think harder about how their careers will serve others, and in particular those who are less privileged, seems to be more important.

Influencing how people think about their careers and what they turn their skills towards is not only achieved by giving direct advice, or by Socratic questioning. The content of what professors teach, the kinds of conversations they choose to have informally with students, and whether they choose to have such conversations at all also influence students. My suggestion is not that professors attempt to indoctrinate students to enter public service, or attempt to induce class guilt. Both things would be inappropriate uses of the authority teachers have even if, as is unlikely, they would be effective. But, in courses where this is appropriate, it makes sense to cover content designed to prompt reflection on the design of social structures and obligation, as well as to require (increasingly popular) service learning that exposes students to the needs of diverse parts of the populations and the challenges of helping to meet them. Just as business and industry-oriented courses require students to have direct experience of what they will be doing in business and industry, it makes sense for courses in the social sciences and the humanities to require students to become directly acquainted with aspects of society and the human condition that are not those which they have experienced in childhood. For overseas students, it makes sense to try and prompt reflection on the structure of the societies that they come from and questions about their obligation to that society and others like it. It also makes sense to prompt questions about their obligation to the less advantaged within the society that is hosting them.

But the ethic I am proposing is more demanding than just involving professors in career guidance and ethics. Many professors have, or could develop, knowledge and skills that enable them to play a part in the wider world. The ethic does not require that each, individually, turn part of their efforts to having a beneficial impact beyond the university, but it does require both that some do so and that others support those who do so, recognizing their efforts as part of the collective mission. A professor who engages in local school reform efforts, or in educating local politicians in how better to devise policies to reduce infant mortality rates, faces an opportunity cost in terms of their time spend contributing to basic research; others should not merely tolerate such work but regard it as something that they share ownership of. To deflect any misunderstanding, I should say that the attitudes I recommend as required by the ethic I am proposing are attitudes I know well, because they are the attitudes that the colleagues in my own Philosophy department have displayed towards my own work outside of Philosophy, to their great credit, and to my great benefit.

What would the professional ethic I am recommending mean for a college itself? One obvious consequence is institutional support for acting on the ethic I describe. To give an excellent real-world example, consider Stanford University's 'Hope House Scholars' Program' (Stanford University, 2009):

> Since spring quarter of 2001, Stanford faculty, staff and students have been engaged in a unique project in Redwood City. Each quarter, two Stanford faculty members offer a course in the humanities to the residents of Hope House, a residential drug and alcohol treatment facility for women who were recently incarcerated. Focusing on such themes as ethics, social justice, and moral responsibility, the women of Hope House engage in college-level course work as part of their rehabilitation and recovery ... each Hope House resident receives a certificate from Stanford Continuing Studies

that verifies two units of credit earned. Along with Continuing Studies, these units are recognized by Canada College and are entirely transferable to other educational institutions. In addition to the units, Stanford Continuing Studies awards each graduate with a voucher to take one continuing studies course in the future, free of charge (estimated value $350 each). Every quarter, approximately 16 women complete the Stanford class.... Utilizing Stanford's greatest resources – our faculty and students – we offer unique opportunities for the residents of Hope House. By challenging their minds, we offer a non-traditional avenue for the women to deal with their addiction, recovery, incarceration, freedom, and reunification with their children. (Stanford University, 2009)

A great, and wealthy, university whose students are almost exclusively drawn from and destined for the elite of their own societies can nevertheless contribute a great deal directly to the well-being of the less advantaged, and can influence the students themselves by engaging in such contributions; and professors, by engaging in work at Hope House, not only provide a direct benefit, but also influence the attitudes and decisions of students.

A different model, engaging undergraduate students in a more systematic way, is Lehigh University's South Side Initiative in Pennsylvania:

The mission of the South Side Initiative is to bring the Lehigh University community and the people of Bethlehem together to learn about changes now taking place in the city, including those associated with the redevelopment of the former Bethlehem Steel site. By promoting informed, democratic dialogue based on critical study, SSI seeks to foster positive collaborations and forms of development that will benefit those who live and work in Bethlehem.

Under the auspices of SSI, eighteen courses (and numerous independent study projects) were rostered in 2007–8 [the first year of the program] in the humanities, social sciences and natural sciences, focusing on the city of Bethlehem and issues related to its history and current transformation.

Courses were offered in nine departments and interdisciplinary programs, including English, History, American Studies, Sociology & Anthropology, Political Science, Earth & Environmental Science/Environmental Initiative, Creative Writing, Art & Architecture, and South Mountain College 'Investigations.' ... SSI [thus] enabled hundreds of Lehigh students to understand the ways in which complex issues such as globalization, democracy, urban development, industrialization and deindustrialization, ethnic conflict, consumerism, economic inequality, environmental degradation and injustice matter in the classroom because they have so decisively shaped our communities and the lives that we can live, here and now. (Lehigh University, 2008)

The Lehigh SSI has several purposes, but two of the central purposes are to make the resources of an elite university available to a working class community that has not always treated its neighbours well, and to prompt students to reflect upon their goals and to equip them with some of the knowledge and skills needed for pursuing public service.

Universities can also use loan-forgiveness and scholarship programs to influence decisions of students, and to reward some of the decisions they make. For example, some wealthy Law Schools forgive loans if students enter public service law firms and stay in them for long enough. Schools of Education could forgive loans for students who decide to work in urban, or poor rural, school districts; the University of Michigan, Ann Arbor, is currently working on an ethics policy which will suffuse the teacher education program, which endorses, facilitates, and valorizes decisions by prospective teachers to prepare themselves effectively to work in high need schools.[4] Nor are all the examples domestic. Many governments in developing countries pay for study abroad on condition that the students return to work in their home country for a specified amount of time on graduation. It is impossible for the colleges where they study to enforce such an obligation, but they could create incentives for students to do so, or to work in the public sector. Officials of one private college I know of noticed that domestic students received Federal Guaranteed Student Loans (which they'd have to pay back) but that similarly needy international students received grants from the college (which they wouldn't have to pay back) because they were, being foreign, ineligible for the loans. This seemed unfair. So they turned the grants into loans, which are forgiven in full if the student takes a public sector position for a specified amount of time on graduating.

▶ Concluding comments

One natural objection to the idea that academics should develop an ethic is that, on the contrary, being an academic is just a job; like other workers, professors are hired for a wage and have no obligation to go beyond the contractual demands of their job. This is unconvincing. The claim, sometimes made by workers who are low in the status order, that one has no obligation to go beyond contractual demands, gets traction from the fact that low-status jobs are often very fatiguing and that the worker has few other realistic options in how to make a living. Neither is true of academics at elite universities, who typically have jobs which give them a great deal of control over the shape of their working lives and who, early in their careers usually, and even later in their careers frequently, have other career options that would create social benefits without demanding huge sacrifices of them (notably, school teaching or working at lower status institutions where they could teach less advantaged students).

Another objection is that academics have an overriding duty to produce high quality research; a very demanding duty that requires most of the time and energy that they should have at their disposal. This objection has more power than the previous one, but not enough. Consider two possibilities. In the first, the university, as its stated top priority, the production of top quality research, and academics feel bound by the mission. My analysis of the role of the university in sealing advantage for its students, though, suggests that universities are not morally entitled simply to stipulate their own missions; given their role in the production of private benefits to the students they admit, they incur obligations to benefit those people whom they harm by not admitting them. I have not given much of an argument that these obligations are stringent and extensive (though I believe that they are). But however stringent and extensive they are, academics have a duty collectively to carry them out, and should spare time and energy from their research to contribute to that task; or should turn their research to the ends specified by that task. Consider, now, the more realistic possibility, in which the university chooses a much broader mission, which includes educating students well, and contributing to the public good through research and service. In that case, academics cannot hide behind the duty to produce excellent research; they must, in addition (collectively) educate students and contribute to the public good, and my contention is that educating students well includes preparing them for a life of service and that the public good is not served well unless the less advantaged among the public are served well.

Finally, someone may object that professors at public universities, and perhaps even at private universities which receive significant public funds, should accept the democratically specified framework to guide their use of their worktime. My guess is, in fact, that few academics would want to advance this objection, because they do not want to validate the sense of legislators that they have legitimate power over what universities and their employees do. Despite that, the objection has considerable power, because no institution that receives substantial support from the government to pursue public purposes (as almost all universities in developed countries, public and private, do) should be, or think of themselves as, unaccountable to the public. But there are two good responses to the objection. First, democratic decisions can be illegitimate, so do not have full weight; a university that was charged by a democratic government with pursuing pernicious ends would, rightly, resist. My contention is that pressure to ignore the imperative to provide benefits to the least advantaged would be pernicious in the circumstances that prevail today. Second, on the contrary, many, if not most, universities actually face democratic pressures to do *more*, and not less, to serve the broader community. Certainly, some of those pressures are strictly about serving economic growth; but many are not, and those few academics who are moved by this last objection can find considerable space within the demands of the public to adopt the ethic I am proposing.

In the absence of radical restructuring of the University, society, or global governance, I have recommended that the liberal conception of higher education can serve as the basis for an ethic for professional academics, an ethic that is consistent with their role as researchers and teachers with pastoral responsibilities to their students, but which commands their attention to those who do not benefit directly from higher education. All I have offered are some vague strands of thought as to what that ethic might include and what it might require academics to do in their professional lives. The case for the ethic having been made, a profession needs to develop a wide-ranging dialogue to work out the precise details.

▶ Notes

1. I'm grateful to the editors, and to the participants in the Globalisation and Higher Education conference at the Institute of Education for comments on earlier versions, and to Paula McAvoy, Jaime Ahlberg, Lynn Glueck, and Mike McPherson for very valuable discussions of the issues. I'm especially grateful to Elaine Unterhalter and Geoff Whitty for prodding me, several years ago, to be a little more daring. Given the content of the chapter, it is perhaps worth saying that to a considerable extent my thoughts have been developed in conversation with, and in response to inspiration from, some of my former and current undergraduate students. The person who has most transformed my understanding of my job and the role of the university is Cory Mason IV, who expressed controlled outrage at my academic attitude when he took two classes from me about 10 years ago, and has prodded, nudged me forward, and inspired me since that time.
2. I arrived at this figure by deducting in-state tuition from out-of-state tuition for undergraduates, and multiplying by four. Of course, the real subsidy for a particular student depends on their course of study, because the university charges tuition at a flat rate in order not to distort course-taking choices.
3. For US figure see William Bowen, Matt Chingos, and Michael McPherson *Crossing the Finish Line* (Princeton University Press, 2009); for UK figures see *Education at a Glance 2008* (OECD, 2008), specifically *the Briefing Note for the United Kingdom*. This document puts the *graduate rate* at 39 per cent; the participation rate must be significantly higher, hence my assumption that it is over 40 per cent.
4. http://www.soe.umich.edu/tei/seminarseries/

► **References**

Bhargava, V. K. (2006) *Global Issues for Global Citizens* (Washington DC: World Bank).

Bok, D. (2006) *Our Underachieving Colleges: A Candid Look at How Much Students Learn and Why They Should Be Learning More* (Princeton: Princeton University Press).

Borland, J., Dawkins, P., Johnson, D. and Williams, R. (2000) *Returns to Investment in Higher Education: Report to the Vice Chancellor, the University of Melbourne* (Melbourne: University of Melbourne).

Careers Service Unity (CSU) (2001) *Graduate Market Trends Spring 2001* (Manchester: Careers Service Unity).

Cheeseman Day, J. and Newburger, E. C. (2002) *The Big Payoff: Educational Attainment and Synthetic Estimates of Work-Life Earnings* (Washington DC: US Census Bureau).

Halsey, A. H. (1993) 'Trends in Access and Equity in Higher Education: Britain in International Perspective', *Oxford Review of Education*, 19(2), 129–140.

Halsey, A. H., Heath A. F. and Ridge, J. M. (1980) *Origins and Destinations: Family, Class and Education in Modern Britain* (Oxford: Oxford University Press).

Higher Education Statistics Agency (HESA) (2008) *Performance Indicators in Higher Education in the UK 2006/7* (Cheltenham: Higher Education Statistics Agency). http://www.hesa. ac.uk/index.php/content/view/1169/141/ (accessed November 2009).

Institute of International Education (2004) *Open Doors 2004, Report on International Educational Exchange* (New York: Institute of International Education). http://opendoors. iienetwork.org/ (accessed December 2009).

Krueger, A. and Dale, S. (2002) 'Estimating the Payoff to Attending a More Selective College: An Application of Selection on Observables and Unobservables', *Quarterly Journal of Economics*, 117(4), 1491–1527.

Lehigh University (2008) *South Side Initiative Annual Report for Academic Year 2007–08* (Bethlehem, Pennsylvania: Lehigh University).

Lowe, R. (2004) *The Welfare State in Britain Since 1945* (Basingstoke: Palgrave, Macmillan).

National Statistics (2004) *Participation Rates in Higher Education* (London: National Statistics).

NCI Higher Education (1997) *Report of the National Committee* (London: National Committee of Inquiry into Higher Education/Department for Education and Employment). http://www.leeds.ac.uk/educol/ncihe/ (accessed May 2009).

Organisation for Economic Co-operation and Development (OECD) (2002) *Education at a Glance 2002 – Chapter A: The Output of Educational Institutions and the Impact of Learning* (Paris: Organisation for Economic Co-operation and Development). http://www.oecd.org/document/52/0,3343,en_2649_39263238_2763124_1_1_1_1,00.html (accessed May 2009).

Stanford University (2009) *Hope House*. http://ethicsinsociety.stanford.edu/community-outreach/hope-house/ (accessed May 2009).

Taylor, M. (2005) 'English Universities Target Cash from 35,000 More Foreign Students', *The Guardian*, 8 February. http://education.guardian.co.uk/students/news/story/0,1408062,00.html (accessed March 2009).

Uchitelle, L. (2007) 'The Richest of the Rich, Proud of a New Gilded Age', *New York Times*, 15 July. http://www.nytimes.com/2007/07/15/business/15gilded.html (accessed May 2009).

Wikipedia (2005) Kenneth C. Griffin. http://en.wikipedia.org/wiki/Kenneth_C._Griffin (accessed May 2005).

Wolf, A. (2002) *Why Education Matters* (London: Penguin).

Zemsky, R., Wegner, E. and Massy, W. (2004) *Remaking the American University* (New Brunswick: Rutgers University Press).

Index